*Pioneer Settlers of Grayson
County, Virginia*

BENJAMIN FLOYD NUCKOLLS

PIONEER SETTLERS OF GRAYSON COUNTY, VIRGINIA

By
Benjamin Floyd Nuckolls

With an index by
Veronica Schofield

CLEARFIELD

Originally published
Bristol, Tennessee
1914

Reprinted, with an added index, by
Genealogical Publishing Co., Inc.
Baltimore, Maryland
1975

Reprinted from a volume in the George Peabody Branch,
Enoch Pratt Free Library, Baltimore, Maryland

Copyright © 1975
Genealogical Publishing Co., Inc.
All Rights Reserved

Library of Congress Catalog Card Number 74-18309

Reprinted for Clearfield Company by
Genealogical Publishing Company
Baltimore, Maryland
1994, 2007, 2012

ISBN 978-0-8063-0640-7

Made in the United States of America

Dedication

THIS book is dedicated to the memory of my father and mother, Clark Nuckolls and Rosa Bourne Hale Nuckolls; and also to other kindred and friends, many of whom have gone before, and many who are on their journey to the Mansions of Rest. ¶We have lived and labored and loved together, and we hope to meet at last in the kingdom of our Lord and Saviour, Jesus Christ, who will finally gather all his faithful ones into their Heavenly Home.

INTRODUCTION

It is with unfeigned pleasure that I write these lines to introduce this modest volume to the reading public. I have known the author and the people of whom he writes for more than a half century. The author himself is of one of the old pioneer families who, by their courage and stalwart virtues, made Southwestern Virginia the garden spot of the world—"The land of the free, and the home of the brave." He was brought up among them, and is by blood akin to hundreds of them. He writes what he knows, and knows what he writes is true. The book is a recital of facts with but little embellishment—a garner for preserving for posterity, a history of the brave doings of the men and women of the generations gone by. This is clearly the author's purpose in writing it, and as such it is worthy of the hearty endorsement of the children of a noble ancestry. And it will be read by this and coming generations, not only in the happy homestead, the hills and valleys of Southwestern Virginia, but in many other states, for the sons of this hill country are spread far and wide over the South and West. Many men and women in the far off western plains will read with thrilling interest story after story of the early days of their fathers and grandfathers who felled the forests and drove the wolves and bears from their lurking dens, and built their log cabins by the spring. The springs of laughing waters are still there, but the log cabins of the pioneers are gone—and beautiful homesteads, waving harvests and lowing herds tell of the comfort and good cheer of the country. The ramshackle school house, in which the children learned their a b c's in the years long gone, are replaced with academies and high schools of architectural taste and adapted to educational purposes. And instead of the log cabin or humble private home of the settlers in which the "circuit-rider" used to conduct divine services, now the "church-going-bell" in every neighborhood calls the people to worship in elegant houses of worship.

This book tells the how of all this change, and the worthy author merits the hearty thanks of all for putting the story in permanent form for preservation. I cordially commend it to book lovers of the day.

Knoxville, Tenn.   D. SULLINS.
    October, 1913.

PREFACE

The times, opportunities, and surroundings have changed so much since the early settlement of this country that the people of the present generation do not realize what were the labors, privations, cares, and anxieties of their ancestors. They were such as try the nerve, strength, and fortitude of mankind.

History proves to us beyond a doubt that our noble ancestors, by strenuous labors and perseverance, changed the face of this country, which they found wild and uncultivated, and that we now enjoy the fruits of their labor, while they "Rest from their labors, and their works do follow them."

They cut down the forests, built their log cabins and stables, cleared up the low-lands and swamps, cleaned up the hills and mountain sides. Their cattle, sheep, and hogs lived on the range, but had to be brought in at night near the cabin to protect them from the ravenous wolves and other wild animals that were plentiful then.

Bells were put on the cattle and sheep so that they could be found when they strayed away. The rich weeds and pea-vines and other vegetable growth afforded feed for the stock, and hogs fed on the mast, and foraged in the woodland. Pens were made, and the stock was driven into them at night, and often large log fires had to be built to keep the wolves away.

We are not attempting in this book to give sketches of all the families that have helped to make our section of the country what it now is, but will give some items of history and tradition that we think will be of interest to many and that have not hitherto been recorded.

We hope that those who scan these pages will not read with the eye of the critic but with appreciation of the facts and items that have been gathered together.

INDEX

ASBURY, BISHOP FRANCIS	171
ANDERSON, MAJ. JAMES	67
ANDERSON, ORVILLE, Clerk of Court	10
BOURNE, WILLIAM, first Clerk of Grayson	17
BOURNE, STEPHEN G.	17
BLAIR, THOMAS, SR.	26
BLAIR, JOHN	26
BLAIR, LORENZO DOW	51
BRYAN, FRANCIS	163
BRYAN, JOSEPH	131
BRYAN, LEWIS H.	132
BRYAN, MORGAN	132
CANUTE, KING OF ENGLAND	162
CANUTE, WILLIAM	163
CANUTE, COL. ELI	163
COLTRANE, COL. IRA B.	123
CORNETT, JUDGE GEO. WASHINGTON	164
COOLEY, BENJAMIN	186
CARICO, REV. WILLIAM	100
COX, JOHN, of revolutionary fame	167
DOW, LORENZO	51
DICKEY, MATHEW	189
DICKEY, JOHN, SR.	188
DICKEY, DR. JOHN R.	184
DICKENSON, COL. MARTIN	54
DICKENSON, JOHN	55
DAVIS, COL. ALEXANDER M.	56
EARLY, JOHN, SR.	205
EARLY, JAMES	203

EARLY, JOHN, JR. ... 203

FELTS, CREED N. ... 51
FELTS, THOMAS, Detective ... 52
FULTON, REV. CREED ... 160
FULTON, SAMUEL ... 160
FULTON, JUDGE ANDREW ... 16

GARLAND, LANDON CABELL, LL. D. ... 143
GARLAND, CHARLES ... 142
GARLAND, MARY ... 142
GARLAND, DAVID S. ... 144
GARLAND, SAMUEL ... 146
GARLAND, HUGH A. ... 146
GARLAND, AUGUSTUS H. ... 146
GARLAND, REV. JAMES POWELL, D. D. ... 147
GARRISON, ISAAC ... 155
GARRISON, DAVID ... 155
GOODYKOONTZ, DAVID ... 193
GOODYKOONTZ, REV. ALFRED M. ... 197
GWYN, JAMES ... 58

HALE, LEWIS, ancestor from Kent, England ... 107
HALE, EDWARD, ancestor from Kent, England ... 104
HALE, JUDGE GARLAND ... 121
HALE, COL. STEPHEN, SR. ... 114
HALE, CAPT. LEWIS, JR. ... 112
HALE, CAPT. PEYTON N. ... 113
HALE, CAPT. FIELDEN LEWIS ... 118
HALE, MAJ. PEYTON G. ... 127
HALE, ELI C. ... 116
HALE, MASTEN ... 73
HALE, PROF. W. STEPHEN ... 116
HASH, JANE ... 173
HANKS, JOSHUA ... 16

Pioneer Settlers

Hanks, "Nancy"	158
Hanks, Creed L.	158
Isom, David	118
Jones, Admiral John Paul	148
Jones, Churchill	153
Jones, Maj. Minitree	153
Jones, Maj. Spotswood	153
Jones, Maj. Churchill	153
Jones, Maj. Abner	156
Jones, William	155
Johnston, Capt. Robert	61
Johnston, James B.	69
Johnston, Mary	61
Kyle, Judge William	52
Kenny, William	205
Kenny, Robert	205
Kenny, William, Jr.	205
Kenny, John A.	205
La Rowe, Louis	206
Lenoir, Gen. William	58
Lundy, Fielden J., Clerk of Court	17
McCamant, Col. Samuel	59
McCamant, Dr. Thomas Jefferson	60
McCamant, Thomas Jefferson, Jr	60
Moore, Col. Alfred	82
Moore, Spotswood J.	157
Moore, Churchill F.	157
McMillan, Col. John	173

NUCKOLLS, JOHN, JAMES, WILLIAM, York, Eng. 65
NUCKOLLS, CAPT. ROBERT G. 72
NUCKOLLS, CHARLES 66
NUCKOLLS, NATHANIEL 90
NUCKOLLS, GARLAND 71
NUCKOLLS, JOHN, S. C., Killed by Tories, 1780 91
NUCKOLLS, EZRA 84
NUCKOLLS, STEPHEN FRIEL, Member of 46th Congress 86

OGLESBY, WILLIAM 89
OSBORNE, ENOCH 171
OSBORNE, SOLOMON 171
OSBORNE, ZACHARIAH 171

PENDLETON, EDMOND, "Jurist" 146
PERKINS, TIMOTHY 24
PERKINS, JOHNSTON 48
PUGH, STEPHEN 25
PUGH, JOHN 116
PHIPPS, BENJAMIN 173
PHIPPS, JOSEPH 173
PHIPPS, COLUMBUS 174
PHLEGAR, JUDGE ARCHER A. 199
PIPER, COL. JAMES 180

REEVES, GEORGE 176
REEVES, JOHN 176

SWIFT, COL. FLOWER, Ancestor from England 98
SMITH, GEN. ALEXANDER, of "Stuarts," Eng. 180
SCOTT, JAMES, of Ireland 126
SHEFFY, REV. ROBERT SAWYERS 70

THOMAS, JONATHAN 24

THOMAS, STEPHEN B.	24
THOMAS, DR. FLEMING	175
VAUGHN, NATHANIEL	16
VAUGHN, REV. JOHN	16
VAUGHN, REV. THOMAS C.	138
WARD, BALLARD E.	73
WORRELL, JAMES	159
WORRELL, ESAW, SR.	159
WORRELL, CAPT. JOHN	160
WORRELL, CHURCHILL	160
WAUGH, CAPT. JOHN BLAIR	48
YOUNG, EZEKIEL	50
YOUNG, FIELDEN	175

INDEX OF ILLUSTRATIONS

Benjamin Floyd Nuckolls	Frontispiece
Dr. David Sullins	vii
The Old Kitchen	1
The Old Nuckolls Homestead	9
Frances Bourne	17
Mastin Hale	21
Nuckolls Springs	25
The Hale Brick Residence	33
Elizabeth Blair Waugh	37
Cliffside	41
Residence of Captain John B. Waugh	49
Elizabeth Thomas	53
Col. Samuel McCamant	57
Matilda Dickinson McCamant	65
Nuckolls Cemetery	69
Clark Nuckolls and Wife	73
Residence of B. F. Nuckolls	81
Ballard E. Ward and Wife	85
James Stuart Ward	87
William Swift Nuckolls	89
Susan B. Hale	93
Margaret Swift	99
Martha Nuckolls	101
Hale Coat of Arms	105
The Hale Monument	113
Eli C. Hale	117
Lucinda Hale	121
Amanda J. Hale	125
Stephen Friel Nuckolls	129
Lucinda Bourne	133
Sophia P. Hale	135
Major Peyton G. Hale	137
Garland Coat of Arms	141
Landon C. Garland, LL. D.	145
The Garret Cemetery	147
Benjamin F. Nuckolls and Wife	195

THE OLD KITCHEN
Built by Lewis Hale, Sr., in 1770. Old Servants, Clarke and Charlotte

CHAPTER I

The portion of Southwest Virginia embraced in Grayson and Carroll counties, bounded by New River and Wythe county on the North, and by the Blue Ridge and state of North Carolina on the South, was first known as Botetourt District, afterwards, as Washington and Montgomery Districts.

New River was first called Woods River and afterwards changed to New River. A Mr. Woods discovered the river, and set up claims on lands on the waters of Crooked and Chestnut Creeks. Other boundaries were secured by Buchanan. Some of the titles to land on which the town of Galax is built run back to the old Buchanan papers.

In 1720, Spottsylvania was formed from portions of Essex, King William, and King and Queen counties, and was named for Col. Alexander Spottswood, who was one of the colonial governors of Virginia.

Orange was formed from Spottsylvania in 1734; Augusta from Orange in 1738; Botetourt from Augusta in 1769; Fincastle county was formed from Botetourt in 1772, and covered far more than half of the present state of West Virginia, all of the present state of Kentucky, and all of what we now know as Southwest Virginia.

In 1776, the county of Fincastle was abolished, and out of its territory three new counties were formed, to-wit: Montgomery, Washington, and Kentucky.

Montgomery was formed from Fincastle in 1776; Wythe from Montgomery in 1790; Grayson from Wythe in 1792; Carroll county from Grayson in 1842.

When Wythe county was formed from Montgomery in 1790 it included a large boundary reaching to the North

Carolina line on the South, and embracing what is now known as Grayson and Carroll counties.

Evansham (afterwards changed to Wytheville) was selected as the place to hold courts and elections, and all free holders were required to go there to vote.

The early settlers had selected land along New River and its tributary creeks, as they were most productive, and were rich with wild pea-vine and other vegetation for the stock.

They did not like to have the county seat so far removed from them, so they called for a county on the south side. Flower Swift was one of the magistrates of the Wythe court. He, with others, made an effort to get a county cut off from Wythe, but was met with violent opposition.

William Bourne was a candidate for the Legislature, but was not elected on account of his known intention to secure a new county. When the Legislature met, Bourne was there as a lobby member, and succeeded in carrying out his wishes. Mr. Grayson, of Montgomery county, gave much help in securing the new county, and in recognition of his services the county was named for him—"Grayson".

The first court was held in William Bourne's barn on Knob Fork of Elk Creek. Flower Swift, Minitree Jones, and Nathaniel Frisbie were appointed magistrates.

The members of the first court were Flower Swift, Enoch Osbourne, Minitree Jones, Nathaniel Frisbie, Philip Gaines, William Bourne, Nathaniel Pope, Matthew Dickey, Lewis Hale, and Moses Foley. William Bourne was appointed clerk of the court.

Records of the first court held in Grayson county, in William Bourne's barn, May 21st, 1793, and partial proceedings of some subsequent courts:

GRAYSON COUNTY, VA.   3

Be it remembered that on the 21st day of May, in the year of our Lord, 1793, at the house of Willaim Bourne, in the County of Grayson, a Commission of the Governor, Henry Lee, of the Commonwealth of Virginia, for the County aforesaid, directed to Flower Swift, Enoch Osbourne, Minitre Jones, Nathaniel Frisbie, Phillip Gaines, William Bourne, Nathaniel Pope, Mathew Dickey, Lewis Hale, and Moses Foley, Gent., bearing date the 10th day of December, 1792, was produced as being read, and thereupon Flower Swift took the Oath of Allegiance to the Commonwealth, the Oath to support the Constitution of the United States, the Oath of a Justice of the Peace, and the Oath of a Justice of the County Court in Chancery, which Oaths were administered to him by Minitree Jones and Nathaniel Frisbie, and then the said Flower Swift administered all the aforesaid Oaths to the aforesaid Enoch Osbourne, Minitre Jones, Nathaniel Frisbie, Phillip Gaines, William Bourne, Nathaniel Pope, Mathew Dickey, and Lewis Hale, who took the same.

A Commission from His Excellency, Henry Lee, Governor of the Commonwealth, to Phillip Gaines to be Sheriff of the County of Grayson to take effect from and after the 13 day of this instant, was produced by the said Phillip Gaines and Read, and thereupon, he, together with William Bobbitt and John Stone his Security, and entered into and acknowledged their bond for the said Phillip Gaines due performance of his Office, which is Ordered to be recorded and Flower Swift and Enoch Osbourne administered to the said Phillip Gaines the Oath of Allegiance to support the Commonwealth of the United States, and also the Oath of Sheriff.

At a Court held for Grayson County the 27th day of May, 1793.

                    Present:
                        FLOWER SWIFT
                        ENOCH OSBOURNE
                        NATHANIEL FRISBIE
                        NATHANIEL POPE
                        MATHEW DICKEY
                        LEWIS HALE
                            Gentlemen, Justices.

The Court proceeded to appoint a Clerk. Whereupon William Bourne was chosen to that office, and thereupon, he together with Thomas Blair, Jeremiah Stone, and John Stone, his Security, entered into and acknowledged their bond according to law for the said Bournes due performance of the duties of his said office, and the said William Bourne thereupon took the Oath of Allegiance, the Oath to support the Constitution of the United States, and the Oath of the Clerk of a County Court.

Present:
MINITRE JONES,
Gent.

Phillip Gaines, Esq., is Nominated as Surveyor, and it is Ordered that the same be certified to the president and professors of William and Mary College.

Alexander Smyth, Gent., produced License Signed by Richard Carey, Henry Taswell, and Edmond Winston, permitting him to practice as an Attorney in the Inferior and Superior Courts within this Commonwealth, and having taken the Oath prescribed by law, is admitted to practice in the Courts.

The Court adjourned until 10 o'clock tomorrow.

FLOWER SWIFT.

At a Court continued and held for the County of Grayson on the 22nd day of May, 1793.

Present:
MINITRE JONES,
NATHANIEL FRISBIE,
MATHEW DICKEY,
LEWIS HALE,
Gent.

William Drope is admitted a Deputy Clerk to this Court, whereupon he took the Oath prescribed by law.

Ordered, that for the purpose of appointing Commissioners to value property taken by E, the County be divided into two Districts, that part eastward of Meadow Creek and New River to form one end, and the residue of the County the other.

William Bobbitt, Jacob Colyar, and George Martin are appointed Commissioners to value property in the lower Eastern District; and Enoch Osbourne, David Cox, Stephen Goast, in the upper or Western District, and it is ordered that they be served with notice to qualify according to Law.

Present,
FLOWER SWIFT,
ENOCH OSBOURNE,
NATHANIEL POPE,
Gent.

The Court proceeded to fix upon a place of holding Courts, and fixed upon a place known by the name of Rose's Cabins, or within one mile thereof, and appointed the house wherein Court now sits as the place of holding Courts until publick buildings shall be erected.

Minitre Jones and Enoch Osbourne, Gent., entered their dissent to the order fixing the permanent place of holding Courts.

Absent, Flower Swift, Gent.

Charles Nuckolls, Flower Swift and Phillip Gaines, Gent., in Court agree that they will Convey to trustees for the use of the Courts, 100 Acres of land at the seat of the public buildings, one-half thereof to be laid out into Lots and Streets, and establish a Town; the balance to be Common, Reserving three half-acre Lotts at their choice after the Lotts were laid off.

Minitre Jones and Mathew Dickey, Gent., are appointed Commissioners on behalf of the Courts to fix on the situation for the publick Buildings within the District aforesaid, to receive from the proprietors of the Lands there a conveyance there of, or an Obligation for the Same, and to contract with an undertaker for the erection of the necessary buildings according to plans to be by them prepared, and finally to lay off a Town at the place; provided that the auction of the buildings shall be let by auction to the lowest bidder, on some Court day, on public notice.

Present,
FLOWER SWIFT,
Gent.

On motion of Phillip Gaines, Esq., David Vaughn is admitted a Deputy Sheriff in the County, whereupon he took the Oath prescribed by Law.

Alexander Smith is appointed Deputy Attorney for the Commonwealth, in this Court, which is ordered to be Certified to; And it is further ordered that he be allowed the Sum of Twenty pounds in the levy the present year, as a compensation for his services for one year from this time.

The Court also appoints Minitre Jones and Mathew Dickey to hold elections for overseer of the poor, the election to be held at the Forge on the 12th day of June next.

Ordered that Shadrack Greer and Tobias Phipps be recommended as Justices of the Peace for this County.

The Court appoints the officers for the regiment of Malitia; Ordered that Flower Swift be recommended as Leut. Col., Minitre

Jones, Major of the first Battalion, Avery Henick, Captain of Rifle Company, first Battalion, John Wilson, Leut., William Chaffin, Ensign.

James Anderson, Captain of Rifle Company, Second Battalion, William Vaughn, Lieut., and Geo. Levesy, Ensign.

There are 3 Companies for first Battalion, Three Captains, Nathaniel Pope, John McCoy, John Pickerell.

Second Battalion, Three Captains, Jonathan Ward, Abner Jones, George Howell.

Court adjourned until Court in Course.

FLOWER SWIFT,
Gent.

Court 10th of June, 1793:

A deed from Flower Swift and Mary his wife, to Mathew Dickey, proven by Minitre Jones, and Redmond Cody.

Ordered that Revd. Moses Foley be admitted to solemnize the rights of matrimony, agreeable to the rules of his church, so soon as he shall enter into bond according to law.

Ordered, that a road be opened from Blair and Dickey's furnace to the county line, From the Furnace to the ground where the Courthouse is to be erected, thence to the Forge, thence to William Jennings, Joseph Mill, Nathaniel Pope, James Cock, and William Williams (Wagoner), views the grounds to County line.

Dennis Fielder, Rubin Cornute, and William Long, who were at the last Court, appointed to view Different ways petitioned for by the Inhabitants of Elk Creek, upon their Oaths do say there may a waggon Road be made from Jeremiah Stones to Hale's Meeting house, from thence to the Widow Roarch Cabin, from thence to Richard Wrights, Sen., to Richard Wrights, Jun., and that the Survey of the same keep it in Repair according to Law.

Ordered that John Nash be allowed for the killing one Old Wolfe out of present County Levy.

Ordered that Joseph Fields be allowed for the killing one Old Wolfe out of present County Levy.

At a Court Continued for the Examination of a Negro man named Natt, the property of James Cox, on Suspicion of his Feloniously taking from Thomas Blair one Duck Blanket to the value of fifteen Shillings.

The above named Natt was led to the Bar, and upon Examination, denieth the Fact, Wherewith he stands charged, upon which several Witnesses were Sworn and examined, and the prisoner heard in his own Defence; On Consideration of which of the Circumstances relating to the Crime, the Court are of Opinion that he is guilty of the fact wherewith he stands charged, but the things being of Small Value, and the prisoner praying Corporal punishment, it is ordered that he Receive fifteen Lashes at the publick whippin post of the County on his bare back, well laid on, and it is said to the Sheriff that Execution thereof be immediately done.

Ordered that this Court adjourn until Court in Course.

FLOWER SWIFT.

A Suit on Bond given by Phillip Gainer.

Martin Dickenson...................Plf.
               v
Daniel Sheffy..........................Dft.

Upon a bond for the forthcoming of the property at the day of Sale upon an Execution obtained from Court.

Robert Sayers proved two days attendance as on evidence in the Suit Baker vs. English, and 16 miles traveling here, and the same returning each Day.

Baker vs. English Judy for £3. s15. 6 and cost.

The Court proceeded to Lay the County Levy, and find the Claims for and against the Same as follows, viz.:

To the Clerk's Publick Services the present year............. ....25 Dol.
The Sheriff same ... ...25 Dol.
To Clerks and Surveyor Book, &c,..50 Dol.
To Alexander Smith Att. Com.. ... .66.67.
To Creditors for Wolfe heads........... ....50 D.
To Clerks for examining Com. Books........ ....5 Dol.
To account for Delinquents..... .... 25.33 D.

Ordered that the Sheriff Collect the Levy and give Bond in the Clerk's Office in ten Days.

The Court proceeded to fix the rates to be observed by Ordinary keepers:

(You will see this Order on p. 35 in the old records of the first Courts for Grayson County which belongs to the Clerk's Office at Independence, Va. William Bourne, first Ordinary Keeper, at his house. B. F. N.)

COURT RECORDS
(See page 35)

The Court proceeded to fix the rates to be Observed by Ordinary keepers, viz.:

PIONEER SETTERS

	£	s	d
A breakfast with Coffee	0	1	3
Ditto Without Coffee	0	1	0
Dinner Warm, if good	0	1	6
Cold	0	1	3
Lodging Clean for 1 in bed	0	0	6
2 in bed	0	0	4
More than 2 in bed	0	0	0
Stableage pr night	0	0	6
Do pr 24 hours	0	0	9
Do. for less than 24 hours	0	0	6
Pasturage in Season pr night	0	0	6
Do. pr 24 hours	0	0	9
Corn pr. Gallon	0	0	8
Oats pr. Gallon	0	0	6
Wine Madera pr. quart	0	8	0
Do. inferior	0	5	0
West india rum pr half-pint	0	1	0
Cosbert Do per Do	0	0	6
Taffia Do pr. Do	0	0	6
French brandy pr. Do	0	0	9
Peach Do. per Do	0	0	6
Gin pr. Do	0	0	8
Whiskey pr. Do	0	0	6
Good Cider pr. qt	0	0	8
Good Beer pr. Do	0	0	6
Small beer	0	0	4

At a Court held for the County of Grayson on the 24th Day of June, 1794.

Present:
FLOWER SWIFT,
ENOCH OSBOURNE,
MINITRE JONES,
MATHEW DICKEY,
LEWIS HALE,
Gentlemen Justices.

Ordered that Joshua Cox be allowed in the next County Levy for the Killing of five Young Wolves."

"Ordered that this Court adjourn from the house of William Bourne to the New Courthouse, Court in Course". Last Court. Wm. B.'s House.

FLOWER SWIFT

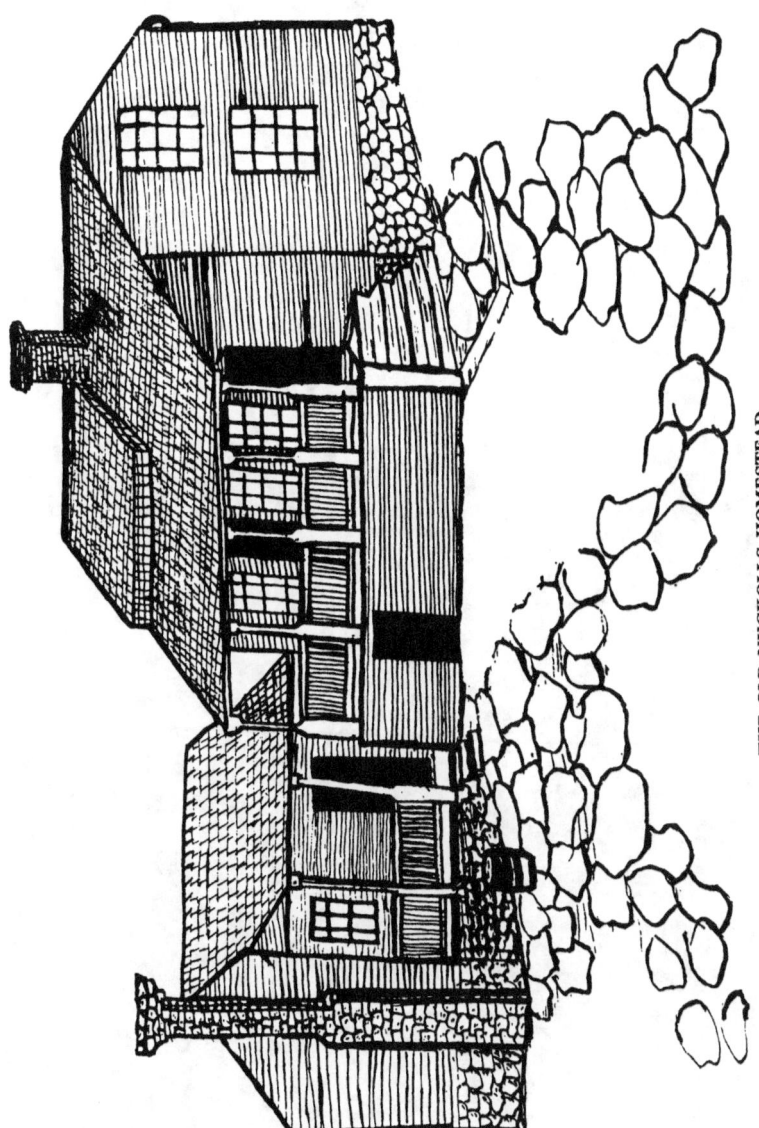

THE OLD NUCKOLLS HOMESTEAD
Built by Robert Nuckolls and Charles Garland in 1805; now owned by Stephen Nathaniel Nuckolls

GRAYSON COUNTY, VA.   9

First Court, N. C. House:
   At a Court held for the County of Grayson on the 22nd day of July, 1794.

                    Present:
                       FLOWER SWIFT,
                       NATHANIEL FRISBIE,
                       NATHANIEL POPE,
                       LEWIS HALE,
                                        Gent. Justices.

   Ordered that the Stock Mark of George Martin be Recorded a half Crop off the Left ear, and a half penny out of the right ear, viz.: the half Crop out of the upper side of the left and the half penny out of the underside of the right.
   A Deed from Mathew Dickey and Rebaca Dickey his wife to Thomas Blair, proven by the Oath of Greenberry McKinzie, and ordered to be Certified.
   A Deed from Flower Swift, and Mary his wife, to Jessie Williams was proven by the Oaths of William Allin, John Williams, and Augustus Webber, three of the witnesses there to, and O. R.
   On the motion of George Ring and Richard Hale, a certificate is granted for obtaining letters of administrations on the Estate of Martin Ring, and Whereupon they entered into with William Hale, Lewis Hale, Dudley Hale, and Jacob Spraker, their Securities, and qualified according to law.
   Ordered that John Fielder, Elisha Bedsaul, and Martin Dickenson be appointed to appraise the personal property and make report there of to Court.
   Ordered that Dudley Hale be appointed Overseer of the road in place of Timothy Roark, and that he, with the usual hands, keep the same in repair.
   On motion of Robert Nuckolls, who, having produced the receipt of the Clerk of this Court for the sum of Twelve Dollars and fifty Cents, a license is granted him to keep an Ordinary at his house in Greenville, One year from the first of May last, Whereupon he entered into bond with Security accordingly.
   A List of Insolvent Tythes for the year 1810 was produced in Court and allowed by the Court, aud proved by the Oath of Abner Jones.
   A Commission from his Excellency, James Wood, Leutenant Governor, in the absence of the Governor, appointing Abner Jones

and John Robertson Justice of the Peace for Grayson County in Chancery.

This closes the copies from the first Book of Record for the Courts of Grayson county. Said book begins with the date of the 21st day of May, 1793, and closes with the 31st of May, 1811.

First court held in new courthouse, on 22nd of July, 1794. Second courthouse built about 1838. County divided, and Carroll cut off of east end of Grayson, in 1842. (For record of First Court for Carroll, June, 1842, see F. L. Hale's obituary.) Independence was chosen as the county seat of Grayson, in 1850 or 1851. Orville Anderson was clerk. He moved to Independence, and died there soon after moving.

The following, in reference to the laying of the cornerstone of the M. E. Church at Fries, Virginia, is taken from The Roanoke Times of November 27th 1902:

NOTABLE DAY FOR FRIES

"The gods have indeed been kind to our infant city on this day of days in her history. The laying of the corner-stone of any pioneer church of any settlement is a vital event in the history of that place, and the people of Grayson, Wythe, Carroll and other counties, have beyond question shown their appreciation of this fact, as demonstrated by their large outpouring today. The occasion which gathered so many hundreds of noble women and men within the corporation of Fries today was the laying of the corner-stone of the M. E. Church, South. The ceremonies were entirely in the hands of the Masons and Odd Fellows and conducted in their very impressive style, each and every officer being in good voice and all were men of high intelligence and fine personal bearing. The Order of Rebekah, with its queenly membership, was in good evidence, and under command of its noble grand, Miss Donna Fielder. Marshals of the day were Dr. Koontz and R. L. Dickenson.

"Lodges were represented from Wytheville, Crozier, Ivanhoe, Hillsville, Old Town, Independence and Pulaski. Dixie Lodge, of this city, has for its worshipful master, Judge Padgett, of Grayson county court. The noble grand of Fries Lodge of Odd Fellows is J. D. Baley.

"Deposited in the corner-stone is a list of Old Town Lodge, No. 68, A. F. & A. M., names of charter members and names of members at this time; a list of members of Dixie Lodge, and time of organization; also a list of Fries Lodge, No. 39, I. O. O. F., with time of organization; a list of Fries Sunday-school; an account of the massacre of the Bartlett family and others by four runaway negroes on the 11th of August, 1851; list of trustees of the church; list of members of the church at this place; paper giving time of organization of Washington Mills and names of directors, copies of Holston Conference Annual, Methodist Discipline, Holston Methodist, Grayson Gazette, Grayson Journal, Virginia Odd Fellows, Christian Advocate, Wytheville Dispatch and Roanoke Times.

"The church building has brick foundation and is to be of wooden super-structure, with a seating capacity of about 800. It will be completed by spring and will have practically no debt hanging over it, due to the liberality of Col. Fries and the public. The church will be, as it now is, under the charge of Rev. T. C. Vaughan, a man of christian zeal and noble personality.

"Rev. E. F. Kahle, presiding elder of this conference, delivered the oration of the day. In clear, well modulated tones and classic style he portrayed the building of Solomon's temple, injecting the thought that, after the colossal work was done it fell short of the humblest meeting house of this era. Since it never knew the Savior of man. His masterful address received the closest attention and will be treasured a long time by those who heard him.

"Within a hundred feet of the church stands the public school, which, when completed, will accommodate 500 children.

"These buildings are under the architectural guidance of Capt. R. P. Henry, who has charge of the extensive and difficult building of this city.

"After the ceremonies matters were handed over to the tender care of a committee of ladies, who undertook, with happy result, the feeding of the vast multitude, serving a splendid dinner and supper.

"More anon from this strenuous little city."

The first trial held in the new court-house in Independence was that of the four negroes who were engaged in the fight of which an account is given below:

"An account of a fight or massacre that occurred with the Bartlett family, John Clements, William B. Hale and Currin C. Hale and four runaway negroes, on the grounds now occupied by the Fries Company, which fight or massacre took place on Monday morning, about 10 o'clock, August 11, 1851.

"William Bartlett and Elizabeth Paschel, his wife, moved to New River, Grayson county, Va., in 1834, with their two sons and one daughter—Samuel Bartlett, Alfred G. Bartlett and Matilda Bartlett, wife of Cyrus Wilcox.

"William B. Hale moved to the adjoining farm east on the river, with his son, Currin C. Hale, about 1838.

"John Clements moved to the mill west of Wm. Bartlett's, on the river, about 1847.

"In the Year 1849 two men came into the county of Grayson by the names of Bacon and Cook. These men claimed to be Methodist preachers from Ohio. They traveled over the county and preached. But it was soon known that they were "abolitionists" and that they were interfering with the negroes, talking with and advising them to run away and go to Ohio, and that they would help them get through.

"On Sunday night of the 10th of August, 1851, four negro men started for Ohio. Two of them, Simon and Lewis, belonged to John Reeves, and the other two, Jack and Henry, belonged to a man named Cox.

"These negroes got a canoe, armed themselves with butcher knives and scythe blades, and started down the river for Ohio. Their instruction from Bacon was to travel down the river at night and lay by in the daytime, and that he would meet them at the Kanawha Falls and take them across to Ohio. They reached the falls near the Clements' mills about daylight Monday morning, August 11, 1851, tied up their canoe and went up into a ravine in the woods and started a fire. The smoke was discovered by John Clements, who went into the woods and found the negroes in camp for the day.

"Mr. Clements sent Calvin Bobbitt for help to take the negroes. Samuel Bartlett, Alfred G. Bartlett, Cyrus Wilcox, William B. Hale, Currin C. Hale and Leftrick Hill came, with guns and a bulldog, and demanded their surrender.

"At once two commenced the fight, the other two running for the river. Samuel Bartlett was struck with a scythe blade and his head cut open. John Clements was cut on the head. Alfred G. Bartlett was struck on the head, cut on the wrist, and his thumb nearly cut off in his efforts to keep off the blows.

"The fight was then between A. G. Bartlett, Cyrus Wilcox and the two stout negroes. Wilcox seized one of the negroes and threw him to the ground. Alfred shot at the other, but failed to hit him, and the negro ran to

Wilcox and stuck the butcher knife through his neck, just missing the jugular vein. Bartlett struck the negro Simon across the back with his gun barrel, having broken the breech of his gun in the fight.

"In this severe and desperate struggle Bartlett and Wilcox so disabled these two negroes that they surrendered. The other two were pursued by W. B. and C. C. Hale. Several shots were fired at them without effect. Currin Hale struck at one with his gun barrel and bent it. Jack threw a rock and struck William Hale on the neck. The other did not attempt to fight, but ran into the river and was caught by the bulldog.

"Thus the bloody struggle ended for the day. Sam'l Bartlett lived about six hours. John Clements afterwards died in Nebraska of his wounds. Cyrus Wilcox recovered; also Wm. Hale and Alfred Bartlett. Only two are now living who were in this bloody and dangerous fight— Alfred Bartlett and Currin Hale. Hale lives in Nebraska. Bartlett remained at the old home until he sold to the Fries M'f'g Co., and now lives near-by. He has by his energy and enterprise reared a large and respectable family, and amid his affliction and disabled condition continues as one of Grayson county's best citizens.

"Two of the negroes left at the camp—Simon and Lewis —revived, tied up their wounds and started again for Ohio, but after several days were captured in Bland county—one in a house stealing something to eat—the other in a corn field stealing corn. The other two—Jack and Henry—went back to their home. They were all brought to Independence and tried in court. Henry was released, as he did not fight. Simon, Lewis and Jack were condemned to hang, and were executed on Friday, Nov. 1, 1851, at Independence, Grayson Co., Va.

"After this massacre the county was in a state of excitement and men gathered from Old Town, Elk Creek,

Knob Fork and other places to search for the man Bacon, who had caused the trouble and bloodshed, as he had told these negroes to fight their way through. Bacon was found at Amos Moore's, but before the men could catch him he ran to Iron Mountain and got away. If he had been caught he would doubtless have been hanged at once. Cook had disappeared before this time.

"The foregoing facts are known to many of us, but have not gone into history.

"We therefore desire these facts to be placed by the hands of Alfred Bartlett in the corner-stone of the church, to be laid at Fries on Nov. 21, 1902, as this M. E. Church, South, is being built on the former Bartlett estate and on the ground where Sam'l Bartlett lived at the time of his being killed in the fight.

"Given under my hand, and by the assistance of Alfred G. Bartlett, an eye witness and actor in this distressing piece of history. Written on the 16th day of Nov., 1902.

"BEN FLOYD NUCKOLLS,
"Minister of M. E. Church, South."

Carroll county was named for Charles Carroll, of Carrolton, Maryland, who was one of the signers of the American Declaration of Independence. He survived all the other signers by six years, and had been dead only ten years when Carroll county was formed.

The following was copied from the record of Carroll's first court:

First order: "Be it remembered that on the sixth day of June 1842, a commission of the peace for the county of Carroll from John M. Gregory, Lieutenant Governor of the Commonwealth of Virginia, acting as Governor, under the seal of the Commonwealth, directed to Joshua Hanks, John Blair, Benjamin Cooley, John Cocke, William Lindsey, John B. Mitchell, Hugh Currin,

William Raines, William C. Hall, and John Vaughn, and bearing date March 29th, 1842.

"Whereupon, the several persons named above appeared and took the several oaths required by law as Justices of Carroll county, which said oaths were administered to them by Thomas McCabe, a justice of the peace in Floyd county."

The record then recites that these justices opened court in the house of James Stafford, in Hillsville, Virginia. Harold Mathews was appointed clerk pro. tem. of the court. A. S. Fulton, Benjamin R. Floyd, Richard T. Mathews, Archabald Stuart, Samuel McCamant, William H. Cook, Madison T. Carter, and Joseph C. Spalding were admitted as attorneys to practice law in the court. William Lindsey was then elected clerk of the court, and Harold Mathews qualified as his deputy. James L. Mitchell was appointed county surveyor, and Robert Kenny, coroner. Nathaniel W. Vaughn, Franklin Clements, Joshua Hanks, Jr., Jonathan R. Sumner, Joshua G. Mabey, Thomas Dalton, Lacy Bobbitt, William Lewis, and John Webb were appointed constables for the county. The court remained in session for two days and adjourned to meet again on the 30th of June (1842) at the house of Parks Ashworth in Hillsville, Virginia.

FRANCES BOURNE
Daughter of William Bourne, Sr., and wife of Stephen Hale, Sr.

CHAPTER II

THE BOURNE FAMILY

From the account given of the formation and early history of Grayson county, we learn that William Bourne was a man of much force, and had a large share in developing the county.

Following is a copy of the family record of William Bourne and Rosamond Jones, his wife, in the old Bourne Bible, now the property of Mrs. Elizabeth D. Lundy, widow of Fielden Johnston Lundy, and youngest daughter of Stephen Bourne and wife, Patty Mays: "Stephen Bourne (Grey) was the son of William Bourne and his wife, Rosamond Jones. Rosa Jones, wife of William Bourne, was a daughter of Minitree Jones, Sr., who married Miss Spottswood. Rosa Jones had three brothers, Minitree, Jr., Spottswood and Churchill, all of Revolutionary fame."

BIRTHS AND DEATHS

William Bourne, born August 23, 1743.

Rosamond, his wife, born Feburary 14th, 1750.

Rosamond, wife of William Bourn, Sr., died 16th March, 1821, age 71 years.

William Bourn, Sr., died June 8th, 1836, aged 88 years.

Stephen Bourn, G., departed this life April the 29th, 1849, on Sunday, 12 minutes after 8 o'clock in the morning.

Patsy Bourn, his wife, departed this life, April the 29th, 1849, on Sunday, 35 minutes after 9 o'clock in the morning. (Only 1 hour and 23 minutes after her husband.)

Children of William Bourn and his wife, Rosamond Jones, were seven daughters and two sons, as follows:

First, Patience, November 18th, 1770. Married Jonathan Thomas.

Second, Milly, March 7th, 1773. Married Jessie McKinney.

Third, Charity, November 7th, 1775. Married John Blair.

First, Stephen, February 26th, 1779. Married Patsy Mays.

Fourth, Mary, January 5th, 1782. Married Martin Dickinson.

Fifth, Elizabeth, March 20th, 1785. Married Capt. Lewis Hale.

Sixth, Frances, June, 5th 1788. Married Stephen Hale, Sr.

Seventh, Celia, December 25th, 1790. Married Robert Johnstone, Roaring River, Wilkes county, N. C.

Second, William, May 4th, 1794. Married Mary Johnstone, Roaring River, Wilkes county, N. C.

The seven daughters and two sons lived to be old, and brought up large families; also raised a number of negroes.

The seven daughters were all widows, at the same time, and by their energy and perseverance managed their estates well. None of the family married the second time.

The following is copied from the Southwest Virginia Enterprise of March, 1912:

"The following paper was read by Miss Bertha Nuckolls of Galax at a meeting of the Women's Missionary Society held in the Galax Methodist Church March 1st, 1912. We clip from the Post-Herald:

"The first missionary woman of Grayson county was Rosa Bourne. Rosa Jones was a descendant of James Jones, brother of Admiral Paul Jones and lived on a large grant of land near Fredericksburg, Virginia.

"About the year of 1765, Rosa Jones was married to

William Bourne in Hanover county, Virginia, near Richmond. Soon after their marriage they left the old colonial home and moved out into the wilderness of New River, which was then Botetourt and Washington district, but now Grayson county.

"On their move they came as far as Fort Chiswell in wagons, and from there they packed their baggage on horses across Iron Mountain to Knob Fork, and settled on the waters of New River, and commenced to open up this country. At that time there were but eight settlers in this part of the country.

"They built cabins and other temporary buildings and cleared out the best portion of the land. Soon after they came here, they discovered iron ore and in addition to his other work, Wm. Bourne began to work the ore in a crude way and finally developed the mineral. He built forges, and also a furnace for moulding castings at the fall of Peach Bottom Creek, near what is now Independence. There are marks where the old furnace stood. There is now at this place an electric plant and the electricity is used to run the mills and light the town of Independence.

"When William Bourne and young wife started their married life in the wilderness of S. W. Virginia, they possessed foresight and perseverance, and prepared the way for progress and civilization, and did much to make this wilderness blossom as the rose. Their descendants have been and are yet found among the foremost men and women of this country. By perseverance and energy they opened the way for usefulness and prosperity for the coming generations.

"Rosa Bourne was always kind to their negroes and provided well for them. She was their doctor when sick, their comfort in trouble, a Christian woman and would say to the sick all around about her, 'You must pray to the Lord for help, and I will pray for you and help you all I can.' She would go to all her friends and neighbors and help them in time of need.

"They had two sons and seven daughters, all married and settled in this country, reared large families, who have been representatives both in church and state over 150 years past; in fact their generations have settled this part of the country.

"Rosa Bourne was born February 14th, 1750.

"William Bourne and wife lived and died on Knob Fork and are buried where he built his first house. His land estate was inherited by his youngest son, Wm. Bourne, Jr., who, having brought up his family there, sold 2700 acres to Dr. Gage. Since then his home has been owned by some of his descendants, and is now held by Prof. F. R. Cornett, and son, Glenn, whose wife, Agnes Phipps, daughter of Columbus Phipps, is a direct descendant of Patience Bourne.

"Rosa Bourne died March 16th, 1821, age 71 years.

"William Bourne died June 8th, 1836, age 88 years.

"Their graves are marked with large tombstones made by hand of soapstone. These tombstones and the inscriptions were the works of John Blair who married Charity Bourne, daughter of William and Rosa Bourne."

The following clipping was printed in a Marion paper several years ago:

"Ballard E. Ward, Esq., who is the owner of one of the largest and best farms in Grayson county, has an old log barn upon his farm, in a good state of preservation, in which the first county court of Grayson county was held after the county was formed. The old barn is very large and to cover it requires 36,000 shingles. On the same farm there is a very old graveyard, which has been abandoned for many years as a burying ground. On one

MASTIN HALE
Eldest Son of Stephen Hale, Sr., and wife, Frances Bourne, and the First of Thirteen Children. He died in his ninety-eighth year

of the tombstones appears the following singular inscription, which was done about 53 years ago:

> Here Rosa Bourne's body laid
> of whom in truth no harm was said.
> Her Sovereign will was much obeyed
> While here with us on Earth she Stayed
> Because that her deportment made
> through perfect love, all feel afraid.
>
> the Man who wrote these lines to tell
> of her character knew her well
> He put these lines upon the Stone
> To make it to the readers Known,
> That they like her may do the same,
> In order to obtain a name
> And to perpetuate their fame.

Among the household goods of William Bourne was a "Grandfather Clock," a sketch of which is given below:

THE OLD BOURNE CLOCK

This clock was brought to what is now Grayson county, about the year 1770. This was the first clock that was brought to this upper part of the New River Valley and was the property of William Bourne and his wife, Rosa Jones. After the death of William Bourne and his wife (1836) it passed into the hands of Stephen Bourne, their son; from him to his son, Martin Bourne; from him to his son, Montgomery Bourne; from him to Benj. Floyd Nuckolls, great grandson of William Bourne and wife, and from him to Ruth Nuckolls Johnston, Cleveland, Tenn. The clock is running and keeping correct time, in this the year of 1913. It is all made of the best material, and the case and works show the ingenuity and taste of an honest workman.

The case of the clock is made of mahogany, and stands eight feet, three inches from the floor to the tip of the central brass knob on top of the clock. The trimmings are of brass, and there are rows of different colored blocks of wood inlaid around the case.

The wheels and pendulum are of brass, and the weights are cast iron. It is an eight-day clock, and is wound with a brass key.

There is no date on the clock but it was brought to Grayson county about the year 1770. The following is copied from a card that was tacked inside the case when the clock arrived in Grayson.:

Common House Clocks, Table Spring Clocks. Time Pieces of different Conftructions.

MADE BY
AARON WILLARD
Boston

Directions for fitting up the clock:

Firft, plumb up the cafe and hang on the pendulum and weights obferving that the heavieft weight be put on the pulley marked "S". Wind up the lines on the barrels, taking care that they run regularly in the grooves, then put the pendulum in motion.

To make it go faster, screw the pendulum up; slower, screw down.

On the face of the clock is the following:

WARRANTED FOR
MR. BENJN. STETSON.

YARON WILLARD,
BOSTON.

The clock is now in the possession of Ruth Frances Nuckolls Johnston, who was named "Frances" for her great-grandmother, Frances Bourne.

She is the fifth generation from William Bourne and she says this old clock, which must be one hundred and fifty years old, is the best time-keeper in the house.

At the time William Bourne settled here, there were no mills nearer than over the Blue Ridge in North Carolina, at the foot of the mountain, then called "Over in the

Hollow." The grain to be ground for bread had to be carried in sacks on horses. There was only a bridle path across New River and the mountain—frequently on the old Indian trails. Wm. Bourne would make these trips with his negro men, each with a sack of grain to have ground for bread (mostly corn.) At one time, on their return from the mill, one man caught his sack of flour against a limb near the path on the mountain, tore the sack, and spilled some flour. From that circumstance, the place was called Flour Gap. It still bears that name. It is near the crossing of the Blue Ridge at Pipers Gap. For years the Flour Gap was the only place for crossing the Blue Ridge. The first road across that part of the Ridge was at this place; trimmed out in a straight course up and down the mountains.

These trips to the mill had to be made in the fall of the year; and, at one time, when the men had gone, there fell a deep snow, and kept them longer than usual, and the family was without something to eat. Rosa Bourne got up early one morning, called a negro woman, and said to her, "We must hunt for something to eat." They took the rifle gun and butcher knife, and started out; and soon found a large deer, sleeping in the snow under a fallen tree top. Rosa raised her gun and fired; the deer jumped up, struck its head against a limb, and broke its neck. She, with the negro woman, ran with the butcher knife and cut the deer's throat, dragged him to the house on the snow, and the family lived on venison and hominy until the men returned with meal and flour.

In that day, all the clothing was made out of wool, cotton and flax. Leather was tanned in a big trough, for shoes and moccasins; nails, hinges, and all tools were made in blacksmith shops. At one time, William Bourne, when he was a member of the Legislature in Richmond, went down in a wagon loaded with fur skins and sold them. A negro woman and little girl were put on the block for sale; he bought them, paid for them, and sent them back home in the wagon. The woman's name was Granny Beck. The girl's name was Aimy. I have heard Aimy say that she and her mother were sent for one evening to go and stay all night with a woman. Sometime after dark, someone came to the door and called. This woman told her to open the door; she did so, and two men came in and caught her and her mother, tied cloths over their mouths, carried them off and put them in a ship, and brought them over the ocean. They came from Africa and proved to be very valuable servants.

Granny Beck, after she came here, took charge of the cattle and stock out on the range; salted and watched after them. She could not count the number, but if one of them were missing she could tell it. She would describe its colour or its size, etc., and would hunt until she found it.

Aimy was the house girl, waited on her master and mistress as long as they lived, and was very much attached to all the family.

William Bourne, in his last will stated that "Aimy has been a faithful, good servant, and has raised for me 18 children. She is not to be sold or taken in, in the divide." With his children, she should be free to go where she pleased. She came to Old Town (then Grayson C. H.), and lived with Mrs. Mary Dickenson. Mrs. Dickenson owned "Mourning," one of the 18 children. After Mrs. Dickenson's death, Aimy went to Elk Creek to my grandmother, Frances Hale, who owned "Winny", who was also one of the 18 children. Aimy died there, and is buried in the Hale family cemetery.

First daughter, Patience Bourne, married Johnathan Thomas; First son, Stephen, married Rebecca Perkins, daughter of Timothy Perkins and wife Miss Anderson.

NUCKOLLS SPRINGS
(Lithiated Iodo-bromo, Arsenic Water) Discovered by B. F. Nuckolls in 1886

Stephen lived on North Fork (now Creston), Ashe county, N. C. Second son, William Thomas, married Mary Pugh; one son, Stephen lived on Wilson Creek, afterward moved west. William Thomas and Mary Pugh had five daughters:

Ann, married Mr. Reeves; Susan, married Enoch Cox; Ludema married Alexander Phipps (See Phipps family); Amelia married Andrew Young of Wilson; sons: Dr. S. E. Young, Baywood, Va.; Dr. Robey Young, of Florida; Floyd Young, of Wilson; one daughter married Mr. Jones, of Ashe county, N. C.

Randolph and Johnathan were sons of Johnathan Thomas and wife, Patience Bourne. Randolph first settled on Bridle Creek, Va. Johnathan settled on Fox Creek, Va., married Miss Grabill. The daughters of Johnathan Thomas and wife, Patience Bourne, were Mary, Elizabeth, Rosa. Mary married Robert Pugh, lived on Wilson; had one daughter, Rosa, who marr ed Calvin Senter; one daughter married Mr. Reeves. One son, Stephen Pugh, who lived on Wilson.

Elizabeth Thomas married Samuel Cox and lived on Bridle Creek. (See Cox family.) Rosa B. married Shadrach Greer; they lived on Wilson Creek, Va.,

Milly Bourne married Jessee McKinney, settled on Arrat River, near Mt Airy, N. C. First son, William McKinney, remained at the old home near Buffalo Shoals, Arrat River, N. C.

Second son, Winston, married Miss Fulton; sons: Jessie and Cleveland.

Third son, Willis, married Miss Mollie Hale, daughter of Eli C. Hale and wife, Miss Frances Scott, of Elk Creek, Va., no issue. One daughter, Miss Polly McKinney, died single; one daughter, Ada, married.

Charity Bourne married John Blair, son of Thomas Blair and Rebecca Andrews. His ancestors came from Scotland.

John Blair and his family were quite prominent in the development and improvement of this country. Mr. Blair was for several years a Representative in the Virginia legislature. One of his old negro slaves used to say frequently, "Old Massa gone to Richmond to make de laws."

He was candidate for re-election when the vote was taken to cut off the county of Carroll from Grayson. John Carl was his opponent for the new county, and was elected over Blair. A slander suit was brought by John Carl, or Carroll, as he claimed to be, and John Blair wrote the following, which he called an "Epistle," and had it printed as it appears below:

The Epistle General of John Blair
Dedicatory to David McComes, Esqr.

JOHN BLAIR. The preacher—(so denominated at the Field's Precinct election in Grayson County in 1842, by a man, who then, and for some time previous assumed the name of John Carroll. "Insomuch as I am the Apostle" of the Protestant Democrats in my diocess, "I magnify my office.") To David McComas, Esqr. intended for the benifit of the community.

In Greenville, in the street
When there we last did meet
How I progress'd in rhimes you enquir'd?
As I then was not well
And did not stand to tell
These many answers, what you then desired.

I rhym'd as I design'd
And still kept the same mind,
Not to have Popery to rule our nation;
I thought we'd incur blame
If a Popish great name
Should be vaunted in our generation.

GRAYSON COUNTY, VA.

Charles Carrol was so great
With such lordly estate,
No title the United States carried
That was high enough styl'd.
To match with his grand child,
She was sent to England to get married.

She was handsome and young
And was high fam'd among
The celebrated belles of our nation;
But our democrat plan,
Afforded not a man
That was high enough styl'd for her station.

So she yielded her hand
To a Lord in England;
The Lord Marquis of Wellesly in splendor;†
Third rank next to the King,
Such high honors would bring
That her heart she resolved to surrender.

He was ugly and old,
But high titles and gold
Does with Catholic cure all defection;
For so their practice tells.
Gold can save them from hell,
And for heaven insure their election.

Charles Carroll's brother John,
Was to England sent on.*
He went there for to get consecrated
Implicit faith to fit
He became Jesuit.
An order democrats always hated.

Carroll's were noble blood
That cross'd the briney flood,
When, in England King Charles rul'd the nation;

†Said to be 65 years old.
*See Libers, Encyclopedia under title Carroll.

He money for to gain.
For to help conquer Spain,
Sold to Papists Maryland plantation.‡

Some twelve hundred came o'er,
Under Lord Baltimore,
And a Catholic coloney planted
Without faith or hope,
But what came from the Pope.
In the land, by King Charles to them granted.

Of whom Carrolls came,
Rais'd in opulent fame.
Till the colonies form'd a new notion,
That a government free,
Uncontroll'd beyond sea,
They would have on this side of the ocean.

Charles Carroll for some cause,
Perhaps to gain applause,
In government, to advance his station;
Or permanently fix
All rule by Catholics,
In this our North American nation.

A declaration sign'd
Which shew'd he had a mind,
From the crown of Great Britain to sever;
But from everything shown,
Was it not for his own
Roman Catholic views for to favor?

John a vicar was made,
Which was the highest grade
That could be raised by Popish promotion;
With supreme sovereign sway,
In directing the way
Of Catholics this side of the ocean.

‡The early settlements of the colonies were called plantations.

The Pope and Cardinals,
So general history tells,
Claim rule over all in earth and heaven;
What real true democrat,
Has faith to believe that,
Such despotic rule Christ would have given?

When Christ himself has said,
There's no superior grade
No Rabbi to rule over another;
But Christ, master of all,
None else is great or small
But evry one equal a brother.*

Over bodey and soul,
They claim to have control
Assuming to themselves power given,
That for money in their hand,
They have sovereign command,
To consign souls to hell or to heaven.

Have we not cause to fear,
From the news far and near,
Of the Pope's power gaining assendance?
May it not as before,
So increase more and more,
Till it overwhelms all independence?

Do we not hear again
In France like unto Spain,
The freedom of conscience is prevented;
By that old popish plan,
Form'd to rule over man,
By the Devil, thro' priestcraft invented.†

---

*Mathew 23rd and 8th.

†It is not my design to make individuos aspersions but as Christ called Peter Satin, which is an adversary—the prince of hell, or the devil, when he used dissimulation. Mathew 16 and 23 and as he must have been moved by the devil when he swore a lie. Mathew 26 and 72 and again when he dissembled and carried away the people from uprightness and the truths of the gospel, Gal. 2 and 11th to 15th does it not appear that if Peter was the church's foundation, when the devil carried him away the church must have fallen at least without foundation for when he carried away, he was not there, so he must have been gone.

If the ratio holds on
As for twelve months it's gone,
Of the increase of popish ascendance.
Here as in France and Spain,
Nothing free will remain
In a century, but on pope dependance.

Just listen from New York,
How the priest are at work,
And from Canada coming to aid them?
To serve their subtile turn,
All the Bibles they burn
The donations that charity made them?

That time fault reached a pope
Proved an end to their scope
Of infallible sovereign dictation,
And prov'd their scheme absurd
Of pretending Christ's word
Ordained such esseatial to salvation.

Else pope Gregory was right,
And pleasing in God's sight,
When hearing King Charles tolerated
Without any restraints
The destruction of Saints,
Till Protestants were exterminated.*

When the Prodestants blood,
Flow'd on the earth like a flood,
The Pope's joy burst out in acclamation;
And to show his joy more,
Caused his cannons to roar,
And held mass to invoke consecration.

Back to Attilla go,¶
General history will show
As pace for ten cent'ries and longer
The popes tyranic reign'd
Absolute, till restrained
By physical force that was stronger.

*See Buck's Theology under title "Persecution in France."
¶Attilla the first King crowned by the Pope.

How does rule absolute
With democracy suit?
Is it not a complete solecism
To say democracy
Can with tyrants agree
What! a democratic despotism!

Now I cannot agree
Acquiescent to see
A man raised under popish direction,
Take such sway in our land,
As to boast, he can stand
To defy other men in election.

When report of his fame
From Lynchburg, whence he came,
Lacks much of what is good reputation,
So I think the best way
Whare he is let him stay
Least we partake of his degradation.

If Squire Lindsey swore true,
And captain Worrell too*

---

*Capt. Jesse P. Worrell's deposition before commissioners appointed by Grayson court was as follows:

Question by John Blair—what do you know of John Carroll, having a ticket of your vote at the last Presidential election at Baskerville precinct'?

Ans. I wrote my name on a ticket, on the morning of the Presidential election, and gave it to Col. Carrol, who remarked that he (Col. Carrol) would take the ticket to the election, and see if it would not do, but observed that he did not think it would be legal.
                                                                Jesse P. Worrell.

William Lindsay, after being duly sworn deposeth and saith:

Question by John Blair—what do you know of John Carrol having a ticket of Jessee P. Worrell vote at the last presidential election?

Answer. Col. Carrol asked me on the day of the Presidential election, previous to the commencement of the election if a vote could be taken by a man sending his ticket, and stated that Jessee Worrell had sent his to the election. I told him that the vote could not be legally taken in that way. After the commencement of the election, I heard Jessee P. Worrell's vote cried; how it came into the sheriff's hands I know not. The vote was challenged, an erased from the poll book. Question by same—was Col. Carrol a commissioner to superintend the election at that place? Ans. He was.
                                                                William Lindsey.

Thomas Blair after being duly sworn deposeth and saith;

Question by John Blair—was you the sheriff that conducted the election at the Baskerville precinct? Ans. I was.

Question by the same—was Jesse P. Worrell's ticket handed to you and if so by whom? Ans. It was handed to me, and my impression is that it was handed to me by Col. Carrol; and I cried it and it was entered on the poll book; and I cried no vote but what was handed to me by the Commissioners or voters; and after the vote was cried and entered, it was objected to by Mitchell, erased off the poll book.
                                                                Thomas Blair.

And Thomas Blairs oath with theirs be respected;
As commissioners took,
And wrote down in a book,
As by Grayson court record directed.

What of it can you make,
But his oath did he break,
When he swore he'd have all votes prevented;
Except legally brought
Yet illegal he thought
Was a vote he himself had presented?

What those three did dispose
Was the truth to disclose,
That at the presidential election
After kissing the book,
To swear none should be took,
But votes legal under his inspection?

Did John Carroll there present,
A ticket by him sent,
Illegal as he himself said he thought it;
Being doubtly apprised,
By his council advised,
Should evince that he could not have forgot it.

What John (called) Carrol tho't.
Can you think he forgot,
If leaving Captain Worrell's he thought it,
When he started to go
To Baskerville's, we know;
On the road he could hardly forget it.

If so when he got there,
Oath of office to swear,
He consulted Squire Lindsey about it;
Then what did he thare do
But swore what proved not true
Can reason be tortured to doubt it?

THE HALE BRICK RESIDENCE
Built by Eli C. Hale in 1854

Illegal, then he brought
A ticket so he thought,
With him from Captain Worrell that morning;
Contrary we find both,
To sacredness of oath,
And contrary to Squire Lindseys warning.

Did he then violate
His oath unto the state?
Willfully and corrupt did he break it,
If such should appear plain,
Why trust his oath again?
What more then would prevent him to break it?

Then how would John Carrol stand;
In a civilized land,
Where truth and real honor is regarded?
Whose end to enjoy,
Disdained vice to employ,
Nor wonld have else but virtue rewarded.

Would it not be a shame
To evry voter's name.
If it was proved to a demonstration,
That the representative,
Made by the votes they give,
Maintained such — a **** reputation?

John Carl's fame to know,
Just back to Lynchburg go,
To men who are with him well acquainted
Go there when your're amind,
His character you'll find
In glowing colors well represented.

Go there when you think fit,
His character you'll get
As well as it can be given by men;
You need not further go
Than to Jacob Rumbough,
John R. D. Payne and David R. Lyman.

There's a lawyer named Brown,
Near the road you go down
To Lynchburg near Staunton you'll find him,
Who can tell you Carl's fame,
Ere he altered his name,
And the character he left behind him.

Thare's a man whom we know
Oft to Lynchburg doth go,
By the name of Andrew Jackson Durnal,
Who could tell if he would,
That Carl's fame there was good,
Or the reverse if was infernal.

Creed Nuckolls could relate,
What men generally state,
When hearing Grayson was represented
By a man of such fame
As follows John Carl's name,
By men of old best with him acquainted.

Friel Nuckolls, too as well
As Creed the same could tell,
From trav'ling to Lynchburg and thro' it,
His chance was just the same,
To hear of John Carl's fame,
From men who in former times well knew it.

Squire James Waugh you all know,
Has to Lynchburg to go,
To get goods to suit his ocupation:
He passing to and fro,
Did hear as much for to show
How John Carl's fame would suit Legislation.

On my rights to intrude,
By John Carrol I'm suad;
By him who is not found in our nation;
Just because that foresooth,
I did publish the truth,
That voters might have due information.

GRAYSON COUNTY, VA.

Can there be any ground,
Till a plaintiff is found,
For a verdict in any court given
Was the like ever known.
Or in all history shown
On record in court under Heaven?

What is life worth to me
To value property
If from freedom of speech I must lose it?
If my country says so,
n God's mame let it go;
For freedom of speech I'd rather choose it.

Though I yield in God's name,
It clears no one of shame;
For in his great day of retribution,
When he displays his might.
He will bring all things right
For in his plans he'll have no confusion.

Read for that freedom took,
For it in history look,
Of that country from which Carl migrated;
You'll see thousands of lives.
Children husbands and wives,
Lost for it in that history related.

Then why should I be slack,
And faintly fly the track,
That martyrdom had marked for example;
No! I will not give back,
But stand up to the rack
Though my country should my fodder trample.

I would have my rhimes seen
Ostensively to mean,
To keep our realm from popery prevaded;
That pure Democracy,
Might keep our concience free
From crouching under despots degraded.

In a canvass speech made,
John call'd Carrol has said,
As to God, and the people was praying.
That he'd wish for to be
Governed by popery,
For this was the purport of his saying.

Now who among you all,
Could so wish for to fall,
Under control of one man's dominion;
Who would doom you to hell
If you pleased him not well,
Can Demo's entertain such an opinion.

A despot for to find
Of most tyranic mind
Need we pass by the pope for to find him;
Who claims sovreign control
Over bodey and soul
Wheres the true democrat who'd thus mind him.

Before he'd hazzard all,
For to stand or to fall;
Would he not hazzard his blood and treasure;
Before it should be said,
He, himself would degrade
To crouch into such vassal-like measure.

On the hypothesis,
That CARROL god's mouth did kiss,
To swear he'd odject all votes not lawful;
Then poll a vote he brought,
As unlawful he thought
To good concience, does not it look awful?

While English language meant
To define represent,
As likeness of the thing represented:
And voters such to see
I'd like they'd show me
How votes such is from shame prevented?

[The Bible being God's word 2nd Thessalonians, 2nd and 8th must it not proceed from his mouth:

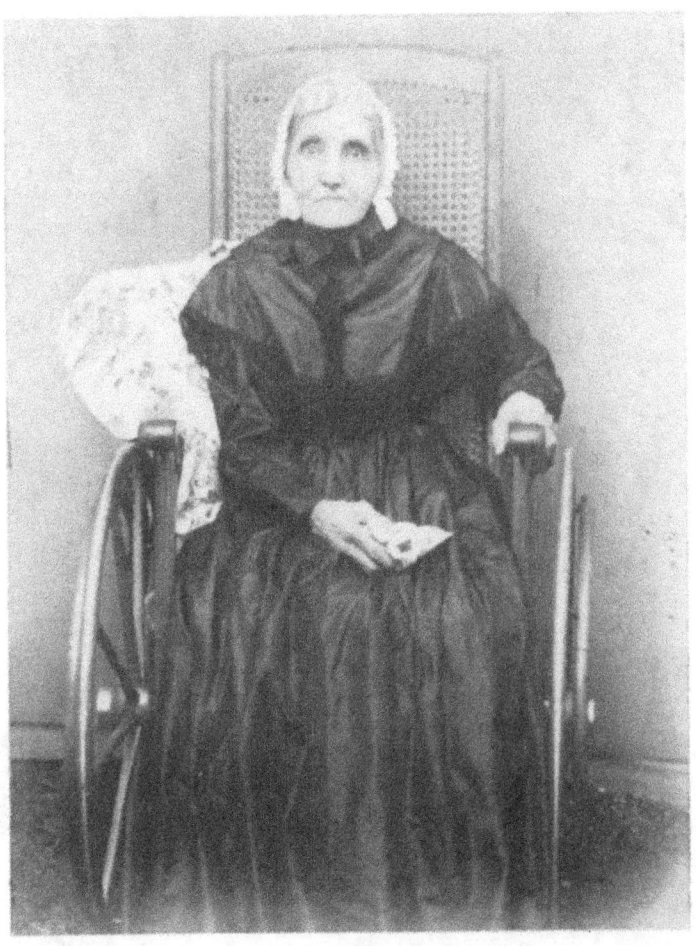

ELIZABETH BLAIR WAUGH
Daughter of John Blair and wife, Charity Bourne, and wife of James Waugh

If such vice we promote,
Are we not a scape goat,†
Bearing sins of him who represented us;
Now you can by your vote,
From that most grevious tote,
From that infamous shame may prevent us.

I set out with intent
The Popes power to prevent,
To that end I would spend and be spended,
My course looks dredful hard,
But I look for reward,
Perhaps not till all labors are ended,

I mean to do my best,
The Pope's power to arrest.
That free concience may be tolerated;
And pure Democracy
Make our whole country free,
With all despotic rules abrogated.

To sacrifice my all
Or obey virtues call,
I have set my determed resolution.
Determed not to draw back
Or to fly virtues track,
What ere the result in conclusion.

I'm resolved full intent,
For to spend and to be spent,
If circumstances should so require
Not to fly virtues track,
Nor dastardly look back,
If God helps me: not even through fire.

This rule I embraced young,
To view all things as dung.*

†Leviticus 16th and 20th.
*Philipians, 3rd and 8th.

Great Jefferson did see,
God made man to be free,
And so pen'd in our constitution;
Inviolate I'm bent,
To keep that instrument;
And, so set my determ'd resolution.

First our grand bill of right,
In which my soul delights,
Formed by democratic resolution;
Afterwards was adjoin'd
And so fitley combin'd,
In our great glorified constitution.

So come woe, or come weal,
To that poll I'd appeal;
Not to violate it in a fraction,
So come peace or come war
Its my polar star,
And the magnet of my souls attraction.

As with tears in my eyes,
I solmnly advise
My country not to be represented,
By a man of such fame,
That might load us with shame,
By your votes you might keep such prevented.

When Carl, to our land came,
Did he record his name,
And his oath for his naturalization;
In Amelia county
May you that record see,
The first name gave himself in our nation.

Was not that still his name,
Till to Lynchburg he came
To fix it on his sign to shew it;
Over his door to tell,
He had goods there to sell,
That all wishing to purchase might know it.

That to prevent what duty should require;
To desert that rule now
Would be like the washed sow,
Returning to wallow in the mire.¶

Far as with Christ I list,
That far bound to persist
To have honor and truth propigated,
I'll fall short as a saint
If from duty I'd faint,
In what Christ by example dictated.

So at hazzard I'll try,
With duty to comply;
Such as Christ by example assigned me;
Nor kick against the pricks—
God, in concience did fix;
Though my country in penalties bind me.

As God made man's soul free,
No distinction there to be.
As by God's word in Scryptures we find it,*
Whoever would be great,
Or attain to that state,
Must serve all as Christ's word has enjoined it.

So real democrats pure,
Cannot despots endure,
Nor the dupes under popish dominion;
But as God made them free;
They're determ'd so to be,
This is Democrat, John Blair's opinion.

He'd have no man called great,
Either in Church or state—
'Till the people discover'd his merits;
And declare by their voice,
They had made them their choice,
Regarding his democratic spirit.

¶2nd Peter 2nd and 22nd.
*Mathew 23d 8. 12 h verses.

Where writings of all kinds,
That name he still sign'd
Till it got into bad reputation;
When he thought the best way,
There no longer to stay,
He would change both his name and his station.

So to Grayson he came
When he changed his name,
And ere his character was detected;
By a rare circumstance†
It so happened by chance
That a delegate he got elected.

Was John Carl drunk or not,
When a drunkard he fought,
Who marked him in his right ear by biting;
Which is but an effect,
Temperance men might expect,
When two drunkards like dogs gets to fighting.

Perhaps God so design'd,
As Carl was hard to find.
By the mame that was first given to him;
That as he had mark'd Cain,
He'd mark Carl now again,
That when he changed his name all might know him.

Though an unpleasant task
The question I must ask,
Why William Parks, withdrew a petition;
Or at least documents
To maintain its contents,
That there existed more than suspicion.

That an oath Carl did take,
He did corruptly break
To defeat Harrison, in election;
My aim now is to see
Whether so it can be,
That Parks' object was for Carl's protection.

†Many candidates near the middle and the upper end of the county, and in the extreme lower end prejudice and amulation prevailed.

"CLIFFSIDE"
Residence of Thomas L. Felts, Built by Him in 1908, Ethelfelts, Virginia

If the affirmative,
To my problems you give,
On reflection what will you make of it;
But had I such a mind,
As holily inclin'd
As one had Jeremiah the prophet.

I'd cry Oh! that my head
Were waters to be shed,
From my eyes in fountains of tears flowing;
That in spirit contrite,
I might weep day and night,
In grief from my people to be going.

That in the wilderness
I'd find a lodging place.
Of way-faring men with spirits greater,*
Than basley to decend
So accomplish their end,
To select and combine with a traitor.

Recolect as you go,
Observation will show,
Scarsce a word positive I have stated
But all hypothetic,
Or as problematic,
A proviso is still indicated.

THE APPENDIX

I am now sued again,
To augment loss and pain.

---

*See Jeremiah, chap. 9th.
[Except relating to Popery against which I go might and main.

N. B. I was raised a Presbyterian and learned the shorter catechism the first question is, Q. What is the chief end of man?
Ans. To glorify God, and enjoy him forever. Now I cannot see any better way for me to glorify God than to subject all my means, mental, and pecuniary to prevent his attributes,—truth and candor, from being as it were trodden down, on which to establish the glory of perfedy, fraud and falsehood.
JOHN BLAIR.
Wytheville December 8th 1846

It is not more than I had expected;
It is not less or more
Than I looked for before,
Our delegate was last time elected.

Hard through life I have wro't,
To procure what I have got,
It peirces to the 'marrow' to lose it†
If my country says so
In God's name let it go,
Rather than serve mamon I'd so choose it.*

If my treatis a'nt true,
Should not all concern'd sue,
If true, how will Carroll's voter's bear it;
If they cant bear truth's test
But, to hide it think best,
They can pull it down cut smear and tear it.

As some has done before,
They can still do so more,
From such might not the like be expected.
Admitting that they knew,
My treatis to be true
And still by their vote keep him elected,

If they cant bear the light,
That brings truth to their sight
Is it not as Christ once did make mention;‡
That darkness they have chose,
Least the light should disclose,
"Evil deeds" they had in their intention.

If such wretches be found,
To cast truth to the ground,
Phœnix like t'will rise resusitated¶
As, from ashes, again

†Hebrews 4th and 12th.
*Mathew the 6th and 24th.
‡John 3rd and 19th.
¶Phœnix is imagioned with the Arabians a bird to live 500 years, only one at a time, then, build a nest of combustable which the sun kindles and burns it; out of the ashes of which a new phoenix survives, so, always keeps a phoenix.

It, new life will sustain,
Truth, must not be thus annihilated.

What has Grayson come to
Or might not Carroll do,
If a delegate they have elected;
Who too true for a joke,
His oath corruptly broke,
From them what might not then be expected.

As I was sued before,
Let me now be sued more,
All I have wrote; if I do not maintain it;
Then, 'so God do to me.'
'And more' and let it be
All I'm sued for, let them that sues gain it.

Why did our delegate,
Until August court wait
To indite me for a demonstration
Against granting him leavè;
From the clerk to receive
Our documents just at his discretion.

Least, as he did before,
He might, still do so more
With forgeries, give then a wrong direction;
With deceit, and with fraud
Circulate them abroad;
Aiming by such to gain his election.

Where Paul, popery defines,
Wrought by satin with 'signs
Decievableness and lying wonder,'
By pontific control,
Over bodey and soul
Kept by popes sovereign dictation under,

To Thesolonians turn,
There this truth for to learn

1st Kings 2nd and 23rd Ruth first and 17th.

Second book, second chapter you'll find it,
How popes power is portrayed,
By 'wondors' as Paul said
By signs lying as satin design'd it;

Should this not satisfy,
Revelations then try,
Seventeenth, saint John corroborated;
Rome a figure, he made§
Of Babylon portray'd.
The spiritual whordom God hated.

As Luther once did say
I'm resolv'd the same way,
'Though devils, thick as tiles may beset me;'*
Like him lawfully called,
And like him sore enthrol'd
In dificulties my truths do get me

Is a sentance, or word
Of this false and absurd;
Or with truth and propriety clashes;
My clothes I will not rent,
But my heart, and repent†
As envelop'd in sac-cloth and ashes.‡

Does it or not shew plain?
That I am sued again,
For countenance in our legislature;
For to make it appear
Like this treatis was near
Efusions of malignant nature.

For if members should view,
My treatis to be true,
Which one of nice feelings would abide him;
In social company,
And conversation free,
In good fellowship to sit beside him.

§Observe the 7 hills called mountains, on which Rome stood; and now partly stands. Rome, was 50 miles round it; Babylon was 60. Worcester's Gazeteer.
*Luthers commentarys page 10.
†Joel 2nd and 13th.
‡Ester 4 and 13.

Had we now the same way;
As in Josiah's day;
Of expressing our mortification;
Might we not our clothes tare§
Till our bodeys were bare,
When we behold our great degradation.

A papist may perplex
And by law suets sore vex
And with costs, and fatigue, sore oppress me;
Yet a promise I've got.

He also wrote the inscriptions for the tombstones of William Bourne and his wife, Rosa Jones. They were given on a preceding page.

John Blair and wife, Charity Bourne, lived at Blair's Forge, near what is now Blair Depot, Carroll county, Va.

From this union there were three sons and six daughters: First son, Thomas Blair, married Sally Patton; one son, John Blair, was killed by a slide in a mill race on Chestnut Creek; one daughter, Catherine, first married James Leonard, second married John Roberts, son of Thompson Roberts and wife, Seraphina Currin.

A. Sidney Blair, youngest son of John Blair and wife, Charity Bourne, married Mildred James, sister to Emeline James, who married L. D. Blair. Sidney Blair settled first at the old Blair Forge, on Chestnut Creek; afterwards bought the farm at Hale's Ferry from William B. Hale, and since that time it has been known as Blair's Ferry on New River, near Fries and Washington Cotton Mills. To A. S. Blair and wife were born three children; two died in infancy. One daughter, Rosa B. was drowned in the dam at the old Blair Forge. She, with her nurse, was playing near the dam, and saw some flowers blooming near the water, and in her effort to get the flowers, fell into

§2nd Chronicles 34th and 27th a good king in Israel.

the water and was drowned before she could be recovered. There is a memorial window in the Methodist Church at Fries, put in by Mr. Blair and his wife, in memory of themselves and their children. They were both members of the Methodist Church, South.

There were six daughters born to John Blair and his wife, Charity Bourne: Polly, Rosa Bourne, Rebecca, Celia, Elizabeth, and Lucinda.

Polly Blair lived to be quite old, never married; Rosa B. married John Hale, son of William Hale and wife, Lucy Stone, of Elk Creek. They lived on Rock Creek and brought their farm up to a high state of cultivation. To them were born thirteen sons: Alfred, Warner, James, Lorenza D., Thomas B., William, Sidney, John, Stephen, and the names of the others I cannot give; some died young, but most of them lived to rear families in Grayson county.

Rebecca Blair married William Stone. They settled on Chestnut Creek, cleared up and made a nice farm on part of the Blair lands. They had a large family: Sons, Hamilton, George, William, Thomas, Lorenzo Dow, John; daughters, Elizabeth, Jane, and Mary.

William Stone, with his wife and all his children, sold out here and moved to Missouri.

Celia Blair married Maj. Minitree Jones, Jr.; she was his second wife. They had one son and one daughter. Thomas B. Jones, who lives at the old Jones homestead at Mouth of Elk Creek on New River, is the son.

Charity B. Jones, the daughter, married Mr. Delp, of Smyth county, Va. They had one son, Minitree Delp who married first Miss Blanch Dickenson, daughter of Col. John Dickenson. He settled on New River, afterward moved west.

Elizabeth Blair, fifth daughter of John Blair and Charity Bourne, married James Waugh, from Pennsylvania.

To them were born three sons; first, William Peaden, who married Miss Sallie L. Hale, daughter of Rev. Wiley D. Hale and wife, Miss Martha Mitchell. To Wm. Waugh and Sallie Hale were born one son, Emmett, who died young; and five daughters: first, Lenora, died young; second, Eugenia, also died young; Martha and Elizabeth (twins). Martha married Edwin A. Wolfe; two daughters, Gladys, Juanita; one son, Eugene. Elizabeth married Edward Reeves, son of George Reeves and wife, Caroline Thomas, of Jefferson, N. C. They lived in Jefferson a while, then bought a farm near Washington City. Mr. and Mrs. Reeves and Mr. and Mrs. Wolfe both own farms and live near Washington City.

The third daughter of William P. Waugh, Laura, married Dr. J. H. Dunkley. They live in Roanoke, Va., and have had two children; one died in infancy, the other died when a few years old. The parents put a beautiful memorial window in memory of the child, Ruth Waugh Dunkley, in the Southern Methodist Church at Galax, Va.

After the death of William P. Waugh's first wife (the mother of the above-named children), Mr. Waugh married Lelia Burt Nuckolls, daughter of William Swift Nuckolls and Susan B. Hale. From this union there was a son, Swift, and a daughter, Susan B. After the death of William Waugh, his widow sold the Waugh homestead at Old Town, and moved to Galax, Va., where she and her children now reside.

William P. Waugh went out as a Confederate soldier in the first company from Grayson county—the "Dare Devil Company"—with Peyton N. Hale as captain. In the first battle of Manassas, Capt. Hale was killed, leading his company in a charge. Several of his men were killed and wounded. Among the number of wounded was William P. Waugh. He was shot through the thigh, and the minnie ball lodged in the wound. In gathering up the wounded, he was found, but being so badly wounded it was thought there was no chance for him to live, so they left him for the night on the battle-field. During the night there came a shower of rain and wet him, and allayed his fever. He was found alive next morning and taken to the hospital, and finally his wound healed, and the bone grew together. Some time after he was brought home he had the ball taken out of his thigh. He was always lame, but lived for thirty years after the close of the war. He died a member of the Southern Methodist Church, and rests in peace.

Capt. John B. Waugh, second son of James Waugh and wife, Elizabeth Blair, entered the Confederate army later than his brother. He was elected captain in the Sixty-first Regiment. His regiment was in the battle of Missionary Ridge, Chattanooga, Tenn. He continued in the war until the close and returned to Old Town, Va., and his father turned over his mercantile business to him. He continued in business there until the town of Galax commenced building, and he moved his stock of goods there, where he has been the leading merchant. The firm is now known as J. B. Waugh & Sons.

In 1877 he was married to Miss Jennie Perkins, daughter of Johnson Perkins and wife, Catherine Johnson, of Helton, N. C. From this union there were three sons: Charles P., Dan Blair, Richard G. These sons are with him in the mercantile business at Galax at the present time.

There was one daughter, Berta Carson, who was a bright, beautiful girl. She was educated at Mary Baldwin, Staunton, Va., and Hollins Institute. While at Hollins she contracted a cold, which resulted in tuberculosis, from which she suffered three years. And while her family tried every available cure she never recovered, but died in February, 1906, at the age of 22. She was buried in

RESIDENCE OF CAPTAIN JOHN BLAIR WAUGH
Built by Him in Galax, Virginia, 1912

the cemetery at Old Town, Va. A beautiful tombstone of Mt. Airy granite with marble slab marks her resting place.

Her mother is devoted to her memory, and keeps fresh flowers on her grave constantly.

When young she joined the Methodist Church at Old Town and lived a devoted Christian life and she rests in peace.

Her mother gave a communion set of sterling silver of six pieces, to the Methodist Church of Galax, in memory of Berta. This communion set was presented through the missionary society, of which Berta was a member.

James Waugh, Jr., son of James Waugh, died young. He was accidentally scalded with hot water, and died from the effects of it.

James Waugh and wife, Elizabeth Blair, had three daughters: First daughter, Flora, married Dr. William R. Dufphey; they lived at Old Town, Va., had two daughters and one son. First daughter, Ella, married Dr. Benjamin S. Dobyns. They now own and live at the Oglesby farm, between Old Town and Galax, Va. They have one son, William; two daughters: Alma and Ruth. One daughter, Aileen, died young, and the parents put a memorial window in the Methodist Church at Galax, Va.

Josephine, second daughter of Dr. Dufphey, married James Witherow. He is a druggist in Galax, Va., and lives there. They have two sons, Fred and Eugene. One daughter died young and the parents put a window in the church in memory of her.

These three children, in whose memory the windows were placed, are great-grand children of James Waugh. Although young, these little children had been taught to know and love the Christ who loves all children.

One little girl was particularly impressed with the picture of Christ as "The Good Shepherd," and loved to be told about him.

Knowing the rough places on life's road, and that fierce storms often gather, "The Good Shepherd" gathered these "lambs" in his arms and carried them through the gates of Paradise, there to await the coming of their loved ones.

Dr. Dufphey and wife, Flora Waugh, had one son, James, that died young. He was a bright boy, and his death was a sore affliction to the family.

The third daughter of James and Elizabeth Waugh was Emma Amelia Waugh; she died at Old Town, of diphtheria, when about ten years old. Mary, the second daughter of James Waugh and Elizabeth Blair, married Fields McMillan Young, son of Ezekiel Young and his wife, Evelina McMillan. They had two daughters:

First daughter, Virginia Young, died of typhoid fever while attending school at Sullins College, Bristol, Tenn.

Second daughter, Mattie, lives with her parents at Edgewater, on Wilson Creek, N. C.

One son, James, died young; is buried at Old Town, Va.

The youngest daughter of John Blair and wife, Charity Bourne, was Lucinda Blair. She married Thomas Howard; they had one son and one daughter. John B. Howard married Miss Kyle, daughter of Madison Kyle of Woodlawn, Va.

Mary B. Howard married Samuel Kyle, son of Madison Kyle. They had three sons and three daughters. Following is an account of the death of one of their children:

"On Sunday the 20th, as she was returning from church at Woodlawn, Miss Stella Kyle was thrown from her horse and received injuries from which she died on Tuesday following.

"She and her cousin, Miss Mamie Houseman, were both mounted on a spirited saddle horse belonging to Mr. L. A. Houseman. The horse became ungovernable and Miss Houseman jumped off escaping almost unhurt while Miss Kyle was thrown on her head fracturing her skull and rendering her unconscious. She was carried home and Drs. Tipton and Robinson, were immediately summoned, but her life was despaired even at the first. She never rallied or regained consciousness.

"She was thirteen years old and a daughter of Mr. and Mrs. Sam D. Kyle of Woodlawn. She was a bright girl and a favorite among her schoolmates.

"She is survived by father, mother, three brothers and two sisters.

"The remains were interred yesterday in the cemetery at Woodlawn near the school and church she had always attended."

Mrs. Lucinda Howard inherited from her father's estate, the old homestead at the Blair Forge, with an interest in the Iron Ridge mineral land. This property passed down to John B. and Mary B. Howard; they sold it and bought good farms near Woodlawn, where they now live.

Lorenzo Dow Blair married Miss Emeline James. They have two sons and three daughters. Their son, William, married Miss Martha Watson; their son, Lorenzo Dow, has several daughters; they live near Galax, Va.

John Blair, son of Lorenzo Dow Blair, married Miss Queenie Lynthecum. They had one son, Walter Blair, who married Miss Laura E. Felts; issue: two sons, Ivy Earl, John Harold; two daughters, Hazel Claudine and Gladys Blair.

Walter Blair is cashier of the First National Bank of Galax, Va., and lives in Galax. John Blair's daughter married Leander Felts.

Lorenzo Dow Blair and wife had three daughters: First, Elizabeth, married Rev. Phillip P. Kinzer. They had one child, who died in infancy. Elizabeth died, and Philip Kinzer married her younger sister, Emma Blair. They have a son, Sidney Blair Kinzer, who married Miss McKnight; they have two sons. S. B. Kinzer is in the hardware business in Galax, Va.

The third daughter of Lorenzo Dow Blair married William Houseman. They live at Blair, Va., near the old Blair Forge, and have sons and daughters. Their first son, Lorenzo Houseman, married a daughter of Judge William Kyle; he is in the lumber business. The second son, Walter Houseman, married Miss Farmer, and went West.

William Houseman's first daughter, Elizabeth E., married Thomas L. Felts. He is partner in the Baldwin-Felts Detective Agency, and is president of the First National Bank of Galax, Va. They have one son, Gordon Felts, and live at Blair, Va. Thomas Felts owns several farms near Galax, Va., and is a public-spirited man, and a great help to the community.

Sallie Houseman, second daughter of William Houseman, married Mr. John James, of Yadkinville, N. C. They have two sons, and live in Galax, Va. Mr. James is a successful business man.

Eugenia, third daughter of William Houseman, married Robert Eversole. They have one son, and live in Galax, Va. Mr. Eversole is editor of the Galax Post-Herald.

Stephen Bourne married Patsy Mays, and lived on Knob Fork near his father's home. He cleared land and improved it until he had a valuable farm. They reared a family of five children, and he and his wife died on the same day, and were buried in the same grave on his farm.

Following are given the ages of Stephen Bourne's children:

ELIZABETH THOMAS
Daughter of Patience Bourne Thomas, and wife of Samuel Cox
(See Cox Family)

GRAYSON COUNTY, VA. 53

Elizabeth Bourne was born June the 24th, 1802. Married James Dickey, Esq., son of Mathew Dickey and Rebecca Wiley, his wife (see Dickey family).

Cynthia Bourne was born October 23, 1803; married Mr. Pugh; moved to Missouri; has a family there.

Martin Bourne was born February 26th, 1806; married Sarah Smith, of Smyth county, Va.

Matterson Bourne was born September 25th, 1808; died, March 2nd, in the year of our Lord, 1826; age seventeen years, five months, and seven days.

William Bourne, Jr., born May 12th, 1810; married Margaret Scott, of Smyth county, Va.; three daughters and two sons.

Nancy Bourne, born Sept. 17th, 1818; married Spencer James, of Smyth county, Va.; three sons, Dr. Ezekiel, Friel, and Stephen.

Martin Bourne and wife, Miss Sallie Smith, had one son, Montgomery Bourne, who married Miss Olive Hale, of Elk Creek, Va.; they had sons and daughters.

His first daughter, Talitha B., first married Tivis Hale; two daughters, Amelia and Sallie; the second time, Talitha B. married Charles Hale; two daughters: Flora and Ella Hale.

Jane B., the second daughter, married John P. Byrd; had sons and a daughter, Sallie, who married John Welch; live at Summerfield, N. C.

Floranza B., third daughter, married Johnston Bourne; moved to Texas.

Cynthia, the fourth daughter, married Joseph Phipps, of Saddle Creek, Va.

The fifth daughter, Julia Ann Bourne, married Carson Andis, and lives at the old homestead; no issue.

The sixth daughter Amanda, married first, Lockett Cooper; second time, Alexander McMillan.

William Bourne (3), son of Stephen Bourne, married Margaret Scott, daughter of William Scott and wife, Miss Elizabeth Porter. Two sons: Andrew, died in Confederate war, single; John A. Bourne married Mrs. Jane Gose; no issue. Three daughters: Elizabeth, married Rufus Perkins; one son, Rev. J. L. M. Perkins, of Holston Conference. Matilda married Mr. Spraker; Cynthia married John Foster. After the death of William Bourne, his widow, Margaret Bourne, married David Gose.

Mary Bourne married Martin Dickenson and lived at Grayson, C. H., now Old Town, Va. Their children were: three sons, James, John and William; daughters: Charlotte, Jestena, Jane, Rosamond B., Matilda and Elizabeth Caroline.

James Dickenson married Miss Julia Thurmon; settled on New River, afterward moved to Mississippi. James Dickenson was murdered in his home by Federal soldiers during the war. Had one son, Martin, who died single; three daughters: Sallie, Mary and Amelia. Sallie married Hugh Gwin; Mary married Richard Gwin, and Amelia married Thomas Gwin, all three sons of Richard Gwin, Sr., and wife, Miss Elizabeth Hunt, of Elkin, N. C.

Hugh Gwin was principal of a school in Mississippi; died there; no issue. His wife, Sallie D., married the second time, Hugh Wright; had one daughter, Julia Wright,

Richard Gwin, who married Mary Dickenson, lived at Elkin, N. C., one of the owners of the Elkin Cotton Mills. They had two sons; Charles G., married Miss Bettie Perkins, of Hilton N. C.; they have three daughters; one son, Ernest, died single; one daughter married Mr. Chatam.

Thomas Gwin first lived at Elkin, one of the owners of the Elkin Woolen Mills. Gwin and Chatam afterward moved to Elk Creek, Grayson county, Va., and bought the Col. Stephen and Capt. John M. Hale farm; built a Roller Flour Mill, and improved the farm and buildings.

Thomas Gwin was representative in the legislature, and was a member of the Convention that met in 1912 to amend the constitution of the state. In the latter part of 1912, he sold his farm on Elk Creek, and moved back to Elkin, N. C., where he now resides. Two daughters were born to Mr. and Mrs. Gwin; the first daughter, Sallie, married Mr. Poindexter; they have one son, Gwin, three daughters.

Col. John Dickenson, second son of Col. Martin Dickenson and wife, Mary Bourne, married Rosamond Hale, daughter of William Ha'e and wife, Lucy Stone. They had four sons and three daughters. First son, Dr. Martin Dickenson, married Miss Mattie Phipps; they had four sons and two daughters. The first daughter, Lelia B., married Judge Robert C. Jackson; issue: two or three children. Lelia Jackson died, and Judge Jackson married the second time, Marian Early, daughter of James Early, Jr., of Hillsville, Va. They have children and live in Roanoke, Va.

Second daughter, Rosa, (of Martin Dickenson and Mattie Phipps) married Mr. Reeves of Wilkes county, N. C.; two sons Albert and Martin.

James Piper Dickenson married in North Carolina and moved to Oregon. Rush Floyd was helpless; died young.

The youngest son, Alexander Martin, marr ed Minnie Dickey, daughter of John M. Dickey; one son, McCamant married Miss Wilson, Blue Springs Gap, Va.

John Dickenson's daughter, Elizabeth, married Dr. Huffman; one son, Eddie Huffman. Married second time, Mr. Lapop, of Charlottesville, Va.; two daughters.

The second daughter, Lucy Dickenson, married William Edwards; daughters and one son.

The third daughter, Mary Dickenson, married Col. Alex. M. Davis; they had several children; Joseph died single, others died young. Garnet Davis, the youngest son, married Miss Mattie Dickey. He has four sons, and lives at the Davis homestead, Independence, Va.

Col. John Dickenson married the second time, Miss Margaret Ellen Andis; from this union, two sons and two daughters; First son, Robert L. Dickenson, married Miss Olive Ring; sons, Roy and one daughter.

Robert L. Dickenson is an enterprising, good citizen and lives on the Garrison farm on New River.

John Dickenson, Jr., married Miss Sallie Ring; lives at the Dickenson homestead. He is a good farmer and useful man; has children.

The two daughters were, Sallie, who married C. H. Edwards, supervisor for Grayson county; one son, Robert, married Miss Collins; four daughters; a nice family.

The other daughter, Miss Blanche Dickenson, married Minitree Delp; had one son, Horace Delp; she died young; her son went West.

Col. John Dickenson was a useful citizen of the county; he owned a large landed estate on New River, was in public office, and in the mercantile business when there were but few stores in the county. The firm of Dickenson and Nuckolls had stores at Old Town, Elk Creek, and Bridle Creek. The goods were then hauled from Lynchburg on wagons. There were but two other stores in the county; they were at Grayson C. H. (now Old Town). At that time, all the goods and groceries came to Lynchburg on the canal, and were hauled out into these western counties in six horse wagons.

William B. Dickenson, youngest son of Martin D., married Miss Mary Edmondson of Glade Spring, Va., and lived at Grayson C. H. with his mother who kept hotel there for a number of years. They had four

COL. SAMUEL McCAMANT

daughters and two sons; three daughters and two sons born at Grayson C. H. He later moved to Glade Spring Depot. One daughter born at Glade Spring. Eugenia, the oldest daughter, married Robert Blair; Ellen married Mr. Thurman; Nannie and Mattie; Robert married Miss Gardner; John, the youngest son of William Dickenson, died suddenly at his home in Glade Spring, Va. The family then all moved to California.

Elizabeth Caroline, the youngest daughter of Martin D. and his wife, married Benjamin Martin, of Lee county, Va. For some years they lived at Jonesville, Va. Mr. Martin was educated at Emory and Henry College, when Dr. Collins was president. When they were married, Dr. Collins performed the ceremony. They were married at the Dickenson Hotel, Grayson C. H. Mr. Martin had three sons, Clarence, John, and Beverly. Beverly died young at Old Town, and is buried there; they had one daughter, Mary; the family moved from Lee county to Texas.

Col. Martin Dickenson's mother was a Miss Bryson of North Carolina. He died in 1833. His wife survived him nearly thirty years, dying in September, 1860. For these thirty years she managed the estate which Col. Dickenson left, and did it successfully. She kept the hotel open and made money.

Charlotte Dickenson married Col. Stephen Hale of Elk Creek, Va. The follwing was written of her by an admirer:

"Colonel Stephen Hale, of Elk Creek, married Miss Charlotte Dickenson, a christian lady, who adorned the family circle. She offered up public prayer and delivered earnest exhortations. Col. Hale and wife and their family were devoted members of the Methodist Church. If every family lived as Col. Hale's this would be a happy world. Col. Hale married the second time, Mrs. Lenora Gwin

Mitchell, who was first Miss Lenora Gwin. She was a noble christian woman, gave peace and happiness in the love of God to the home of these good people, where their sun of ife sat beneath a cloudless sky to rise in the resurrection morning."

As the foregoing sketches give a number of the names of the Gwin family, I will insert here a sketch of one of the ancestors of the Gwin family, General William Lenoir. He resided in Wilkes county, N. C. His life, character, and services have been recorded by an able and familiar hand. The following is an extract from the Raleigh Register, June 22nd, 1839, and recorded in Wheeler's history of North Carolina: "This venerable patriot and soldier died at his residence at Fort Defiance in Wilkes county on Monday, May 6th 1839, aged 88 years.

"Gen. Lenoir was born in Brunswick county, Va., on the 20th of May, 1751, O. S.; descended from poor but respectable French ancestry. When about eight years old, his father removed to Tar river, near Tarboro, N. C., where he resided until his death, which happened shortly after. Gen. Lenoir received no other education than such as his personal exertions permitted him to acquire. When about twenty years of age, he married Miss Ballard, a lady possessing those domestic and heroic virtues which qualified her for sustaining the privations and hardships of frontier life, which it was her destiny afterward to encounter. In 1775, Gen. Lenoir moved his family to the county of Wilkes.

"James Gwyn married a daughter of Thomas Lenoir, a soldier in the Revolutionary war. Gen William Lenoir was a resident of Wilkes county, owned and cultivated a large farm on the Yadkin River. He was a good citizen, brought up a family whose piety and devotion to christianity will leave fruits to ripen in eternity."

His younger son, Rufus Lenoir, married Miss Sallie Gwyn of Elkin, N. C., daughter of Richard and Elizabeth Gwyn.

Jestena Dickenson, daughter of Col. Martin Dickenson, married James Meek. They lived at the Stone house in Washington county, Va., had two sons; first, Joseph Meek, married Miss Clark and settled in Burk's Garden, Va. James also settled in Burk's Garden. They owned a fine landed estate in the Garden. Their daughter, Jane Meek, married Dr. William Hoge. Their family is in Bland county, Va.

Mary Meek married Phillip Snapp, and lived near the old homestead. Their son lives at Snapps Siding on N. & W. R. R.

Sophia Meek married Mr. Edmondson. He and his wife died of yellow fever in Mississippi; two children; the youngest daughter, Caroline, married Alex Golahorn; lived near Saltville, Va.

Mrs. Jestena Meek married the second time, Col. Strother, of Washington county.

Matilda Dickenson married Col. Samuel McCamant from Pennsylvania. He was prominent as an attorney; was a representative in state senate, and in all movements for the good of this county. He lived at Grayson Old Court House, reared and educated his family, and he and his wife both died and are buried at Old Town, in the Dickenson graveyard. They had seven sons and three daughters. The sons: Alexander Smith, James Martin, John D., William B., Samuel, Thomas Jefferson, Emmett. The daughters: Charlotte Virginia, and two daughters who died in infancy.

The daughter, Charlotte Virginia, was a lady of fine intellect, culture, and refinement; also a fine christian character. She married Rev. Charles M. Howard, an Evangelist in the Presbyterian Church. She lived at the old homestead; died without issue and is buried at Old Town, Va.

Alexander S., John D., and William B. McCamant, all married daughters of Thomas Gardner in Texas. James Martin and Emmett also went to Texas and married there. John D. had two daughters, Hattie and Lizzie. They lived in Fort Worth.

Lizzie McCamant married Rev. Carter, who belongs to the Texas Conference. He is a Methodist Minister and was educated at Emory and Henry College, Va.

Samuel McCamant, Jr., married Miss Nancy Kitchen. He died during the war; no children.

Thomas Jefferson McCamant married Miss Ellen Hale, daughter of Maj. Peyton G. Hale and wife, Jane Bourne, of Elk Creek, Va. They had five daughters: Blanche, Lizzie, Clyde, Josephine, Myrtle. Josephine and Myrtle died young. Blanche married Clayton Higgins; one son, McCamant Higgins. They own and live at the McCamant homestead at Old Town, Va.

Lizzie McCamant married Fred Armfield; they have two daughters. They live at the old Governor Franklin homestead on Fish River, N. C.

Clyde McCamant married Marvin Vaughn, son of Rev. Thomas C. Vaughan and wife, Lucy Hale. They live at Spring Valley, Grayson county, Va.; have one son, Thomas Jefferson.

Col. Samuel McCamant had one brother, Thomas Jefferson McCamant, who studied medicine in Pennsylvania and came to Grayson C. H., and lived with his brother. The doctor never married; died about 1860, and is buried in the Dickenson graveyard, Old Town, Va.

Miss Rosa B. Dickenson married Hugh Gwin, and they live near Mt. Airy, N. C. They have four sons: First son, Martin, married Miss McComas, and lived near Mt. Airy, N. C.; one son married Miss Johnston. John Gwin married Miss Crockett and lived in Rich Valley. One daughter, Mary, married Mr. Morgan; lives at Seven Mile Ford.

Elizabeth Bourne married Capt. Lewis Hale, Jr., and lived on Elk Creek. (See Hale history, p. 104.) They had four sons: Jackson, Washington, Rufus, Capt. Peyton N. Hale; four daughters: Millie, Celia, Elvira, Rosamond B. (See Capt. Lewis Hale, Jr.)

Frances Bourne married Stephen Hale, Sr., and settled at the Hale homestead, Elk Creek. (See Hale history, page 117.)

Names and number of their sons and daughters follow:

Eight sons: Mastin, Warner, William B., Martin, Fielden Lewis, Chapman G., Clark, Eli C.

Five daughters: Lucinda, Rosa Bourne, Mary, Amanda Jane, Sophia P. (See Stephen Hale, Sr.)

Celia Bourne married Robert Johnstone and settled on Roaring River, Wilkes county, N. C. This Johnstone of Revolutionary fame was in the battle of Kings Mountain. There were sons and daughters of this family in Wilkes county N. C., but I cannot give their names.

William Bourne, Jr., married Mary Johnstone, sister to Robert Johnstone. He settled at the old Wm. Bourne homestead, on Knob Fork, Va., and brought up his family there. Their daughter, Rosa B., married Stephen M. Hale, son of John Hale and Mary Hale, his wife. They had sons and daughters. Their son, Alexander Hale, married Miss Sallie Roberts, daughter of Thompson Roberts and wife, Seraphina Currin; one son, Friel; one daughter, Nannie; and one daughter, Malinda Hale, married Stephen Whitman, son of David Whitman and wife, Elizabeth Hale.

Stephen M. Hale and his wife, after living in Grayson some time, moved with their family to Texas, from Independence, Va.

Malinda Bourne married Robert Currin, son of Maj. George Currin and his wife, Martha Swift. They had a son, William B. Currin, and a daughter, Mary J. Currin; all moved to Oregon.

Rachel Bourne married James P. Waugh; they first lived at Grayson C. H.; afterward moved to Jefferson, Ashe county, N. C.; died there; no issue.

Jane Bourne married Peyton G. Hale, son of Wi.liam Hale and wife, Lucy Stone. (See Ha'e history.) They lived and died at the Wm. Hale homestead on Elk Creek, Va.

Lucinda Bourne married Stephen Friel Nuckolls, son of Ezra Nuckolls and wife, Lucinda Hale. They both died in Salt Lake City, Utah. They had sons: William, Paul, Rupert (See Nuckolls Family). Rupert Nuckolls now lives in Butte, Montana; is cashier of the State Savings Bank there.

Harvey Gordon Bourne married Miss Frances Nuckolls, daughter of Ezra Nuckolls and wife, Lucinda Hale. They have one daughter, Mary Bourne, and two sons, William, and Houston Bourne.

Johnstone Bourne married Floranza Bourne, daughter of Martin Bourne, of Knob Fork, Va. They live in Texas.

Following are the descendants of L. W. Bourne, the third son, and eighth child of William Bourne, Jr., and Mary Johnstone Bourne.

L. W. Bourne was born January 13th, 1832; married Julia Fulton March 12th, 1857. From this union there are five children, two girls, and three boys. Pinkie Bourne was born March 7th, 1859; Cleveland Bourne was born August 18th, 1861; Robert Bourne was born September 26th, 1867; William Stephen Bourne was born October 28th, 1873; Chloe Bourne was born November 1st, 1877.

Pinkie A. Bourne was married to John H. Skinner, December 5th, 1873. From this union are four boys and two girls: Lute Skinner was married to Ella Corn, January 10th, 1897. To this union are three girls and two boys, Eunice, Verna, Ellie, John, and George. They live at Nogal, New Mexico.

Conda Skinner, the second son, married Ethel Greer, August 24th, 1904. From this union are one girl and one boy, Brooksie and Christa, who live at Nogal, New Mexico.

Floy Skinner married May 15th, 1907, to Alice Zumwalt; one girl is added to this union, Elsie Bly; live at Nogal, New Mexico.

Roy Skinner, the fourth son, was married to Clara Adams, March 12th, 1911; home, Carrizozo, New Mexico.

Alice Rosa Skinner, the first daughter, was married to Ben B. Parker, May 3rd, 1891. To this union are three boys and three girls; Carl Parker, aged eighteen years, married Ethel Roth, September 4th, 1910. Live in Sacramento, Cal. Rolla, Bryce, Pinkie, Hattie, and Ella live in Carrizozo, New Mexico.

Effie Julia Skinner married Bowen Zumwalt, February 13th, 1898. To this union are four boys and one girl, Clifton, Floy, Wayne, Murray, and Chloe.

Chloe Bourne, second daughter, and youngest child of L. W. Bourne and Julia Bourne, married W. R. White, February 28th, 1898; no issue.

Cleveland Bourne, eldest son, was married to Lula Henley, October 10th, 1885. To this union are four girls, Minnie, Midge, Julia, and Etta; four boys, William, Thomas, Milton, and Lute. All yet under the parental roof, at Tularosa, New Mexico.

Robert Bourne, second son, married Josephine Pfingsten, December 30th, 1891. To this union, one son, Emmett. Robert Bourne is owner and manager of the Telephone line, and living at Duran, New Mexico.

William Stephen Bourne, third and youngest son, was married to Annie Zumwalt, January 27th, 1901.

To this union are two sons, Creed and Rex; home, Carrizozo, New Mexico.

L. W. Bourne, father, grandfather, and great-grandfather, of this large family, is living with his eldest daughter Mrs. John Skinner, Carrizozo, New Mexico.

Julia Fulton Bourne, wife of L. W. Bourne, died September 21st, 1908. Was buried, at Ever Green Cemetery, Carrizozo, New Mexico.

William Bourne (3), youngest son of William Bourne (2), and wife, Mary Johnstone, died single, at Independence, Grayson county, Va.; a fine young man, in the prime of life.

Capt. Richmond G. Bourne, son of William Bourne and wife, married Miss Mary Wagoner of Tennessee, daughter of David Wagoner and wife, Miss Celia Perkins, daughter of Timothy Perkins, of Grayson county.

Mary Ann Bourne, youngest daughter of William and Mary Bourne, married Preston Reeves; one son, Richmond G. Reeves, married Miss Hall, on Rock Creek, Va.

Capt. R. G. Bourne entered the war between the states as an officer in the Grayson Cavalry Company, Dr. Wm. H. Bramblett as Captain, in the 8th Regiment of the Cavalry. After the first year, Dr. Bramblett resigned, and Capt. Bourne took charge as captain, and was captain when the war closed. After his marriage, he lived at the old Bourne homestead on Rock Creek, near Independence, Va. He had two sons: William married Miss Wiley; Charles married Miss Dickey. He also had two daughters: Callie married George W. Simmerman of Wythe county, Va. Addie married Mr. Barton, Independence, Va. Capt. R. G. Bourne did much for his country and was a useful citizen.

MATILDA DICKENSON McCAMANT
Daughter of Col. Martin Dickenson and wife, Mary Bourne, and wife of Col. Samuel McCamant

CHAPTER III

THE NUCKOLLS FAMILY

The early history of our country tells us that the first permanent English colony in America was established on the coast of Virginia in 1607. Montgomery's English history says, "A London joint stock company of merchants and adventurers or speculators established the first permanent English colony in America on the coast of Virginia in 1607, at a place which they called Jamestown in honor of the king."

The tradition in the Nuckoll's family is that three Nuckolls brothers came from York, England, in this company of colonists. They were merchants, and their names were John, James and William. From one of these brothers, John Nuckolls of Louisa county, was descended. John Nuckolls married Mary Garland about 1776. Mary Garland was the daughter of Robert Garland (4) of Louisa county. Robert (4) and Edward (4) were sons of John Garland of Garland's Neck, and were the founders of the Louisa branch of the Garland family (see chapter on Garland family). Mary Garland was a member of the Episcopal Church, and her prayer book, which was printed in MDCCLXI (1761), has been handed down to her children and grandchildren until it is now in the possession of the author of this book, who is her great-grandson. In this prayer-book there is a record of the time of births of Mary Garland and John Nuckolls, and the names and time of births of their nine sons and one daughter. Following is a copy of the record:

"Mary Garland, born March 20th, 1755.
"John Nuckolls, born July 12th, 1755.

"The ages of children born to John Nuckolls and wife, Mary Garland:
"1st. David Nuckolls, born October 26th, 1778.
"2nd. Rhodes Nuckolls, born June 11th, 1780.
"3rd. Robert G. Nuckolls, born August 7th, 1782.
"4th. Peter Nuckolls, born June 18th, 1784.
"5th. Elisha Nuckolls, born September 4th, 1786.
"6th. Nathaniel Nuckolls, born January 12th, 1789.
"7th. Samuel Nuckolls, born December 26th, 1790.
"One daughter, Patsy Nuckolls, born November 27th, 1792.
"8th. Asa Nuckolls, born February 11th, 1795.
"9th. Ezra Nuckolls, born March 28th, 1798."

There is also a record given of the births of fifteen negroes belonging to John Nuckolls, and twelve negroes belonging to Mary Garland. Of this number, none were sold out of the Nuckolls family, except two men who were sold to men who owned the wives of these two negro men. Several of the descendants of these negroes are now living with and working for the descendants of John Nuckolls and Mary Garland.

All the children of John Nuckolls and Mary Garland were born in Louisa county, Va.

In 1780, Charles Nuckolls moved to Southwest Virginia and entered one thousand acres of land on New River and Cripple Creek, and others of the Nuckolls family followed him. About the year of 1790, John Nuckolls' family came from Louisa county and settled on New River and Meadow Creek near Greenville or Grayson C. H. At the same time, Charles Nuckolls, who was a cousin of John Nuckolls, moved from Cripple Creek to Meadow Creek, near Greenville.

The land entered by Charles Nuckolls on Cripple Creek is now owned by John P. M. Simmerman and others. Nathaniel Nuckolls, son of John Nuckolls, owned a part of this land, lived there, brought up his family, and died in Wythe county.

Charles Nuckolls married first a Miss Garland of Eastern Virginia; they had ones on, Robert. His second wife was Mary Black. From this union there were three sons: John, who moved to Kentucky; James, who moved to Missouri, and Charles, who died single; and five daughters, Betty, Sally, Polly, Susan, and Nancy.

At that time this country was Washington and Montgomery District. Wythe county was formed in 1790, and in 1792 Grayson was formed from Wythe, taking in the south side adjoining the State of North Carolina. (See records of the first courts of Grayson county, 1793.)

Charles Garland, brother of Mary Garland Nuckolls, came with his sister's family from Louisa county to Grayson. He died single and is buried in the Nuckolls cemetery in Grayson county. John Nuckolls and his wife, Mary Garland, went back to Louisa county, died, and are buried there. Of the nine sons of John Nuckolls, seven of them settled in Grayson county. The daughter, Patsy, or Martha, married Maj. James Anderson, of Albemarle county, Va. They established a home and reared a family in Grayson. Both are buried in the Anderson cemetery near Galax, Va. Descendants of Maj. James Anderson live on the Anderson estate near Galax, Va.

Rhodes, the second son of John Nuckolls and Mary Garland, and Peter, the fourth son, moved from Grayson to Kentucky; Elisha, fifth son, and Samuel, seventh son, also moved to Tennessee and Kentucky. Asa, the eighth son, died single, and is buried in the Nuckolls cemetery. Nathaniel Nuckolls, sixth son of John Nuckolls and Mary Garland, first married a Miss Garland of Louisa county, Va.; issue, three sons: Lee, Garland, and Andrew; and two daughters: Sena and Allie. The first son, Lee, married Miss Lydia Painter. They lived near Ivanhoe, Va., and had no children. They are buried near Ivanhoe.

The second son, Garland, moved to Missouri in 1830.

The third son, Andrew, married Celia Jones, daughter of Maj. Abner Jones and wife, Hannah Fawbush, of Grayson county; issue: two sons, Calvin and Kent, and four daughters. Two of the daughters moved to Nebraska and died there; the other two daughters are living single. Calvin Nuckolls moved to Nebraska. Kent Nuckolls had four daughters. The first daughter, Cynthia, married James B. Johnson, lived and died in Hillsville, Va. (See following obituary):

"Mrs. Cynthia (Nuckolls) Johnson, widow of James B. Johnson, died Monday, and was buried Tuesday afternoon, age seventy-eight years.

"After a long, busy and useful life, she died as she lived, honored, trusted and loved. She reared her own monuments while she lived, in the hearts of all who knew her. Life completed if work all done, and well done, constitutes completion. Her Christian life was beautiful from its beginning to its close, and through all vicissitudes and sorrows that she met in the way, her faith in God never wavered.

"None ever entered her home without a warm welcome, nor left without feeling the warmth of a genuine hospitality, so characteristic of the people of her ancestry. Disease did not destroy the charm of a kind, indulgent disposition, nor old age diminish unselfish solicitude for her friends and loved ones.

"The deceased was the mother of a large and gifted family. Impressive funeral services were held at the home after which all that was mortal of this grand old mother in Israel was tenderly conveyed to our Silent City, where by the side of a devoted husband she now rests in peace."—Carroll Journal.

PHOTOGRAPHS OF THE NUCKOLLS CEMETERY

"Mrs. Johnson was a daughter of Andrew Nuckolls and Celia Jones Nuckolls. Their ancestors were English, and early settlers of Virginia. Nathaniel Nuckolls, father of Andrew Nuckolls, was one of the pioneer settlers of Wythe county. Maj. Abner Jones, father of Celia Jones Nuckolls, was also a pioneer settler of Grayson county. These families have done much for the development of this section.

"Mrs. Johnson was very much interested in all that was for the interest of both church and state, loved her friends and was kind to all.

"The pall-bearers were her nearest relatives. Four sons-in-law, James Early, Fulton Green, W. D. Tompkins and James Cooley, of Knoxville, Tenn., Judge Robert Jackson, Bernard Early, Rev. B. F. Nuckolls, and Dr. C. D. Nuckolls."

Mr. James Johnson was a successful merchant and useful citizen. Four daughters, Viola, Henrietta, Eliza, Dora, and one son, Heath, were born to James Johnson and Cynthia Nuckolls. Viola, the eldest daughter, died young; Henrietta married Maj. John Rawley; they lived in Richmond, Va., and had two sons, Kent Nuckolls, and Heath. Maj. Rawley died several years ago; the sons are lawyers, and live with their mother in Richmond.

Eliza, third daughter, married James Early, a merchant; they live in Hillsville, Va., and have several children. The eldest daughter, Marion, married Judge Robert C. Jackson and lives in Roanoke, Va. Eliza and James Early have other children—one son, Bernard. The fourth daughter of James and Cynthia Johnston, Dora, married Fulton Green, son of Mr. Jack Green, who married Miss Betsy Fulton, daughter of Judge Andrew Fulton. They have three daughters, Clara, Blanche and Nancy, one son, Ashby. One of the daughters married Gordon Hall.

Heath Johnston, only son of James Johnston and Cynthia Nuckolls, married Miss Sallie Green, daughter of Mr. Jack Green. They had one daughter, Alpha Heath, single; one son, died young, and the father, Heath Johnston, died soon after the death of his son.

Heath Johnston was an exemplary young man. He had taken his father's place in business, and his death was a loss and sorrow to the community, as well as to his immediate family. His widow married a lawyer, W. D. Tompkins. They live in Hillsville, and have children.

Sena, the first daughter of Nathaniel Nuckolls, married the first time, Daniel Sheffey; they had one son, Ezra Nuckolls Sheffey, who was a druggist in Marion, Smythe county, Va. He married first a Miss Preston, second a Miss Rhea; moved to Greenville, Tenn., and died there; he has sons and daughters living in Greenville.

Mrs. Sena Nuckolls Sheffey married the second time, Joshua Jackson. They had one son, Berton, who died in the Confederate army. One daughter, Nannie, who married Melville Fisher, of Cripple Creek, and they now live in Tennessee.

Rev. Robert Sawyers Sheffey was a son of Daniel Sheffey by his first wife, Miss White, of Abingdon, Va. He was a local Methodist preacher of the Holston Conference, a man who had some eccentricities of character, but whose unbounded faith in God, and good works among his fellow-men made him widely known throughout Southwest Virginia. He was a man who had power with God in prayer, and the writer knows of many striking and direct answers to his prayers.

In Robert Sheffey's time there was much illicit distilling of whiskey in the mountains of Southwest Virginia and he was the enemy of the traffic. At one time he prayed for a certain distillery to be removed, and a water spout burst just above it, and left not a trace of the plant.

He prayed for specific things, and God honored his faith by giving him what he asked for. The wicked trembled when he prayed for justice to be meted out to wrong-doers, and many were brought to repentance through the influence of his prayers. Mr. Sheffey first married Miss Swecker, of Wythe county; they have children living in Wythe county. His second wife was a Miss Stafford, of Giles county; they have one son, Edward Sheffey, who lives in Lynchburg, Va. He is a man of fine character, and honors the God of his father. He is superintendent of a very fine Sunday School, and a man of large influence.

Allie, the second daughter of Nathaniel Nuckolls, married Mr. Engledow, of Wythe county, Va. She, with her husband and her brother, Garland Nuckolls, moved to Missouri about 1830. She has a daughter, Mrs. Allie J. Bone, living at Mineral Point, Missouri.

Nathaniel Nuckolls married the second time, Miss Martha Toler, of Wythe county. They had two sons and two daughters; first son, John Nuckolls, lived in Wythe county; second son, Calvin Nuckolls, moved to Tazewell county, Va. First daughter, Elizabeth Nuckolls, married William Pope; they lived on Cripple Creek, Va., and reared a family there; second daughter, Nancy Nuckolls, married Abner Thompson; they also lived on Cripple Creek, Va.; no issue. The plantation on which Nathaniel Nuckolls first settled is now owned by the Catron family. Rev. S. S. Catron, of Holston Conference, was brought up on this farm. The following clipping from a Roanoke paper gives a sketch of Robert Rhodes Nuckolls:

"Richmond, Aug. 11—Information was received here today of the death of Robert R. Nuckolls, well known throughout newspaper, printing and labor circles for more than half a century. His death occurred yesterday afternoon in Louisa county. He was 72 years of age.

"Major Nuckols, as he was called, was a type of the Virginia gentleman. He was born, however, in Alabama, coming to Virginia at the close of the war, when his regiment was disbanded in this state. He was in prison when the war ended, but came to Hanover county. He was connected with the old *"Whig"* and afterwards with the *"State."* He traveled the state for the last named paper, working in its circulation and advertising departments. He had experience in almost every branch of the profession. He was editor-in-chief of the *"Star,"* remaining with that paper until it suspended.

"Nuckols worked with the *Richmond Journal* until health failed him. He married Miss Swift, of Louisa county, after the war. His wife died four years ago. Respected and esteemed throughout the state, where he was widely known, his death is regarded as a loss to the newspaper profession of the state."

Robert Garland Nuckolls was the third son of John Nuckolls and wife, Mary Garland. He was born in Louisa county, Va., August 7th, 1782; he came to Grayson county with other members of the family, and settled on Meadow Creek, one mile from Grayson Old C. H. He married Miss Margaret Swift, daughter of Col. Flower Swift and wife, Mary Bedsaul (See Swift history). Soon after his marriage, Capt. Robert G. Nuckolls opened up an Ordinary, or Tavern, at Grayson Old C. H. (See License for Ordinary in the proceedings of the Court).

To Robert G. Nuckolls and wife, Margaret Swift, were born eight sons and two daughters: first son, Creed Nuckolls; second, Clarke S. Nuckolls; third, James Nuckolls; fourth, George; fifth, Nathaniel Nuckolls; sixth, Thomas Nuckolls; seventh, Hugh Nuckolls; eighth, Andrew Nuckolls. First daughter, Martha Nuckolls;

CLARK NUCKOLLS AND WIFE, ROSA BOURNE HALE

second daughter, Sena Nuckolls.

Creed Nuckolls married Elizabeth Hale, daughter of Mastin Hale, Sr., and wife, Susan Perkins (see Hale history); issue, three sons: Robert G. Nuckolls, married Miss Lucinda Hale, daughter of Maj. Peyton G. Hale and wife, Jane Bourne (see Bourne history); no issue. They live on Elk Creek in the William Hale homestead. Lee Nuckolls, (single) lives with his brother, Robert Garland Nuckolls. Charles Nuckolls married Mrs. Effie Walters; no issue; lives at Speedwell, Wythe county, Va.

Clarke S. Nuckolls married Rosa Bourne Hale, daughter of Stephen Hale, Sr., (son of Lewis Hale, Sr., and his wife, Mary Burwell), and Frances Bourne, (daughter of William Bourne, Sr., and wife, Rosa Jones.) Issue: eight daughters, four sons. First daughter, Amelia Gwyn Nuckolls, married Ballard E. Ward of Speedwell, Wythe county, Va. (son of William Ward and wife, Mary Young). Issue: seven sons and one daughter.

First son, Ellis William Clarke Ward, graduated at Emory and Henry College and took course in Vanderbilt University, Nashville, Tenn. He was licensed to preach by the M. E. Church, South; married Miss Lelia Sparks of Centre, Cherokee county, Ala.; was principal of Elk Creek School, then moved to Centre, Alabama, and commenced the practice of medicine. He died with typhoid fever in Centre, Ala.; one child (died in infancy); both buried at Garrett Cemetery, Ala.

Second son, Floyd Harvey Ward, married Miss Ella Walsh (daughter of Dr. Walsh). First daughter, Mamie, married Dr. Phipps, and lives at Bridle Creek, Va.; second daughter, Laura Ward, married Richard Rowe, Wythe County, Virginia; third daughter, Ethel Ward, married Prof. Crockett Carr, Galax, Virginia.

First son, Ballard E. Ward, married and lives in Pocahontas, Virginia; fourth daughter, Floyd; fifth,

Ida; one son died young; one son, Clarence, single.

Floyd Harvey Ward and family moved to Illinois from Knob Fork, Va.

Frances Laura Ward, only daughter of Ballard E. Ward, married John C. Hale of Centre, Cherokee county, Ala. Issue, one son and two daughters. The son, Ballard E. Hale, died young. First daughter, Stella Hale, educated at Centenary College, Cleveland, Tenn., single; second daughter, Virginia, single, at Centenary College. They live in Centre, Alabama. Mrs. Hale died in Centre, Alabama, January 30th, 1914; is buried in the Garrett cemetery. John C. Hale is son of Clarke Hale and wife, Susan Garrett, of Garrett's Ferry, Ala. Clarke G. Hale was son of Stephen Hale and wife, Frances Bourne, of Elk Creek, Va. John Hale has been a merchant the greater part of his life. He now employs his time looking after the Garrett plantation, a large and productive body of land, on the Coosa river near Centre, Ala.

James Stuart Ward (third son of Ballard E. Ward and Amelia Gwyn Nuckolls), married Miss Alice Varney, of Newfields, N. H.; one son, Varney Stuart Ward.

James Ward died in Roanoke, Virginia, September 17th, 1913. His son, Varney, is a student in the Phillips Exeter Academy in Massachusetts.

Eli Hale, fourth son of Ballard Ward, died young, and is buried at Speedwell Church, Wythe county.

Leonidas Hicks Ward, fifth son, married Ellen Hale (daughter of Charles Hale and wife, Tabitha Bourne). First son, Everett Hale; second, Gwyn; one daughter, Ruth; third son, Leonidas; fourth, Basil. They live at the Charles Hale homestead on Knob Fork.

Dr. Lilburn Ward, sixth son, married Nellie Mahood of Culpepper, Va.; one son. They live in Pocahontas, Va. Dr. Ward is practicing dentistry there.

Herbert Gwyn Ward, seventh son, first went to Centre, Ala., and was in business with his brother-in-law, J. C. Hale. From there he went to Pueblo, Col., and was employed for a while by the Nuckolls Packing Co. He went from there to California, and finally to Minneapolis, Minn. He was drowned in Pike Lake, New Brighton, July 15th, 1905.

Ballard E. Ward's first wife, Amelia Gwyn Ward, died at Speedwell, Wythe county, Va., when her youngest son, Herbert Gwyn Ward, was four weeks old. She is buried at the Speedwell Methodist Church, Wythe county, Va.

Ballard Ward married the second time, Sophia L. Nuckolls, fourth daughter of Clarke Nuckolls and wife, Rosa Bourne Hale. He sold his farm on Cripple Creek, and bought the farm on Knob Fork in Grayson county, where William Bourne and Rosa Jones, his wife, first settled. At that place, a son, Ballard Ernest Ward, was born to them, July 15th, 1877. He is the only child of Ballard Ward and Sophia Nuckolls. When he was an infant, his mother died, and is buried at the Nuckolls cemetery near Old Town, Va. At the request of his mother, Ballard Ernest Ward was taken by her brother, B. F. Nuckolls (the writer of this history), and brought up with his family. He was married to Miss Lucy B. Anderson, Ivy, Va., on June 10th, 1913. He is travelling auditor for the Pocahontas Consolidated Collieries Co., and lives in Pochontas, Va.

Ballard E. Ward married the third time, Mrs. Caroline Frances Killinger of Marion, Va. He died in 1896, and is buried in the cemetery at Ebenezer Church, Spring Valley, near his home in Virginia. His third wife died and is buried in Marion, Virginia; no issue.

Malinda Nuckolls, second daughter of Clarke Nuckolls, died single.

Benjamin Floyd Nuckolls, first son of Clarke Nuckolls and Rosa Bourne Hale, and writer of this history, was born October 20th, 1838, at the old Nuckolls homestead near Grayson Old C. H. When quite young, he clerked in his father's store at Grayson C. H., was educated at the Jefferson Academy, Ashe county, N. C., licensed to preach May 31st, 1861, and admitted to the Holston Conference at Greenville, Tenn., October, 1861.

On the 6th of November, 1865, he married Miss Mary Fletcher Goodykoontz, daughter of David Goodykoontz and wife, Ruth Harter of Floyd county, Va. (See Goodykoontz history.)

From this union there were four children: First son, William David, born in Concord, Tenn., March 16th, 1868, died near Athens, Tenn., and is buried in the cemetery at Wesleyana Church, by the side of the grave of Rev. Carroll Long.

First daughter, Rosamond Ellen, was born near Athens, Tenn., Oct. 20th, 1869, educated in Wytheville, Va., and at Martha Washington College, Abingdon, Va.; married B. G. Witherow, Sept., 1896. They have two sons, Charles, and Benjamin, and live near Galax, Va.

Second daughter, Ruth Frances, was born in the old Goodykoontz home near Floyd C. H., Va., March 5th, 1872, educated in Wytheville, Va., and at Martha Washington College, Abingdon, Va.; married J. E. Johnston of Cleveland, Tenn. They have one daughter, Mary Ruth and live in Cleveland, Tennessee. Their daughter, Mary Ruth, was married on January 7th, 1914, to Dr. Carl Thomas Speck. They reside in Cleveland.

Second son, Isaac Clarke, was born at Independence, Va., Nov. 11th, 1873; died near Old Town, Va., Oct. 10th, 1875, and is buried in the Nuckolls cemetery.

Sarah Frances Nuckolls, third daughter of Clarke S. Nuckolls and wife, Rosa Bourne Hale, married Dr. Brutus

Fleming Cooper and settled at Old Town, Va. Issue: six daughters and one son. First, Emma Cooper, married Stephen Mason Hale, son of Rev. Wiley Dickenson Hale and wife, Martha Gwin Mitchell. They have six sons and five daughters; first son, Willie Hale, married Minnie Burke; second son, Cleveland Hale, single; third son, James Hale, single; fourth son, Scott Hale, single; fifth, twins, died infants.

First daughter, Clara Hale, married Oscar Oakley, of Mt. Airy, N. C.; second daughter, Blanche Hale, married Mr. Banner, Mt. Airy; third, Forrest Hale, single; fourth, Lillie Hale, single; fifth, Alice Hale, single.

Stephen M. Hale and family all live in Mt. Airy, N. C. He and his sons are successful merchants.

Eddie Forest Cooper, second daughter of Dr. B. F. Cooper and wife, Sarah Frances Nuckolls, married James Lafayette Warrick, son of John Wesley Warrick and wife, Ellen Carson. They have three sons and two daughters. First son, Thomas; second, Claude S., third, Paul. First daughter, Bertie, married Mr. Charles Vance, Kingsport, Tenn.; one daughter, Ethel Louisa; second daughter, Ethel, single. All now living at Kingsport, Tenn. Lula, second daughter of Dr. B. F. Cooper and wife, Sarah F. Nuckolls, married James Wiley Dobyns, son of Ben W. Dobyns and wife, Charlotte Hale. They have two sons: first, Benjamin E., second, Stephen Brutus Fleming. All now living at Kingsport, Tenn. Benjamin married Miss Huffard, of Wythe county, Va.

The only son of Dr. B. F. Cooper and wife, S. F. Nuckolls, Johnnie, died young at Old Town, Va.

Fourth daughter of Dr. B. F. Cooper and wife, S. F. Nuckolls, married Alexander Chapman Anderson, son of Friel Nuckolls Anderson and wife, Elizabeth Roberts. They have five daughters and two sons: first daughter, Ruby Elizabeth, died young; second daughter,

Catharine; third, Lula; fourth, Virginia; fifth daughter, Paulina; first son, Edward; second, Daniel.

Fifth daughter of Dr. B. F. Cooper and wife, S. F. Cooper, Lillie Rosa, married Charles Anderson, son of Friel Nuckolls Anderson and wife, Elizabeth Roberts; one daughter, Garnett, died young; one son, Grey. They live in Galax, Va.

Nannie Cooper, sixth and youngest daughter of Dr. B. F. Cooper and wife, Sarah F. Nuckolls, single.

Dr. Brutus Fleming Cooper was born in Wythe county, Va.; read medicine under his brother, Dr. John Cooper, and Dr. Bert Saunders, near Leadmines, Wythe county, Va. Commenced the practice of Medicine at Old Town, Va., 1855.

Sarah Cooper died at the old homestead, Old Town, August 31st, 1909. Dr. Cooper died at Kingsport, Tenn., 1910. Both are buried in the old Nuckolls Cemetery.

William Swift Nuckolls, second son of Clarke S. Nuckolls and his wife, Rosa Bourne Hale, joined the 8th Virginia Cavalry Co. in 1861. His captain was Dr. Wm. Bamblett. Wm. Swift Nuckolls was wounded in Maryland in 1864. He partially recovered from his wounds, and in 1868 was married the first time to Miss Susan B. Hale, daughter of Martin Hale and wife, Jestena Hale, of Leesburg, Cherokee county, Alabama. (See sketch of Hale family.)

From this union, one daughter, Lelia B. Nuckolls, who married William P. Waugh. She was his second wife, and to them were born one son, Swift, and one daughter, Susan. Swift Waugh is being educated at the Virginia Polytechnic Institute at Blacksburg, Va., and Susan is in school at Martha Washington College, Abingdon, Va.

William Swift Nuckolls married the second time Miss Fannie M. Kinzer, daughter of Michael Kinzer and wife, Annie Tunner, of Hillsville, Va.; issue: three daughters, Annie, Susan Viola, Amelia Clyde; two sons, John Michael, Alexander Heath.

Annie married Kemper Hampton, son of Litrell Hampton and wife, Nancy Blevins. They live at Round Meadows, Grayson county, Va., and have three sons, Bernard, Raleigh and Litrell, and two daughters, Selma Frances and Nancy Vera.

Susan Viola Nuckolls married Edwin Dodd of Tazewell county, Va. They live in Galax, Va., and have three sons, Edwin Nuckolls, John, Robert; one daughter, Ruth Nuckolls. Mr. Dodd is manager of the Galax Furniture Factory.

Amelia Clyde Nuckolls married Rudolph Couch; they live in Galax, and have two daughters, Hazel and Ruby.

John Michael Nuckolls married Eliza Hankley of Rural Retreat, Va. They have one daughter, Louise, and one son, Francis. They live in Galax, Va.

Alexander Heath Nuckolls married Ella Lundy, daughter of William Lundy; they have one daughter, Alpha Heath, and live with their mother, Mrs. Fannie Nuckolls, on a part of the old Nuckolls homestead, near Old Town, Va.

William Swift Nuckolls died in February, 1887, and is buried in the Nuckolls Cemetery.

Mary A. Nuckolls, fifth daughter of Clarke Nuckolls and Rosa Bourne Hale, married Churchill Fawbush Moore, son of Isaac Moore and wife, Euphemia Jones, who was the daughter of Maj. Abner Jones and wife, Hannah Fawbush. They have five daughters and three sons:

First daughter, Celia Fawbush, died single; second daughter, Amelia Nuckolls married a Mr. Miller, and lives in Winston, N. C.; third daughter, Rosa Bourne, married Fred Lawson, they live in Ivanhoe, Va., and have one son, Fred Moore; fourth daughter, Leona Nuckolls, single; fifth daughter, Lura, single. First son, William, died single; second son, Glen, died single; third son, Arthur Neal, married Cora Moore, daughter of Orville Moore.

Dorthula Gertrude Nuckolls, sixth daughter of Clarke Nuckolls, married first, Robert Rodgers, of Wytheville, Va. He died in Roanoke, Va.; no issue. She married the second time, Albert G. Umberger, Wytheville, Va.; he died, no issue. Mrs. Umberger now lives in Galax, Va.

Margaret A. Nuckolls, seventh daughter of Clarke Nuckolls, married John A. Ward, son of Lilburn Ward, and wife, Annie Groseclose. They live on Cripple Creek, Va., and have three sons, James Brown, Charles and Robert N. Kent, and seven daughters, Annie, Ella, Rosa Bourne, Susan, Lena, Stella H., and Ruth Nuckolls. James Brown, single, lives in Kingsport, Tenn.; Charles, single, Cripple Creek, Va.; Robert N. Kent, Pocahontas, Va.

Annie married Eugene Kyle; they live on Cripple Creek, Va.; three sons: Ward, Glasgow, James; one daughter, Elma. Ella Ward married Charles Dobyns, son of Samuel Green Dobyns, and wife, Ruth Lawson, of Patrick county, Va.; no children. They live at Speedwell, Va.

Rosa Ward married Rev. Keller Yonce Umberger, a Lutheran Minister. They live in Bluefield, West Va.; one son, Kenneth.

Thomas Fielden Nuckolls, third son of Clark Nuckolls, died of diphtheria in 1862; is buried in the Nuckolls cemetery.

Stephen Nathaniel Nuckolls, fourth son of Clarke Nuckolls, married Leona Mitchell Cornett, daughter of Capt. William Cornett and wife, Linnie Mitchell, who was the daughter of William M. Mitchell and wife, Sophia P. Hale. They have four sons, William Swift, Clarke Hale, Benjamin Winton, Earl Garland, and six

RESIDENCE OF B. F. NUCKOLLS
Built by Him in 1876, Near Oldtown, Virginia

daughters, Maud Forrest, Linnie, Bertha, Pauline, Gay, and Dawn.

Maud Forrest married Dr. Asbury Glen Pless, of Waynesville, N. C. They had two children; one son, Asbury Glenn; one daughter, Maud Forrest.

Mrs. Pless died soon after the birth of her second child, and the child died soon afterwards; both are buried in the Nuckolls cemetery. Dr. Pless married the second time, Miss Shelton, of Richmond, Va. They live in Galax, Va. Linnie is single, lives in Galax. Bertha is single. Pauline died young, is buried in the Nuckolls cemetery. William Swift lives in Wyoming. Ben Winton, Clarke Hale, Earl Garland, Fay and Daron live at home.

Elizabeth B. Nuckolls, youngest child of Clarke Nuckolls, married Geo. W. Todd. They live in Galax, Va., and have three sons, Lance, Emmon, and George W. Clarke, and three daughters, Rosa B., Ila, and Mebus. They are all living in Galax, Va. Rosa is being educated at Martha Washington College, Abingdon, Va.

Martha Nuckolls, first daughter of Robert G. Nuckolls and wife, married John Brown, Jr., oldest son of John Brown, Sr., and his wife, Martha Wood, who came from Yorkshire, England. John Brown, Jr., was born in Yorkshire in 1801. To John Brown, Jr., and wife, Martha Nuckolls, were born three sons, and two daughters. First son, Creed, died single; second son, George, died single; third son, Nathaniel, living, single; first daughter, Sena, married Francis Bryan, no issue; second daughter, Amelia, married Joseph Duphey; lives now at Battle Creek, Nebraska; one daughter, Isabella, single; one son John B., educated in Nebraska, and at Blacksburg, Va.

Sena, second daughter of Robert G. Nuckolls and wife died single; is buried in Nuckolls cemetery.

The Brown family came from Yorkshire, England,

before or about the time of the formation of Grayson county, and bought and entered lands on Meadow Creek, and have held the estate in the family until the present generation. The Browns, like all other pioneer settlers, began in woods. It is said, the first tree was cut down by the Old Man Brown who had never seen a tree cut. He pulled off his coat and silk hat, and commenced to cut all around the tree; at last it fell on his silk hat and coat, and mashed them; but he worked on. He cut a forked limb, and scratched up his ground, planted corn, and raised a crop; and there has been plenty raised on the farm ever since, and now the old homestead is the most valuable farm on Meadow Creek. It is now owned by Mrs. Mary Osborne and her children. She is a daughter of Jane Brown, who married Hiram Williams. Jane Brown was the youngest daughter of John Brown, Sr., and Martha Wood, of England. Mrs. Mary Osborne is the wife of Emmett Osborne, a son of Floyd Osborne and his wife, Rosa B. Hale. Mrs. Mary Osborne has four daughters, Annie, Bettie, Callie, and Hattie, and two sons, Ellis, and Dean Floyd. Their father, Emmett P. Osborne, died at a Roanoke, Va., hospital, of appendicitis in 1911. He was a good man and is greatly missed by all.

The second wife of Col. Alfred Moore was Mrs. Susan Nuckolls Wellington, of Eastern Virginia. Her mother was a Swift. Her son, Mr. Wellington, lives in Richmond, Va.

Nathaniel Nuckolls, son of Robert G. Nuckolls and wife, Margaret Swift, moved to Missouri in 1845, married Sarah Ann Finn; from there he crossed the plains, and was a miner in California; found gold, came back to Missouri and moved his family in wagons to California, and settled there. One of his sons, Clarke, was born on top of the Rocky Mountains, on the journey to California. There were sixteen children born to them, and all settled in California.

Andrew Nuckolls, James Nuckolls, George Nuckolls, and Hugh Nuckolls, sons of Robert G. Nuckolls and wife, Margaret Swift, died single, and are buried in the Nuckolls cemetery.

Thomas Nuckolls, son of Robert G. Nuckolls and wife, Margaret Swift, married Charlotte Jestina Stone, daughter of John Stone and wife, Sarah Leonard; issue: six sons, and two daughters: First son, Hugh, married Ellen Wright; first daughter, Amelia, married Thomas N. Meyers; two sons; Flora W., single; one son, Robert G. Nuckolls, married Miss Bryant, three children.

Second son of Thomas Nuckolls, Nathaniel, married Miss Wall, of Hillsville, Va. They live in Ketchakan, Alaska; two children. He is engaged in mining and shipping. He has traveled all over the west.

Second son, Ellis V. Nuckolls, married Bessie N. Williams; children died. Ellis and his wife are Readers of the Christian Science Church, in El Paso, Texas.

Fourth son, Chester B. Nuckolls, M. D. He graduated in medicine and first practiced in Fluvana county, Virginia He is now located at Hillsville, Va.; has a drug store and also a large practice. He married Miss Carrie Reeves, daughter of Andrew Reeves and wife, Miss Alexander, formerly of Alleghany county, N. C., but now living in Texas. They have one son, Chester Reeves Nuckolls.

Fifth son, Henry C. Nuckolls, married Frances Cooley, of Carroll county, Va.; one daughter, Jessie, died young; two sons now living in Oklahoma. First, Ellis; second, Ben. His wife died in Oklahoma, is buried at Gambetta, Va.

Sixth son, Elbert L. Nuckolls, married Bertie Thornton, of Hillsville, Va.; one daughter, Jessie; one son, died in infancy; one daughter, small. Elbert is a lawyer in Fayetteville, W. Va. He is successful in his practice, and also in his business enterprises.

Two daughters of Thomas Nuckolls and wife: first daughter, Sarah Margaret, died young; Bertie married Robert Wade, of Halifax county, Va.; now living in Oklahoma.

Thomas Nuckolls was a useful citizen and lived a successful life. A marble shaft marks his resting place near the railroad at Gambetta, Va. His wife died at the home of her daughter, Bertie Wade, in Oklahoma, February, 1912, and is buried with her husband at Gambetta, Carroll county, Va.

Ezra Nuckolls, ninth son of John Nuckolls and wife, Mary Garland, came to Grayson county with his brothers, sister, and uncle, Charles Garland, and married Lucinda Hale, oldest daughter of Stephen Hale and wife, Frances Bourne. From this union there were seven sons and six daughters; the oldest son, Stephen Friel, was born in Grayson county, near Grayson C. H., August 16th, 1825; died February 14th, 1879, in Salt Lake City, Utah. He married Lucinda Bourne in Grayson County, Va., daughter of William Bourne, Jr., and wife, Mary Johnstone. Four sons of Friel Nuckolls and Lucinda Bourne: William B. and Bruce are mining in Montana; Paul died nineteen years ago; Rupert B. Nuckolls lives in Butte, Montana. He has been connected with the State Savings Bank for over seventeen years; he is now cashier of this bank. He is married, and has two daughters, Frances and Virginia; one son, Stephen Friel. After the death of his father, Stephen Friel Nuckolls, Rupert B. was sent to Virginia by the Executor of his father's estate, (Dr Fowler, formerly of Bristol, Tenn.) to Roanoke College, at Salem, Va. He afterward returned west and has made a success in business.

The second son of Ezra Nuckolls was Heath, who remained with the family in Virginia until 1853. At that time, the family that remained here moved to Missouri

BALLARD E. WARD AND WIFE, SOPHIA L. NUCKOLLS
Daughter of Clark Nuckolls and wife, Rosa Bourne Hale

and settled at Rock Port. Ezra Nuckolls died there; also his wife died there soon after he died; both buried at Rock Port, Mo.

Heath Nuckolls married Miss Hawk, settled in Nebraska City. He died there and is buried in Nebraska City. His wife and daughter live there.

Columbus Nuckolls also lived in Nebraska City; he married, died, and is buried there; he has a wife and children living there.

Lafayette Nuckolls married in Missouri, afterward moved to Texas; died, and left a family. Houston Nuckolls married in Missouri; he also lived in Nebraska City, and died there.

Emmett, the youngest son of Ezra Nuckolls, married first in Missouri, married second time, his cousin, Miss Ellen Anderson, daughter of Robert Garland Anderson, who had also moved to Missouri from Grayson county, Va. Emmett finally settled in Pueblo, Colorado, established The Nuckolls Packing House in Pueblo. He married the third time in Pueblo and died there, October 12th, 1910.

ANNOUNCEMENT

"It is with deep sorrow that we announce the death in this city on Wednesday, October the twelfth, nineteen hundred and ten, of our President, Emmett Nuckolls, after a brief illness following an injury received while attending to his regular duties at our plant.

"The Nuckolls Packing Co.,
"October 18th, 1910.   Pueblo, Colo."

His last wife still lives in Pueblo, Col. He also has two sons in charge of The Nuckolls Packing Co. there. Of this Company, E. Nuckolls is president; J. M. Nuckolls, vice-president; G. Harvey Nuckolls, treasurer, and W. F. Nelson, Secretary.

Stephen Friel Nuckolls left Grayson Court House and went to Missouri about the year 1848; he came back to Grayson and married, returned to Missouri when Nebraska was a territory. When Nebraska City was located, he planned and laid off the City and was prominent in securing the change of Nebraska from a territory into a state. He lived there for some time. One of the counties in Nebraska is named for him, "Nuckolls county." He was successful in business, made money, and was liberal in every way with his money. When his father, Ezra Nuckolls, moved from Virginia to Missouri, he took with him quite a number of negroes. They moved through in wagons. These negroes were kept at Rock Port, Mo., and at that time John Brown and his Company were on their raids. They carried away two young negro women, "Celia" and "Eliza," that belonged to the family; they took them into Illinois; Stephen Friel Nuckolls followed them, found them in Illinois, and made an effort to take them back. He was arrested and put in prison, and the negro women were taken to Canada. Officers came into the prison to take Friel Nuckolls out to hang him; he placed himself in one corner of the room, drew his revolver, and said to them, "The first man that opens that door, I will shoot him down."

They did not go in, but he had to pay twenty-two thousand dollars to get out of the jail. He was in sympathy with the South, and when the war broke out, he thought best for him to leave the Western country.

He moved, with his family, to Jersey City, New Jersey, and remained there until the close of the war. While he was there, he sent money to the soldiers, and helped many of them who had been captured and were in the Northern prisons. Soon after the surrender he returned to Nebraska, with but little means, but began again to accumulate money. He then moved to Wyoming Territory, and was

JAMES STUART WARD
Son of Ballard E. Ward and wife, Amelia G. Nuckolls

elected from there as a member of the 46th Congress and served this term in Washington as a useful member.

After his return from Congress he moved to Salt Lake City, Utah. At that time there was an effort to move the "Mormons" from Salt Lake, and his object in going there was that in the event they were moved, their property would sell at a low price, and he could make profitable investments. After being well situated there, he concluded to remain, as he had investments in mining and other interests by which he was gathering large profits.

In the year 1875, I wrote him and asked for some help in building a Methodist Church at what was Grayson C. H., but at that time, the Courts being moved, the post office was Nuckollsville. As this was the old place of business for the Nuckolls family, I thought he would be glad to help us build the Church and would perhaps send me $100. I soon received a letter in which he stated if I would promise to raise $1,000, he would send to me $1,000. I wrote him I would accept his offer. He promptly sent the $1,000 in New York exchange checks, stating he wanted us to put up a good building. We finished the building and had it dedicated by Dr. David Sullins in 1876. This Church has been a great blessing to us.

Stephen Friel Nuckolls accumulated a large estate and was a man of wide influence. His wife died in Salt Lake City, and he died soon thereafter, February 14th, 1879.

There were born to Ezra Nuckolls and wife, Lucinda Hale, six daughters; all born in Grayson county, Va.

Polly, the oldest daughter, married Rice Schooler; he was from Eastern Virginia. He and his wife settled near Grayson C. H., afterward moved to Missouri and settled at Rock Port. Their children were born in Grayson county, Va.

Frances, their oldest daughter, married after they moved to Missouri. She married a kinsman, and came back to Roanoke, Va.

Ellis, the oldest son, lives at Rock Port, Mo.; Kent, second son, married in Missouri a Miss Bradley, formerly from Abingdon, Va.; has a family of children in Rock Port. Houston, another son, lives at Rock Port. They have a stock farm in Missouri.

The second daughter of Ezra Nuckolls and wife was Frances H., who married Harvey Gordon-Bourne, son of William Bourne, Jr., and wife, Mary Johnston. Harvey G. and his wife first settled on Little River, in Grayson county, Va.; afterwards, moved to Missouri; both died out west; they had one daughter, Mary Bourne, one son, Houston Gordon. Houston Gordon has one daughter, Mrs. Pearl Bourne Dameron; her husband is a lawyer, the county attorney and council for the A. T. & S. F. R. R.; they live at La Junto, Otero county, Colorado. They have two sons, seventeen and fifteen years old, and one daughter seven years old.

Rosamond B. Nuckolls, the third daughter of Ezra Nuckolls, went to Missouri with her brother, S. F. Nuckolls, and married out there a Mr. Bourchees. They lived at Hamburg, Iowa; both died there; have sons and daughters.

Sena, fourth daughter, married Mr. Martin; lived and died at Colorado Springs, Colorado; have children there.

Elizabeth, fifth daughter, married Thomas E. Metcalf, a lawyer; lives at Long Beach, California. Mr. Metcalf died recently. They have two sons, both lawyers, who live at Long Beach, Cal. Elizabeth Metcalf is the only one of the children of Ezra Nuckolls and wife, Lucinda Hale, who is now living.

Ezra Nuckolls and his brothers were of much help in the formation of the county of Grayson. They had been

WILLIAM SWIFT NUCKOLLS

well educated and had good family training in Eastern Virginia. The men and women were tall in stature, a number of them seven feet in height and well proportioned. Several of them inherited from their Colonial ancestry at Jamestown, a liking for the mercantile business, and with some of the present generation it is still kept up.

Ezra Nuckolls was for a term sheriff of Grayson county. He, with Creed and Clarke Nuckolls, sons of Robert G. Nuckolls, formed a partnership with William Oglesby, and went into the goods business at Grayson C. H., Va. They were the first merchants at the place and had branch houses at Elk Creek and Bridle Creek and continued in business until after the close of the war of 1861-1865. The style of the firm was then changed to Nuckolls and Dickenson. Another firm at Grayson C. H. was Nuckolls and Jennings. James Waugh began the mercantile business at Grayson C. H. before the war. After the war, his sons, William P. and John B. Waugh continued the business. William P. Waugh was in the mercantile business at the time of his death at Old Town, Va., in 1896.

His brother, John B. Waugh, continued in business at Old Town until the North Carolina Extension of the N. & W. R. R. was built to Galax. He then transferred his business to Galax, built a handsome home there and resides there now with his family.

When the county of Grayson was divided and Carroll county formed from the east end, the courts were moved sixteen miles west, to Independence, Va. The firm of Nuckolls & Jennings, of Old Grayson C. H., opened a branch house at Independence. Ezra Nuckolls built the first store house, and also the first hotel at Independence, and continued in business until he sold out and moved to Missouri, about 1853. Robert G. Nuckolls built and opened the first hotel, or ordinary, at Grayson Old C. H. William Bourne built the first clerk's office and was the

first clerk of the courts held first at his house, and later
at the court house. The office is still standing in good
repair after over one hundred years' service. It is a good
oil brick with dressed stone foundation and is now used
as post office and supervisor's office. This building still
belongs to the County of Grayson.

NATHANIEL NUCKOLLS

The subjects of the following sketches are not residents of Virginia, but as they are descended from the Jamestown Nuckolls family, and the history is interesting, we insert it:

Nathaniel Nuckolls, of Muscogee county, Ga., was the fifth child of Thomas and Ann Nuckolls, and was born in Louisa county, Va. One of the brothers, who were merchants in Jamestown, had married a Miss Duke in England. Her father was a prominent physician, came to America with his son-in-law, and practiced medicine extensively in Virginia. Dr. Duke had a large family, and the Dukes have for many years been prominent in Virginia and North Carolina. From this Nuckolls brother, who married Miss Duke, Nathaniel Nuckolls was descended. Thomas and Ann Nuckolls had six sons and four daughters; the sons were Duke, Stephen, Alexander, Samuel, Nathaniel, and George Bias. Duke, Stephen, Alexander, and Samuel were farmers; George Bias was a lawyer; Nathaniel was a mechanic. Two of his sisters were named Mary (Polly) and Lucinda; names of the other two not given. Nathaniel owned an interest in a gold mine in North Georgia, then bought a farm in Alabama, and taught some of his negro men to work at the mechanics trade, and he studied architecture, and planned and built many houses. He was a merchant for a while in Columbus, Ga., and planned and had built for himself there a handsome residence, where he lived for twenty years before his death on

September 17th, 1868. His wife died in June of the same year. They left three sons, Thomas J., Nathaniel A., and James T., and seven daughters, Elizabeth A. Ware, Louisiana A. Hawkins, Mary V. Kyle, Cornelia L. Richardson, Laura C. Freeman, Adella L. Nowlin. The will of Nathaniel Nuckolls was recorded in Muscogee county, Ga., October 5th, 1868, and copied on the records of Cherokee county, Ala. (at Centre, Ala.), in 1911. In his will he gives to each of his three sons, farms valued at six thousand dollars each, and to each of his seven daughters, farms valued at six thousand dollars each, and directs that all of his other property be equally distributed among his children. The will states that the farm given to Mrs. Freeman was deeded to her by Martin Hale, and A. H. Mackey, administrators.

Of the ten children of Nathaniel Nuckolls, there are now only two living—Mrs. Laura A. Freeman, who lives with her son, Thomas N., on her farm near Centre, Ala., and Mrs. Adella L. Nowlin, who lives in Gadsden, Ala. There are a good many descendants, however, living in Alabama, and in different parts of the country.

JOHN NUCKOLLS OF SOUTH CAROLINA

About the years 1765-75, John Nuckolls moved from Virginia to South Carolina, settling near Spartanburg. He was probably a great-uncle of Nathaniel Nuckolls, as William T. Nuckolls (his grandson), was a cousin of Nathaniel Nuckolls. Mrs. C. F. Marsh, of Morristown, Tenn., is a descendant of John Nuckolls, and gave the author the following information: "John Nuckolls is buried at Whig Hill, S. C.; following is the inscription on his tombstone:

"'In memory of John Nuckolls, Sr., who was murdered by the Tories for his devotion to liberty, on the 11th day of December, 1780, in the 49th year of his age.'

'"Rest, noble patriot,
'"Rest in peace
'"The prize you sought
'"Your country won."'

The Revolutionary records of South Carolina were many of them destroyed when Columbia was burned, but one record tells where John Nuckolls was a commissioner of election in 1776. Mrs. Marsh also sent the following copy from the *Carolina Spartan*:

NUCKOLLS AND DAWKINS

Two Famous Families—Whig Hill—Tory Raids— Revolutionary Scenes

"In a recent issue of the *Carolina Spartan* there appears some very interesting local history under the title of Nuckolls and Dawkins. Hoping that it will be of interest to our subscribers, especially the older residents of the country, we publish the piece entire.

"Now and then a question, or a suggestion, sets the train of thought or investigation in motion that keeps moving and widening as it moves. A few days ago a lawyer of the city asked for some information about Elijah Dawkins, who died in Union county in 1834. A lawyer from another State wanted some information about the Dawkins estate. The necessary information was furnished but the investigation did not cease.

"A sketch of General Dawkins and his family would prove most interesting at this time. Elijah Dawkins married Nancy Nuckolls. It must have been between 1793 and 1800. They had eight children, whose names we cannot give in order of birth. They were Elijah, Joshua P., Thomas N., Benjamin F., James B., Susan, Nancy and Elizabeth. All of these married except Elijah. Joshua P. married a Miss Davidson. Both of

SUSAN B. HALE
Daughter of Martin Hale, and wife of William Swift Nuckolls

them are dead, but their two children; Benjamin and Mrs. Nannie Trench are living in Florida. We believe these are the only survivors of this large family. Judge Thomas N. Dawkins married Miss Mary Polton, who is living in Union, S. C. Benjamin F. Dawkins married Miss Elize Cleveland, of Greenville. These died without children. James B. Dawkins married Miss Carrie Taylor and moved to Florida. He is dead, but his wife is living at Gainesville. Susan married Wm. T. Nuckolls, both of whom died years ago without children. Nancy married Gen. James Rogers. She was the tall woman that Major James E. Henry did not wish to be seen walking with in Washington.

"Gen. Rogers and Mr. Nuckolls were both members of Congress.

"Mrs. Rogers had one son, Dawkins, a young man of fine progress, who was killed early in the war. Elizabeth married Abner Benson. He was also a Congressman. She had twins, both of which died young and she soon followed. What became of Abner Benson is unknown to the writer of this sketch. About 1830 it was said that Mrs. Elizabeth Benson and Mrs. Clarissa Henry were two of the handsomest women in the up-country. They were noted for their striking appearance and gracious manners.

"This leads us back to the Nuckolls family. John Nuckolls married Agatha Ballock in Virginia, perhaps in Dinwiddie county. The Nuckolls family came over from England and settled in Virginia. Their history runs back to 1452, when the "War of the Roses" began. They were adherents to the house of York, the emblem of which was the white rose. When the original Nuckolls emigrated to America, he brought a bush of that rose with him. Each member of the family kept a bush of this famous rose. When John Nuckolls and his wife Agatha, came to

South Carolina, they brought the rose with them and planted it at Whig Hill, near Grindall Shoals. From that plant their decendants got cuttings or roots, and several members of the family had the white rose until 1860, when sentiment was knocked out of the hearts of many of our people. If the rose of York is now living, it is at the residence of John D. Jeffries, who owns the W. T. Nuckolls homestead. "Aunt Nancy" Dawkins had the rose until the time of her death, about 1861 or 1862, and T. D. Littlejohn now owns the famous homestead.

"About 1765 to 1775, John Nuckolls and his wife, with some of their older children, came to this state. They settled between Thickety and Pacolet, at the place afterwards known as Whig Hill. There they were living when the war came on. They had accumulated considerable property and owned some negroes. Mr. Nuckolls went into the war at the beginning. Owing to the nature of the service in upper Carolina the patriotic soldiers could often get to their homes and remain a few days, or a few weeks. When the necessity arose they would rally at some appointed place and enter the field again. It was perhaps in the fall or early winter of 1780, just before the battle of King's Mountain, that John Nuckolls visited his home at Whig Hill. The meal tub was nearly empty. He went with his son John, a mere lad, over to a mill on Broad river, about fifteen or eighteen miles from home. This mill was perhaps at the Sam Jeffries mill above Smith's Ford. The distance being so great, Mr. Nuckolls had to remain all night. It is said that millers in those days provided a room in the mill house, or in their dwelling for customers thus detained. Nuckolls was well known and recognized as an uncompromising rebel. On his way to the mill tradition says that a man by the name of M. Keown saw him. Learning that he was going to stay all night, he mustered up a crowd of tories in the neighborhood, getting some of them from the York side of the river, and went to the mill and awoke Nuckolls and killed him. When they aroused him they said: 'We've come for you.' He knew what they meant. He asked permission to wake his son so that he could give some messages for his people at home. They refused and said that if he awoke his son they would kill him also. They then took Nuckolls out a short distance from the mill and prepared to shoot him. He asked permission to pray five minutes. This was granted. He prayed aloud. After he had uttered a few petitions, one of them said: 'If he continues praying that way much longer, we will not be able to kill him.' Some one then fired a ball through his head. He was thrown into a ditch or gully and some rock and brush thrown over the body. Sometime after that Mrs. Nuckolls had the bones gathered up and buried at Whig Hill. The tombstone, which is standing, has this inscription, 'Killed by Tories'. Mrs. Nuckolls, about 1782 to 1785, married Joshua Petty. He was as much loved by the children as if he had been their father. He managed the farm so as to increase the property and gave the daughters the best education possible. He never had any children of his own. The Nuckolls children were Nancy, who married Elijah Dawkins; Susan, who married Charles Littlejohn; Frankie, who married a Goudelock. John Nuckolls was the boy who was at the mill when his father was killed by Tories. He married a Miss Tompson, daughter of gentleman Bill Tompson, and had two children, William T. and Melissa. William married his cousin Susan Dawkins, and Melissa married Major William Norris.

"If one wished to follow out the different branches of this family tree he would get somewhat confused. The Goudelocks, the Morgans, the Littlejohns and one branch of the Jeffries family would come in for consideration.

"As we have said before, W. T. Nuckolls and his wife, Susan Dawkins, had no children. His sister, Mrs. Norris, had four or five children, only two of whom are living. John D. Norris is in Texas and Miss Julia Norris is living with her nephews, children of her sister, who married Major Frank Anderson, of this county. Their home is at Bethpage, Tenn. Of the descendants of Gen. Elijah Dawkins, only two are living. They have been mentioned before in the sketch, and their home is at Gainesville, Fla. Major S. M. Dawkins and his sister, Miss Ophelia, now living in Spartanburg, are descended from a brother of Gen. Elijah Dawkins. Their grandmother was Frankie Nuckolls, daughter of the original John Nuckolls. They were perhaps the only persons in this state bearing the name of Dawkins, except the two children of Major Morgan Dawkins.

"Several times the Tories made raids on Whig Hill. One band of them had their headquarters at Anderson, or Thickety Fort, which stood on the north side of Goucher Creek, about two and a half miles from its junction with Thickety. Col. Patrick Moore, a stalwart Irishman, six feet seven inches tall, was the Loyalist who had command of the fort. There was another band of Tories down on the Enoree, that played havoc with the property of the patriots. The famous raid made on Whig Hill was, in the winter of 1780, a short time before the battle of Cowpens. They made a clean sweep of everything in the house. Mrs. Nuckolls had been well brought up and educated, and she had many pieces of artistic needle work in her house. Everything was taken, and the only bed for the youngest child was a sheep skin used as a saddle blanket. After these raids John Nuckolls and one of his sisters would mount horses and go out and search for their stolen property. At one time they went as far as Lynch's Creek and brought back some stolen negroes.

They also went over into Laurens county and found some of their stock which they would drive home. In one of the searches they entered a house and saw some of the fine work of their mother's hanging in the room. Such were the scenes through which the patriots and their families had to pass during the revolution of 1776.

"This is a very imperfect sketch, dealing only with a few historical facts. Long ago they could have been rescued from oblivion by the pen of a ready writer. But they are passing away and will soon not be remembered by any one. The material for the colonial and early history of upper Carolina is very meagre. We hope by writing this sketch that some one will be induced to continue the subject. We hope there are persons living who will be able to give interesting sketches of Wm. T. Nuckolls and his wife; Gen. James Rogers and his wife, and Aunt Nancy Dawkins. The intelligent readers of the *Spartan* would take special interest in reading about the people who helped to make our early history."

In the preceding sketch reference was made to the "War of the Roses," stating that the Nuckolls family in England were adherents of the Duke of York, whose emblem was the white rose, and that the white rose was brought to America by the Nuckolls emigrants, and that John Nuckoll's family took roots of the rose to South Carolina with them, and planted them at Whig Hill.

John Nuckolls, the ancestor of the author of this history, also brought the rose from Louisa county, Va., about the year 1790, and planted it in Grayson county, and it is still growing on the old Nuckolls home place near Old Town, Va.

CHAPTER IV

THE FLOWER SWIFT FAMILY

The Swift family were Colonial Settlers in America, and are now found in all parts of these United States.

Flower Swift was one of the pioneer settlers of the New River Valley. He came here from North Carolina, secured quite a boundary of land on the river, near the place first selected to build the Court House for Grayson county. Flower Swift and Charles Nuckolls donated one hundred acres of land for the purpose of building the first court house and public buildings for the county, reserving to themselves three choice one-half acre lots, after laying off the lots for the public buildings and the streets. The town was first named Greenville; the post office, Grayson C. H. After the courts were moved, and Carroll county formed, the post office was changed to Nuckollsville. There was already a post office in Scott county, Va., Nickelsville, and the names being so near alike gave trouble with the mail, so the legislature made another change to Old Town, which name remains at the present time.

Flower Swift was a magistrate in Wythe county. He and William Bourne, Lewis Hale and Minitree Jones were instrumental in getting the territory of Grayson county cut off from Wythe county, two years after its formation.

The following is copied from "Proceedings of First Court at William Bourne's house":

"Under a commission from Henry Lee, Governor of the Commonwealth, directed to Flower Swift and others, bearing date of the 10th day of December, 1792, being

MARGARET SWIFT
Daughter of Flower Swift, and wife of Capt. Robert Nuckolls

read, and thereupon, Flower Swift took the oath of Allegiance to the Commonwealth, the oath to support the Constitution of the United States, the oath of a justice of the county court in chancery, which oath was administered to him by Minitree Jones and Nathaniel Frisbie. Then the said Flower Swift administered all the aforesaid oaths to the others." (See proceedings of the first court at William Bourne's House.)

Flower Swift was the leading justice of the courts, as the readers will see from the first chapter in this book, copied from the first book of records of the first court for Grayson county.

He had been living here for some time, as stated before. He came here from North Carolina, secured lands on the east side of New River, and paid for same by the sale of a lady's side saddle. There was also a boundary of land on the west and north side of New River, bought with a flintlock rifle gun.

Flower Swift married Mary Bedsaul. They opened up a field near the bank of the river, one mile west of where Old Town now is, and built a cabin with board roof, weighted on with logs and with puncheon floor. He also built a blacksmith shop, and set out some peach and apple trees. He reared a large family; after his family had grown up, he and his wife and part of his family moved farther west, as the western country was opened up. The family records were taken off with the family, and we cannot give the names of all the sons and daughters. We have the names of four sons, Thomas, John, William, and Elisha; these sons all moved west. There were three daughters who married here: First, Miss Jestena Swift, married a Mr. .... Jones. They moved to North Carolina. Alfred Swift married Miss Julia Jones, daughter of Minitree Jones.

The second daughter, Margaret Swift, married Capt. Robert G. Nuckolls. They opened up the first hotel, or "ordinary" (as it was then called) at the new court house. On the first court records we find the following: "On motion of Robert Nuckolls, who, having produced the receipt of the Clerk of this Court for the sum of Twelve Dollars and Fifty Cents, a license is granted him to keep an Ordinary at his house in Greenville, one year from the first of May last, whereupon he entered into bond, with security accordingly."

Before this, sometime, John Nuckolls and Mary Garland, his wife, Charles Garland, Asa Nuckolls, Ezra Nuckolls, and Martha Nuckolls came to this county from Louisa county, Virginia. John Nuckolls and Mary Garland returned to Louisa county, and died there; the others remained, and bought a boundary of land of about 400 acres, and built on Meadow Creek, one mile from Greenville. This land is still in the Nuckolls family.

Capt. Robert G. Nuckolls and Margaret Swift were married in 1805. Court record by William Carrico, Sr., a Methodist minister, who was also an early settler here, on west side of New River. Rev. Carrico came to the house of Col. Swift to perform the ceremony. He found Col. Swift busy working in his blacksmith shop. Mr. Carrico went into the shop and asked if he had any objection to the marriage. He said, "No, but Bob Nuckolls will carry off my best spinner." She was a good spinner; she spun wool and flax until her old days and died at the age of ninety-one, honored and respected by all.

There were born to them two daughters and eight sons: Creed, Clarke, James, George, Nathaniel, Thomas, Hugh, Andrew; two daughters, Martha, Sena. (See Nuckolls History, page 65.)

The third daughter, Martha Swift, married Maj. George Currin of Montgomery county, Va. They were

MARTHA NUCKOLLS
Daughter of Robert Nuckolls and wife, Margaret Swift, and wife of John Brown, Sr.

married at the same place, one mile from Greenville, on the river.

Maj. Currin and Martha Swift, his wife, bought six hundred acres of land on Chestnut Creek, of the Buchanan Survey; they built, settled, and brought up their family there. Maj. George Currin died, and is buried on his old home place. He and his wife were worthy, useful citizens, and reared a nice family of sons and daughters; his wife, in her old age, moved to Missouri, died there, and is buried on Red River, Mo.

Maj. Currin was a man well educated, and was a representative in the Virginia Legislature and State Senate, for several years. He owned the lands on which the town of Galax is built. His grandsons also own farms on the old tract of land, and his grandson, Thomas F. Roberts, owns the old homestead. There is a Memorial window in the Methodist Church in Galax in memory of Maj. Geo. Currin, Martha Swift, Capt. Robert G. Nuckolls, Margaret Swift, Thompson Roberts, Clarke S. Nuckolls, Surphina S. Currin, Rosa B. Hale. This is a triple art glass window, on the front to Centre street, put in by the descendants of Maj. George Currin and wife, Martha Swift, and Capt. Robert G. Nuckolls and wife, Margaret Swift. The author of this history, B. F. Nuckolls, had put into the brick wall under this window, a walnut chest, in which we expect to deposit family history to be read by future generations.

Of Maj. George Currin and wife, Martha Swift, there were four sons, and three daughters: first, Robert, married Malinda Bourne, daughter of William Bourne, Jr., and wife, Mary Johnstone; their son, William, married; their daughter, Mary, married Mr. Smoot; all went to Oregon. Second son, John, married Miss Swift in Missouri; they now live in Oregon, and have children there.

Third son, William, married.

Fourth son, Hugh, married Miss Young, Oregon; one son, George, married, and owns large ranches and stock farms in Hepner, Oregon. He is a useful, good man, and has been successful in every respect. He sent a check for $25.00 for the memorial window in the Southern Methodist Church at Galax.

First daughter, Ann Currin, married Joseph Fields of Bridle Creek, Grayson county; settled there first, afterwards moved west. They sold their land on Bridle Creek to Joseph Bryant and wife, Sarah Hale. They had two sons: first, Hugh Fields; second, William.

Second daughter, Catherine Currin, married Martin Cooley, son of Benj. Cooley, Sr., and wife, Miss Jane Dickey.

Third daughter, Surphina Currin, married Thompson Roberts, from near Mt. Airy, Surry county, N. C. They bought out the interests of others in the Maj. Currin farm, and settled there, and reared their family. They died and are buried with Maj. Currin in the family grave yard, in Galax, Va. In this family there were seven sons and five daughters:

First son, Currin Roberts, married Frances Bartlett; they have sons and daughters.

Second son, John, married Mrs. Catherine Leonard; she was the daughter of Thomas Blair, Jr.; they have one son, Sidney.

First daughter, Sallie Roberts, married Alexander Hale, son of Stephen M. Hale and wife, Rosa Bourne, who was daughter of William Bourne, Jr., and wife, Mary Johnstone; they have one daughter, Rosa; one son; they live in Texas.

Second daughter, Martha Roberts, died when a young lady with diphtheria in the year 1862. Also three sisters, fourth, Lucy, fifth, Catherine, sixth, Margaret S., all died with diphtheria near same time. Their father died soon after them.

Seventh son, Thomas Floyd, married Florence Cox, daughter of Thos. Cox and Nancy Roberts, his wife; their first son, Charles, died young; second son, Dan; third son, Fred; fourth son, Frank Currin; first daughter, May.

Third daughter, Elizabeth, married Friel Nuckolls Anderson; their first son, Charles, married Lillie Rosa Cooper, daughter of Dr. B. F. Cooper and wife, Sarah Frances Nuckolls. Their first daughter, Garnett, died young; first son, Grey, still living. Second son of Friel Anderson and Elizabeth Roberts, Alex Chapman, married May Cooper, daughter of Dr. B. F. Cooper and Sarah Frances Nuckolls; their first daughter, Rhuby, died young; second, Catherine; third, Lula; fourth, Virginia; first son, Ned; second, Dan; fifth daughter, Pauline.

Third son, Hugh, married Alverda Burrus; no children. Fourth son, Logan, married first Evaline Trimble; they have one daughter, Lola, who married Isaac Pope; they have sons; second, married. Fifth son, William, married Martha Jones. Sixth son, James, married first, Elizabeth Hale, daughter of Warner Hale and Mary Cox; they had one son, Clyde, who married Miss Ballard; one daughter, Ollie. First daughter, Olive, in Oregon. James married second time, Miss Blair, of Wythe county; one son, small.

CHAPTER V.

HALE HISTORY

For the beginning of this history, I will copy from "History of Middle New River Settlements, and Contiguous Territory," by David E. Johnston.

THE HALES OF THE NEW RIVER VALLEY

"This family is of English origin, decendants of the Hale's of Kent. The first American emigrants of the name, coming in 1632, bore the coat of arms of the Kentish Hales. The traditional story in the family of these New River Hales is that the family was quite numerous in Massachusets and Connecticut, and that sometime prior to the beginning of our war for independence there were in one family of their name, seven brothers, all of whom joined the American army. A great part of them served through the war, under General Washington, in and around Boston, in the Jerseys, and in Pennsylvania; that one of the brothers that had a family drifted south to Virginia, some years prior to the beginning of the Revolution, located in what now is Franklin county, Virginia; that this settler had a son, Edward, who served in the American army in the early period of the revolution, and later, in 1779, came across the Alleghenies into the New River valley, and later married a Miss Patsy Perdue, and settled on Wolf Creek.

"Edward Hale was born about 1756, was a man of rather small stature, fair complexion, was a man of information and intelligence, and became a prominent figure on the border in this day, engaging in the Indian wars, fights, and skirmishes.

THE HALE COAT OF ARMS

"He was in the party under Capt. Mathew Farley that followed the Indians in the summer of 1783, after their attack on Mitchell Claig's family, on the Bluestone, at Clover Bottom; and was in the skirmish had with a part of these Indians on Pond Fork of Little Coal River, in which he killed an Indian at the first fire. From the back of this Indian, killed by Edward Hale, William Wiley, who was in the party of pursuers, took a strip of the Indian's hide, which he gave to Hale, and it was used by him and a number of his family for many years as a razor strap.

"Edward Hale marched with Captain Shannon's Company to North Carolina in February, 1781, and was in the engagement at Wetzell's mills on the 6th of March, and at Guilford court house on the 15th day of the same month, 1785. Edward Hale married Miss Patsy Perdue, a daughter of Uriah Perdue, then recently removed from what is now Franklin county, Virginia.

"Mrs. Hale was a sister of the w fe of the Elder, Joseph Hare.

"The names of the children of Edward Hale and his wife are as follows: viz., Thomas, Isaiah, Charles, Jessie, Isaac, Daniel, Elias, and William; and the daughters, Mary and Phoebe."

From the early days down to the present time, the Hale name has been prominent in the affairs of the country. We are all familiar with the story of the heroic martyr, Nathan Hale, the spy of the Revolutionary days, whose monument stands in City Hall Park, New York. Edward Everett Hale's writings are well known and he was for many years the honored and loved chaplain of the United States Senate, to whose halls in later years Massachusetts sent Senator Hale as her representative.

In the preceding pages we state the coming of the Hale family to America, as a Colonial family, from Kent,

England, in the year 1632, and that they bore the coat of arms of the Kentish Hales.

We also stated that one of the brothers drifted south to Virginia, some years prior to the beginning of the revolution, and located in what is now Franklin county, Va. Lewis Hale was from this branch of the Hale family, and married Mary Burwell, who was a descendant from the Burwells of Jamestown, Va. The Burwells were early settlers at Jamestown, and official members of the First Episcopal Church at Jamestown, Va.

Soon after his marriage, Lewis Hale and his family moved from what is now Franklin county, Va., to the upper part of the New River Valley, and settled on Elk Creek, Va.

"At the time he started from Franklin, he and his brother-in-law, John Walden, expected to settle in Kentucky. After they came to the New River valley, they learned that the Indians were very troublesome in Tennessee, and John Walden (as he had no family) decided to go on horse back, look out a place for them to settle, and return.

He took with him some money, disguised himself as a poor traveller and started on his way, but was killed by the Indians, and robbed of his money. Tradition says he was killed and robbed on Walden's Ridge, Tenn., and that this circumstance gave rise to the name, "Walden's Ridge."

When Lewis Hale learned the fate of John Walden, he and his family decided to remain in the Valley of Elk Creek. He reared a family of six sons and two daughters, settled them all in good homes, in the valley near him, and for years Elk Creek was known as the Hale Settlement. The first church was built by Lewis Hale and called the "Hale Meeting-house." When Grayson county was formed in 1792, Lewis Hale was one of the first

Magistrates of the court, appointed by Henry Lee, Governor of Virginia.

The following was written by Judge D. W. Bolen, of Hillsville, Va.:

LEWIS HALE

"The tradition that Lewis Hale was a soldier in the war of the Revolution seems to be well authenticated. I have heard Capt. F. L. Hale say so, and have heard the same thing from various other sources. It is my recollection that Capt. Hale said that his grandfather served under Col. Wm. Campbell. Once when discussing the monument of Gen. Campbell, which is at his grave near Seven Mile Ford, and in sight of the railroad, and which had been pointed out to me from the train, Capt. Hale seemed to know much more about the history of Campbell and his men than I did at that time. It was in this connection that he mentioned that his grandfather had been a soldier and I am nearly sure that he said that he served with Campbell. I find, however, that he was not a member of Campbell's regiment proper. Campbell was colonel commandant for Washington county, while Walter Crockett was colonel commandant for Montgomery county. Lewis Hale evidently belonged to Crockett's command. A few of Crockett's men served with Campbell at the battle of King's Mountain, October 7th, 1780, and a large part, if not the whole of Crockett's command, served under Campbell in the battle of Guilford Court House, March 15th, 1781. At Guilford, Col. Campbell had a very bitter quarrel with Col. Henry Lee (Light Horse Harry) about certain maneuvers on the battle field, and after the battle was over Campbell resigned his commission as colonel, and a few weeks later, Governor Jefferson made him a general, and sent him to command in the east with Lafayette, and a little later he died of pneumonia. Outside of

King's Mountain and Guilford, Campbell's military career was in suppressing Indian raids and local bands of Tories. Lewis Hale was in Crockett's territory (Montgomery county). To my mind the conclusion is almost irresistible that Lewis Hale, as a member of Crockett's command, was attached to Campbell's command, and participated in one or perhaps both of the above named battles."

Lewis Hale cleared up land, built houses, and accumulated property, and was a useful citizen of this once wilderness country. He died July 2nd, 1802, and is buried near his home, which was left to his youngest son, Stephen Hale, and from him, to his youngest son, Eli C. Hale, and now is held by Eli Scott Hale, youngest son of Eli C. Hale.

Lewis Hale was called out in the militia and was in the battle of King's Mountain. His six sons were in the war of 1812, at Norfolk, Va. His third son, Dudley Hale, died while in camp at Norfolk, Va.

Lewis Hale's grave was left unmarked, and in 1902 some of his descendants decided they would not any longer leave it so. They framed the following appeal and sent out to the descendants of Lewis Hale.

"AN APPEAL.

"---------------------------- ----------------------------
"--

"You are a descendant of Lewis Hale, who settled on Elk Creek, in Grayson county, Va., and was buried there, July 2nd, 1802. His grave is in the cemetery on the farm now owned by Eli C. Hale and has never been marked. We have decided to erect a monument at his grave, with his name, that of his wife, Mary Burwell Hale—and their six sons and two daughters. We appeal to you for One Dollar, more or less, to help pay for the monument and thus perpetuate the family history. You are also cordially invited to be present on July 2nd, 1902,—the one hundredth anniversary of his burial—at which time we want to put up the monument. You are requested to make remittance to the member of the committee by whom this is sent.

"COMMITTEE
"REV. B. F. NUCKOLLS,
"PROF. W. STEPHEN HALE,
"E. SCOTT HALE,
"JOHN MCLEAN,
"DR. SAM MITCHELL,
"ROBERT G. NUCKOLLS."

There was a ready response and on July 2nd, 1902, a monument was unveiled at the grave of Lewis Hale, bearing on it the names of Lewis Hale and his wife, Mary Burwell Hale, and the names of their six sons and two daughters.

The following account of the unveiling was written and published in the *Southwest Virginia Enterprise* by John A. Whitman, great-great-grandson of Lewis Hale. Mr. Whitman is editor and publisher of the *Southwest Virginia Enterprise.*

THE LEWIS HALE MONUMENT UNVEILED

"Wednesday, July the second, between two and three thousand people assembled on Elk Creek, Grayson county, Virginia, to witness the unveiling of a monument erected to the memory of Lewis Hale and wife, who died in eighteen hundred and two. The procession formed in a grove near the residence of Mr. W. S. Hale and in charge of Marshals E. Scott Hale, Leon Dickenson, Thomas Cornett and Charles Hale marched to the cemetery. 'Coronation,' led by Mr. F. A. Cornett, was sung.

Then Mr. W. S. Hale thrilled his hearers with an eloquent address containing a fund of interesting information and entertaining facts concerning his pioneer ancestry. The unveiling proper then followed, eight great-great-grandchildren of Lewis Hale taking part in the ceremony—Allie Rose Bryant, Sue Waugh, Ethel McLean, Agnes May Hale, Gwyn Ward, Hale Lundy, Leon Hale and William Scott Hale. A photographer was on the ground with his camera and got a good view of the monument and those of the near relatives who surrounded it at the time. The crowd then repaired to a nearby grove where the exercises were concluded. Several selections were rendered in choruses and a sloo "One Sweetly Solemn Thought" was effectively sung by Mrs. Ruth Nuckolls Johnston, of Cleveland, Tennessee. The memorial sermon was ably preached by Rev. B. F. Nuckolls, of Old Town. His text was Acts, thirteenth chapter and thirty-sixth verse, "For David after he had served his own generation, by the will of God fell on sleep and was laid unto his fathers and saw corruption." During the intermission which followed a sumptuous lunch was partaken of and the hospitality of Grayson county fully p oven by the keen appreciation with which each man solaced his inner self. The reading of the names of the contributors to the monument next won the attention of the listening throng.

"Mr. A. M. Dickenson, formerly of Grayson but now of Marion, discussed 'A Hundred Years of Progress,' citing the advance made since 1802, when the remains of Lewis Hale were consigned to the grave. A song and the benediction concluded the exercises, but the day will live long with those who were present, and will pass into the annals of Grayson county as complete and not to be forgotten.

"A few facts regarding Lewis Hale may be interesting

to the reader. The exact date of his birth is not known, but it was thought he must have been sixty or sixty-five at his death in 1802. In about the year, 1760 Lewis Hale and wife started from what is now Franklin county, Virginia, to Kentucky, but owing to the hostility of Indians they stopped over in Grayson county. They were so attracted by the country and climate that they decided to make it a permanent home. At that time there were but seven families living on Elk Creek; and what is now a beautiful valley dotted with handsome houses, churches and academies, and where progress and prosperity are so evident, was then an almost untenanted and trackless forest. Here Lewis Hale reared six sons and two daughters, and from these descended men who have been prominent in war, church and state, others playing important parts in the country's history. A great many have emigrated to other states and taken foremost places among the people of the country. A large portion of Grayson county's people are their descendants and are noted for sturdiness, uprightness and general worth. The projectors of the plans to thus honor and keep green the memory of these pioneer settlers are to be very much complimented on their success and commended for the spirit of commemoration of the departed to whom they and the country at large owe so much."

LEWIS HALE AND DESCENDANTS

To Lewis Hale and wife, Mary Burwell, were born six sons, and two daughters:

Their first son, Richard, married Elizabeth Stone.

Second son, William, born March 20th, 1771, married Lucy Stone, sister to the above Elizabeth Stone.

Elizabeth and Lucy Stone were daughters of Jeremiah and Susanna Stone.

Third son, Dudley, married Mary Burroughs.

Fourth son, Francis, married Elizabeth Burroughs, sister to Mary Burroughs.

Fifth son, Lewis (2), married Elizabeth Bourne.

Sixth son, Stephen, married Frances Bourne, sister to Elizabeth Bourne.

Elizabeth and Frances Bourne were daughters of William and Rosa Jones Bourne.

Two daughters: First, Elizabeth, married first, Thomas Burroughs, had children; Elizabeth married second time, they had children. One daughter married Hamilton; one son, Rev. Hale Snow Hamilton, of Holston Conference.

Second daughter, Mary, married first, John Hale; had two sons, James, who died young, and Stephen M., who married Rosa Bourne, daughter of William Bourne, Jr.; they had a large family; moved to Texas. Mary married second time, James Atkins; no children.

Richard Hale's children: First, Lewis, Jr., married Celia White and moved to Tennessee; their first son, William, married Miss Russell in Tennessee, Bradley county, near Cleveland, Tennessee.

First daughter, Charlotte, died young.

Second daughter, Talitha, married a Mr. Carden; they had one son, Rev. Wm. C. Carden, of the Holston Conference; one daughter, Sarah Carden.

Third daughter of Lewis Hale, Jr., was Lucinda, born on Elk Creek, Va., August 14th, 1818; married John Wesley Stanton and settled in Georgia, in Murray, now Whitfield county. They had nine children; William Lewis, Celia Elizabeth, Peyton Lisby, Elbert Miller, Chapell Quillian, Sarah Jane, McClure Hale, Mathew Whitfield, and Mary Irene. All living except McCure Hale, who was drowned in 1896.

Second son of Richard Hale, Rev. Jeremiah Hale, married Susan White, lived on Elk Creek; first son,

THE HALE MONUMENT
Unveiled July 2nd, 1902

Tivis, married Telitha Bourne; they had two daughters; first Amelia, married Stephen Clarke; they now live in Wythe county. Sallie married Stephen Cornett; they have children and live on Elk Creek. Second son, John S. Hale, married Susan Troy; lived on Rock Creek.

Third, Oscar, died in the army, 1863; single.

First daughter, Lucinda Hale, married Mr. Byrd.

Second daughter, Jane, married Stephen Clarke; they had two sons, Walter and Oscar; they lived at Independence and Wytheville, then moved to Elizabethton, Tenn.

Sena, daughter of Richard Hale, married Col. Eli Cornett; lived on Elk Creek, near Summerfield.

Their first daughter, Matilda, married James Hale, son of John Hale and wife, Rosa Blair; they had one daughter, Rosa, who married John Roberts; they live in Missouri.

Second daughter, Elizabeth Cornett, first married Samuel Carson; they had one son, Adolphus, who married Ella Scott, and moved to Missouri. Elizabeth, second time, married James Warrick; they had several children.

Third daughter, Amanda Cornett, first married Capt. Peyton N. Hale, son of Lewis Hale, Jr., and Elizabeth Bourne; he was killed in first Manassas battle, leading his Company; they had one son, Emmett, who died young; one daughter, Bettie, who married Basil Horne, Smythe county; they have two sons, William and Basil.

William Hale was the second son of Lewis Hale and Mary Burwell. Their first son, John Hale, married Rosa Blair, daughter of John Blair and Charity Bourne. They had thirteen sons:

First, Alfred, married Elizabeth Jones, daughter of Maj. Minitree Jones, Jr., and wife, Nancy Golden; they reared a large family on Rock Creek.

Second son, Warner, married Mary Cox, daughter

of David Cox and wife, Jane Doughton, had a large family in the west.

Third, James, married Matilda Cornett; moved to Missouri.

Three of these brothers, Lorenzo Dow, John B., and Alonzo Sidney, all married daughters of David Isom and wife, Sarah Choate. Thomas married Elvira Cornett; he also moved to Missouri.

Second son of William Hale, Col. Stephen Hale, married first Miss Charlotte Dickenson, daughter of Martin Dickenson and wife, Mary Bourne, of Grayson Court House, Va.

Their first son, Rev. Wiley Dickenson Hale, married Miss Martha Mitchell; their first daughter, Charlotte, married Ben W. Dobyns; one son, James Wiley Dobyns, married Lula Cooper, daughter of Dr. B. F. Cooper and wife, Sarah Frances Nuckolls; they have two sons: first, Ben; second, Brutus Fleming. Second daughter, Virginia Hale, died single; third daughter, Sallie B. Hale, married William P. Waugh. Their first daughter, Eugenia, died; second, Lenora, died; third and fourth, twins, Elizabeth B. and Martha M.; Elizabeth married Edward Reeves, son of George Reeves and wife, Caroline Thomas.

Martha M. married A. Edwin Wolfe; their first daughter Juanita; second, Gladys; one son, Eugene; fifth daugh er, Laura Waugh, married Dr. Dunkley. He is connected with the Shenandoah Hospital, Roanoke, Virginia.

Fourth daughter, Caroline Hale, married William Scott; they live in Texas, and have children.

Fifth daughter, Emma Hale, married Frank Williams; their first daughter, Leona, married Mr. Scott; they have two children; second daughter, Sallie, married Dr. .... Reed; third daughter, Mary, married ....

Sixth daughter, Alice Hale, married Ellis Lundy, of Independence, Va., son of F. J. Lundy and wife, Elizabeth Dickey; their first daughter married Mr. Rhudy; second daughter married Thomas Cornett; third daughter married Walter Busic.

First son, Clarence, married Minnie Sutherland, daughter of Capt. William Sutherland, of Hillsville, Va. They live at Mt. Airy, N. C.; he is a clothing merchant; they have two sons.

Second son, Fielden Hale, married Rosa Busic; first son of Rev. Wiley D. Hale, James, died in Confederate army, single.

Second son, Stephen Mason, married Emma Cooper, daughter of Dr. B. F. Cooper and wife, Sarah Frances Nuckolls. Their first son, William, married Minnie Burke; second son, Cleveland, single; third son, James, single; fourth son, Scott, single.

First daughter, Clara Hale, married Edgar Oakley; second daughter, Banner; third daughter, Lillie; fourth daughter, Forest; all the family live in Mt. Airy, N. C.

Second son of Col. Stephen Hale and wife Charlotte Dickenson, Reese, married Celia Perkins, daughter of Levi Perkins and wife, Milly Hale; they have a son and daughters in Texas.

Third son, Creed Hale, died single; was killed in First Manassas battle.

Fourth son, Capt. John M. Hale, died single, at Staunton, Va.

First daughter of Col. Stephen Hale, Theresa, married Rev. Russell Rogers; lived in Washington county, Va. Their first daughter, Charlotte, married Mr. Neal; second, Mary; first son, Charles; second son, John.

Col. Stephen Hale married the second time, Mrs. Leonora Gwyn Mitchell, of Mitchells River, N. C.; they had one daughter, Caroline, who died single, a grown young lady. One son, James Gwyn, died single, a grown young man.

Eli C. Hale, youngest son of Stephen Hale and wife, married, first, Miss Frances Scott, daughter of William Scott and wife, Elizabeth Porter; four sons: first, William Stephen, a graduate of Emory and Henry College. He studied law, was a representative in the legislature, superintendent of public schools; also a teacher. He married Miss Mary Booher of Tennessee; two daughters: first, Gussie, married Vivian Hale; one son, William Scott, died young; another died in infancy; one daughter, Mamie, single.

Second son, Robert Clarke, married Mary McLean; one daughter, Gussie, married Jelane Rhudy, Elk Creek, Va,

Third son, Maurice, married Kate Perkins; two children; they live at Blue Springs, Va.

Fourth son, Eli Scott, lives at the old Hale homestead. He married Miss Eva Hale, daughter of Norman Hale and wife, Miss Lillie Thorntorn of Hillsville (daughter of William Thorntorn and wife, Martha Johnston). They have one daughter, Rachel Holmes; one son.

Eli C. Hale married second time, Mrs Lillie Hale, widow of Attorney Normon Hale, Hillsville, Va.; from this union, three children. Two died in infancy; third, Agnes Hale, in E. C. T. School, Elk Creek, Va.

There were seven daughters of Eli Hale's first family: First, Laura, married Dr. Emmett Vaughn; they live in Lynchburg, Va.; one daughter, Alma; two more children.

The second daughter, Emma, married Mr. Barnett; lives in Lynchburg, Va; first daughter, Bessie; also one son and another daughter.

Third daughter, Mary Hale married Willis McKinney of Mt. Airy, N. C.; no issue.

Fourth daughter, Callie Hale married Rev. John Pugh; one daughter, Frances; one died young; other children; they live near Grant, Va.

Fifth daughter, Susan Hale, married George Lambert,

ELI C. HALE
Thirteenth of the Family of Stephen Hale and wife, Frances Bourne

Rural Retreat, Va.; two children.

Sixth daughter, Alvirda Hale, married Mr. Booher; they have children. Seventh daughter, Chatham Hale, married Mr. Booher; they have children. Alvirda and Chatham Booher live near Bristol, Tenn.

Sophia P. Hale and Dr. W. M. Mitchell had five daughters and one son.

First daughter, Malinda M., married Capt. William Cornett; their daughter married Stephen Nathaniel Nuckolls; one son, married in Missouri; children there.

Second daughter, Frances, married Rufus Thomas; no issue.

Third daughter, Mary, married Ephriam Gentry; sons and daughters; New River, Va.

Fourth daughter, Sena, married Dodge L. Phipps, Long's Gap, Va.; two sons, two daughters.

Fifth daughter, Virginia, married Newton Cox; one daughter, married.

Only son, Samuel Hale Mitchell, M. D., lives at the Mitchell homestead, Elk Creek, Virginia. He married Bessie Cornett, daughter of Monroe Cornett and wife, Jane McCarter; children: one son, died in infancy; first daughter, Katie May, teacher in Martha Washington College, Abingdon, Virginia. Second daughter, single.

Stephen Hale, Sr., sixth son of Lewis Hale, Sr., married Frances Bourne, daughter of William Bourne, Sr., and his wife, Rosa Jones; children: eight sons; first, Mastin, married Susan Perkins.

Second son, William B., married Matilda Jones.

Third son, Martin, married Jestin Hale, daughter of Dudley Hale and wife, Mary Burroughs.

Fourth son, Warner, who died young.

Fifth son, Fielden Lewis, married Evalina Anderson, daughter of Maj. James Anderson and wife, Martha G Nuckolls.

Sixth son, Clarke, married Susan Garrett of Centre, Cherokee county, Ala.

Seventh son, Chapman G., married Margaret Isom, daughter of David Isom and wife, Sarah Choate.

Eighth son, Eli C., married Frances Scott, daughter of William Scott and wife, Elizabeth Porter, who was a daughter of Andrew Porter and wife, Miss Gleaves.

OBITUARY OF CAPT. FIELDEN LEWIS HALE

"'Captain Hale is dead!' 'Yes, he is dead!' Often and tenderly these words have passed from lip to lip among the people of Carroll county since the news of the death of Captain Fielden L. Hale, of Florida, reached here a few days ago.

"Capt. Hale was born on Elk Creek in Grayson county, Va., on the 9th day of September 1814, and died at his home in Seville, Florida, November the 5th, 1894, aged 80 years, 1 month and 26 days. His grandfather, Lewis Hale, was a soldier in the war of the Revolution, and from data in our possession it seems nearly certain that he fought in the battle of King's Mountain under Gen. Wm. Campbell. His father, Stephen Hale, was a soldier in the war of 1812. Capt. Hale himself enlisted in the Confederate army and served as captain of a company of volunteers.

"The prime of his manhood was spent in Hillsville. It was here that he had his largest and widest experience. He was here in business as a merchant when the county was formed.

"His store house then stood where D. A. L. Worrell's residence now stands. His name appears frequently among the records of the first court ever held in the county, which was the June term, 1842. B. F. Cooley was then appointed Sheriff and F. L. Hale became his surety; at the same term F. L. Hale, John B. Mitchell, and I. B.

Coltrane, were appointed to superintend the building of the courthouse. On the 1st day of September, 1842, F. L. Hale was commissioned by the governor a justice of the peace and member of the county court for Carroll county. He held this office for several years. At the June term, 1849, he was appointed county clerk to fill a vacancy and held the office for the unexpired term. In 1858 he was elected clerk and held the office a full term. The records of his official life everywhere bear the impress of duty well performed. January, 1861, was ushered in amid such clouds of war as this country never saw before. The Legislature of Virginia on the 19th of that month passed the famous resolution for a peace conference, all the cotton states having just seceded from the Union. The same Legislature called a convention of the people to decide upon the course Virginia should pursue towards the Union. An election of delegates to this convention was held on the 4th of February, and F. L. Hale was elected as the delegate from Carroll.

"The convention assembled at once and Mr. Hale, with a majority of its members, was opposed to unconditional secession. The convention did but little the first sixty days of its session. But the time arrived when it was plain that the peace conference would accomplish nothing. On the 15th of April, President Lincoln issued his proclamation for seventy-five thousand troops, of which Virginia was called on to furnish her proper quota, to suppress the action of the seceding states. This proclamation was accepted by the south as a declaration of war, and three days later the Virginia convention passed the ordinance of secession, and cast her lot with that of her sister states of the South. Capt. Hale voted for and signed this ordinance. His familiar signature to that document may be seen hanging upon the walls of the State Library in Richmond. As an evidence of his sincerity and patriotism in this critical measure, Mr. Hale returned home and though past the military age entered the army and fought for the cause. He staked his fortunes upon the success of the Southern Confederacy and lost. Capt. Hale's record as a private citizen is an interesting exemplary one. The statutes upon the subject of forfeited delinquent lands from 1832 to 1850 were in much confusion. The Ruston grant of 242,000 acres covered all the land in Carroll county north of the Blue Ridge, except a small corner in the southwest corner of the county. This survey in 1839 was declared forfeited for failure to enter it on the land books for the purpose of taxation. It was exposed to sale and purchased by D. Graham, Robert Rapert, F. Allison. As the statute declared the land forfeited, the people believed it was open for re-entry and survey, and numerous indeed were the small grants that were then obtained for lands inside of the Ruston grant. Capt. Hale procured between 50,000 and 100,000 acres of land inside the Ruston grant. He sold these lands in small tracts and people settled upon them in nearly every section of the county. The years rolled along and finally the supreme court decided the Ruston title to be good. This decision created a panic among Hale's purchasers. There were hundreds of them. They had erected homes, laid out plantations, and made large and costly improvements.

"It seemed to them that all was lost. Capt. Hale, though then in failing circumstances resulting from the war, effected a purchase of such portions of the Ruston title as completely protected every person who had purchased from him.

"This was no doubt a very trying period for Capt. Hale. It incurred a responsibility that a man of doubtful integrity would have shirked.

' On one of his last visits to Carroll he referred to it

LUCINDA HALE
Daughter of Stephen Hale and wife, Frances Bourne, and wife of Ezra Nuckolls

and a gleam of honest delight came over his face as he remarked in the presence of the writer that he had never sold a tract of land to a man who lost it.

"At the age of 26 Capt. Hale was happily married to Miss Evelina Anderson. She bore him four sons and one daughter. The daughter died in this town many years ago. She is still remembered by some of our people as a beautiful child; the joy and constant companion of her father; but just as prattling childhood was merging into womanhood her sweet spirit like a bird of spring returned to the bright land whence it came. The wife died in 1855. The sons all grew to manhood and all but Stephen, preceded their father to the grave. In 1859 Capt. Hale was married to Mrs. Elizabeth S. Burt, of Alabama, a lady of the most excellent and estimable qualities. For thirty-five years she bore him sweet companionship and with loving hands and loving heart sweetened his cares and soothed his sorrows.

"The hearts of the people of old Carroll go out for her in tender sympathy in her sad bereavement. As husband and parent no soul was more tender and loving than Capt. Hale. His love for her, and his attentions to his wife and children and grandchildren was proverbial and poetical. Amid the severest calamities and afflictions his face was a ray of light in his home. As a neighbor and friend he was faithful and constant to the end.

"Reverses of fortune, death of his sons, calamities that would have driven other men to madness and death. never soured his nature or caused him to murmur. Envy, jealousy and malice had no place in his soul. He was kind and generous to every creature he met with in this world. He made firm and lasting friendships with people in every rank and grade of society and appreciated the friendship of the humblest creature in our world.

"His intellectual qualities were of a high order. He seemed to know, to comprehend and recollect everything. On his last visit to Carroll he could describe the corners and lines of lands he once owned, but which he had not seen for thirty years, with such accuracy that there was no trouble to go on the ground and indentify them.

"For about 12 years before his death he had made his home in Florida, but usually visited Carroll once a year. His return in the spring or early summer was looked for with delight by our people. He would usually get here by the June term of our court and it was often touching to witness the greetings he would receive from the people on the streets, especially from old soldiers, and from the plain country people that knew him and loved him so long. The time for his departure came and he knew it and felt it. The flowers of youth, and the strength of his manhood were gone; old age came and lingered, but its furrows on his face and its weight upon his head never dimmed or marred the beauty of his character. To look upon his snowy locks and tottering steps was to increase our love. He was a ripe shock and ready for the Master's garner. His peace with God had long been made.

"His faith and trust in the mercies and goodness of the everlasting Father grew and multiplied as his years accumulated; and when the summons came, with the radiance of immortality on his face and eternal life in sight, he went forth like one: 'Who wraps the drapery of his couch about him, and lies down to pleasant dreams.'"

The five daughters of Stephen Hale and wife were: First, Lucinda, married Ezra Nuckolls, son of John Nuckolls and wife, Mary Garland, of Louisa county, Va.

Second, Rosa B., married Clarke S. Nuckolls, son of Robert Garland Nuckolls and wife, Margaret Swift. (See Nuckolls family.)

Third, Mary, who died young.

Fourth, Amanda J., married Col. Ira B. Coltrane. (See Obituary of Col. I. B. Coltrane.)

Fifth, Sophia P., married Dr. William Marshall Mitchell, son of Dr. Zachariah Mitchell and his wife, Elizabeth Newland, of Blue Springs, Smyth county, Va.

COL. IRA B. COLTRANE

"A familiar form passed from mortal view when on the 13th day of May, 1894, at his home two miles west of Hillsville, Col. Ira B. Coltrane peacefully breathed his last, having attained the good old age of 78 years, 11 months and 15 days. Col. Coltrane's life was spent in our midst. He leaves behind him more monuments to his usefulness than perhaps any man that has lived in our section. When a boy fourteen years old he drove a team across the Blue Ridge at the Good Spur. On his return, in company with several wagons, when the foot of Good Spur was reached, all teams were hitched to the front wagon, and by hard pulling and tugging it was taken to the top of the mountain. The teams were all taken back to the foot and hitched to another wagon and it was taken up to the top as the first one was. This th'ng was repeated until every wagon landed safely on the mountain top. While this thing was going on the young teamster looked into the deep gorge just east of Good Spur, where Paul's Creek goes rippling down the mountain, and in his mind located a place for a better road. Years afterward when Virginia had embarked upon the policy of internal improvements, Col. Coltrane was a member of the General Assembly and procured an appropriation to open the Fancy Gap turnpike across the mountain along the very line his boyish eyes had mapped out. He then came home and by genius and skill located and opened the road across the mountain, which is one of the very best, if not the best, crossing of the Blue Ridge to be found in Virginia. This crossing will never be changed, neither its location nor its grade can be improved. It will remain there as a convenience and a blessing to the people of Southwest Virginia and Western North Carolina for ages after the face of its projector and constructor has faded from human memory.

"The bridge across little Reed Island Creek, two miles north of Hillsville, is a model of perfection. It was pronounced by the Chief Engineer of the N. & W. R. R. Co. to be as good a wooden bridge as can be built with human hands. This bridge was built by Col. Coltrane and will long stand as a monument to his memory. The court house at Hillsville is a model of beauty and symmetry. It is universally pronounced to be one of the soundest, most durable, as well as convenient, structures that can be reared. Col. Coltrane was its builder and its architect. Long before it was finished Col. Coltrane saw hat he would lose money on his contract; but he went on to completion without one inferior piece of material or one inferior piece of workmanship going into it. The stone wall and the stone steps in front of the court house and some of the cut stone in the building were not in his contract, but he was unwilling to turn off anything but a good job and so he did this work and received no pay for it. It would be next to impossible to tell how often Col. Coltrane has been appointed to draw plans for buildings, to assess damages, to receive work that was being done for the county and to perform other duties of that kind, but just as often as he was appointed he performed his duties faithfully and well. He drew the plan for the first court house and jail ever built in our county. He was Colonel of Militia, and had served in both branches of the legislature. But of all the monuments he has erected the grandest one is his character for truth and honesty.

AMANDA J. HALE
Daughter of Stephen Hale, Sr., and wife, Frances Bourne, and wife of Col. Ira B. Coltrane

If there was ever a track of falsehood, flattery, deceit, or corruption in his composition it had been carefully rooted out. His manner sometimes seemed rough, and his words sometimes sounded harsh but they were utterances of the plain, unvarnished truth, nevertheless, without affixes, prefixes or adjectives.

"In his legislative life his name was a terror to all lobbyists. He would snap their heads off with as much composure as he would snap the idler who came around him to meddle with his business or his work. A person fond of feeding on flattery could never have enjoyed Col. Coltrane as a companion or associate. On the other hand a person contented with fair dealing, with firm and unyielding friendship unmixed with falsehood or deceit, would love him for his sterling qualities. Beneath his stern exterior there beat a kind and loving heart. Col. Coltrane was married to Amanda Hale of Grayson county, on the 9th of June, 1844. She and seven of the children born to their union preceded him to the grave. Mrs. E. L. Williams is the only child that survives to mourn his death. During the long, long months of his illness she sat at his side and administered to his wants as only faithful woman can do. Several small grandchildren by a deceased daughter, Mrs. G. T. Burroughs, and the children of Mrs. Williams, are his descendants. May the spirit and the mantle of the honest and upright grandfather rest upon them. For some time before his death Col. Coltrane knew that his days were numbered, and that he was lingering at death's door; but he was not afraid. He had not overlooked the subject of religion. He had read and studied the bible; he had examined the creeds and tenets of faith of the prevailing denominations in this section of the country; but he never joined any church. He looked upon his own judgment and the promptings of his own conscience as his safest guide to a correct understanding of his duties towards God and towards man; and these he faithfully followed. He stated in his last sickness that he had yielded himself into the hands of God and trusted Him to do whatever was right. We know that he went into the presence of his Maker with no lie on his lips and no hypocrisy on his soul. He had lived long and no doubt met upon the other bank of the mysterious river thousands whom he had known in this life; but it is safe to say he met no one there upon whom he had committed a fraud, or to whom he had in this life done intentional wrong. One of the largest crowds that ever assembled at our village cemetery gathered around his open coffin to take a last sad look at the face they had known so long and so well and then with loving hands the casket was interred close by his wife and children and among the relatives that for generations have been buried there.

> "Were a star quenched on high,
> For ages would it light
> Still travelling downward from the sky
> Shine on our mortal sight;
> So when a good man dies
> For years beyond our ken
> The light he leaves behind him lies
> Upon the paths of men."
>   B.

James Scott was from Ireland, and married Rachel Holmes. She was of the nobility of Scotland, and there was so much opposition and displeasure with her family that James Scott and his wife emigrated to America, and settled in Rye Valley, near Blue Springs, Va. Their son, James, married Margaret Porter; one son, Rev. Andrew Scott.

Their son, William, married Elizabeth Porter. Elizabeth and Margaret were daughters of Andrew Porter and wife, Miss Gleaves, who was a sister of Maj. James

Gleaves, of what is now Wythe county, Va. The descendants of William Scott and family are given on preceding pages.

Capt. Lewis Hale, fifth son of Lewis Hale, Sr., married Elizabeth Bourne, daughter of William Bourne and wife, Rosa Jones; they had four sons: First, Jackson, married Catherine Isom; second, Washington, married Nancy Hale, daughter of Francis Hale; third, Rufus, married Nancy Hale, daughter of Dudley Hale; fourth, Capt. Peyton N., married Amanda Cornett, daughter of Col. Eli Cornett and wife, Sena Hale.

Four daughters: first, Milly, married Levi Perkins.
Second, Celia, married Mr. Rutherford.
Third, Elvira, married Mr. Davenport.
Fourth, Rosa B., married Charles Daugherty; one son, Lindsey; others in Texas.

Maj. Peyton G. Hale was prominent in the affairs in both Church and State; was a member of the Senate in 1882 when the question of the state debt was discussed, and the question of Funding and Readjusting was coming before the Senate for a vote. Hale and three other members left the house, and were known as the "Big Four." They were Maj. Peyton G. Hale, Judge Lybrook, Mr. Williams and Mr. Newberry. They refused to follow Mahone into the Republican party; did not like Mahone's methods of conducting the affairs of the State.

DEATH OF MAJOR HALE

"Information has been received here of the death, at his home in Grayson county, yesterday, of Major Peyton G. Hale, one of the immortal 'big four' who fought Mahone's methods in the Legislature, and did much towards clinching the nails in his political coffin.

"Major Hale was what Albert Pike would call 'a Virginia gentleman of the olden time.' Honest, brave, patriotic, and true to every trust or responsibility, he was a typical Virginian, and his death will be mourned by all who knew him for his worth."

William Hale and wife had four daughters: first, Susan, married Morgan Bryant, a Methodist minister. Their first son, Shadrack, was also a Methodist Minister; he married Sallie Bryant, his cousin; they have sons and daughters.

Second son, Gideon, died single.

First daughter, Lucy, married Henderson Cheek; they have sons and daughters.

Second daughter, Sarah, married Archibald Edwards. Their first son, William Edwards, married Lucy Dickenson. One daughter married John Murphy. Second, Morgan, married; Wythe county; one daughter married Prof. Gentry; one daughter, Rosa Bryant, married Columbus Fulton, Independence, Va.; one daughter married J. H. Rhudy, lawyer (see children); second daughter married Mr. Couch.

Elizabeth, second daughter of William Hale, married David Whitman, Wythe county, Va.; they had two daughters: first, Caroline, married George W. Gentry, and moved to Texas; second, Nancy, married Peter Gallagher; they had three sons, Emmett, Patrick, Marvin, and three daughters, Mary, Elizabeth, Nannie. Peter Gallagher's wife, Nancy, died while they lived in Wytheville, Va. He was appointed under President Cleveland, and went to Pocatello, Idaho. Emmett is married and lives in the West; Patrick died in the West; Marvin is married, and lives in the West; Mary married and lives in Pocatello, Idaho; they have children; Elizabeth married Mr. Green and lives in Pocatello, Idaho; they have children. Nannie married, and died in California.

One son, Stephen Whitman, married Linnie Hale, daughter of Stephen M. Hale and wife, Rosa Bourne;

STEPHEN FRIEL NUCKOLLS

they live in Texas. Clarke married and moved to Texas.

David, Jr., married Malvina Porter, daughter of Stephen Porter and wife, Margaret McNutt, Cripple Creek, Va.

Mrs. Whitman died in 1882 at the family homestead, and is buried on Cripple Creek. After her death, the family moved to Wilmore, Ky. Their first daughter, Gertrude, married in Kentucky; second daughter, Margaret, married Dr. Haller; they live in Pocahontas, Va., and have children. Third daughter, Jennie, married Mr. A. H. Jordan, a druggist, in Pulaski, Va.; they have two children, Margaret and Elizabeth.

Fourth daughter, Blanche, married Mr. Galloway, cashier of the Bank in Pocahontas, Va. Fifth daughter, Lillie, is a teacher, single. Sixth daughter, Nannie, is a teacher, single.

William Whitman married Miss Sloan, Pulaski, Va. They have a large family of children, and live near Pulaski, Va.

Clay Whitman married Caroline Kegley; first son, John A. Whitman, married Miss Carrie Heuser and is editor of the *Southwest Virginia Enterprise*, Wytheville, Va.

William H. married Miss Gleaves; lives in Loudon county, Va.

Sidney married Rosamond Vaughn, daughter of Rev. T. C. Vaughn and wife, Lucy Hale.

Fifth, George, died single.

Nancy, third daughter of Wm. Hale, married David Gose, Cripple Creek, Va., one son, William, married Susan Umberger; one son, John, is mayor of Bristol, Tenn; one daughter.

First daughter, Rosa, married Lewis Perkins, moved to Texas; Matilda, first married Riley Moore; second time, married Leonard Sutherland, Elk Creek, Virginia; the fourth daughter of William Hale and wife, Rosa, married

John Dickenson; they lived on New River; had sons and daughters. (See Martin Dickenson family history.)

Dudley Hale, third son of Lewis Hale, Sr., married Mary Burroughs; he was a soldier, and with his five brothers, went to Norfolk, Va., in the war of 1812. Capt. Lewis Hale, his brother, was in charge of the company. Dudley Hale died while they were in Norfolk. His wife died in a short time after her husband; his brothers took their children and reared them. There were five sons and five daughters; Preston, Franklin, and James, moved to Cherokee county, Alabama. Burroughs married Miss Sutherland and settled on Elk Creek; their first son, Alexander, first married a Miss Catron. Second wife, Miss Lucinda Wheeler, of Knob Fork. Second son, Eli, married Miss Hampton; one daughter married Hackler. Burroughs Hale's second wife was Miss Clara Houk; two daughters by second wife: first daughter married Hawkins; second, Amanda, married Jacob Thomas, of Elk Creek; one son, Jo, married Bourne; one daughter, marred; Cora, first daughter, married Elbert Ring.

Lewis B. Hale, son of Burroughs Hale, married Margaret Huddle of Wythe county, Va.; their first son, Leftrick, married Miss Hale; Gideon married Jestina Bryant; Peyton died single; John married Miss Bryant; Mastin, Jr., married Caroline Hale; Lewis, Jr., married Miss James, of Wythe county, Va.

First daughter, Keziah, married Ephriam Bourne; their first daughter, Linnie, married Mr. Vaughn; Rosa married James Rhudy; third married Vaught; fourth daughter married John McLean; first son, James, in Missouri; second daughter, Jane, died single; third, Olive, married Montgomery Bourne; fourth, Sallie, James Yontz.

The five daughters of Dudley Hale: first, Mary,

married James Brewer; moved to Georgia; have sons and daughters.

Second, Sarah, married Joseph Bryant, Bridle Creek.

Their first son, Stephen, married Mazie Phipps, daughter of Joseph Phipps and wife, Nancy McMillan; their first daughter, Jennie, married Crockett Mallory; second daughter married, first, John Hale; one son, Wallace Graham. Third daughter married Dan Busic, treasurer of Grayson county.

Second son, William Bryant, married Emmeline, daughter of Isom Cox; they have one daughter, who married John M. Parsons, lawyer and state senator of Grayson county, Va.

One daughter, married Burt Bagwell.

One daughter, married Charles Cox, son of Harden Cox, of Potato Creek, Va.

The three daughters of Joseph Bryant and wife Sarah Hale:

First, Rosa, first married Noah Weaver; lived at Weaver's Ford, New River; second, married Mr. Dixon.

Second, Olive, first married Ed Greer, Grassy Creek, N. C.; second time married Mr. Pierce.

Third daughter, Jestin, first married Gideon Hale, Elk Creek; second, married James Greer, Grassy Creek, North Carolina.

Fourth daughter of Stephen Bryant married Dan Busic; their first daughter married Emmett Cox; lives at Peach Bottom, Virginia; second, Rosa, married Fitzhugh Lundy, Independence; one son, Busic, married Lundy, daughter of Ellis Lundy and wife, Alice Hale, Independence, Va.

One son of Stephen Bryant and Mazie Phipps Kenerly, married Etta Phipps, daughter of Joseph Phipps and wife, Cynthia Bourne. First daughter married Dr. Robinson; lives at Woodlawn, Carroll county, Va.;

second, married R. S. Fulton, second son of Joseph
Bryant; Aaron, died when a young man, in Mississippi.
 Third son, Lewis Hale, married Drucy Phipps; their first
son, Joseph, married Miss Graham. Second son, John,
married Lesbia Phipps, daughter of Columbus Phipps
and Nannie Cox. They have children, and live in Texas.
Third son, Alexander, married Bena Cox, daughter of
Isom Cox and wife, Jensey Phipps.
 Fourth son, I. B. Bryant, married Miss Reeves; one
son, Lewis Preston. I. B. Bryant is Grayson county
court clerk.
 First daughter of Lewis H. Bryant married James
Perkins, lawyer; second daughter married James R.
Hale; live in Oregon. One son, Jo, married Miss Graham,
N. C. One son, Robert, married Con Phipps, daughter
of Joseph Phipps and Cynthia Bourne, Bridle Creek, Va.
Second daughter married Mr. Spicer. Third daughter,
Phoebe, Married Mr. Thompson, North Carolina.
 This family of Bryants is related to William Jennings
Bryan, "The Commoner." Francis Bryan, the father of
Morgan Bryan, was a brother of William J. Bryan's
great-grandfather. Francis Bryan and his sister, Elizabeth, came to Southwest Virginia; first stopped at "Fort
Chiswell," afterward went across to what is now Grayson
county, Va. Elizabeth married John Sutherland; Francis
married Phoebe Woodruff. (See Bryan History by Mrs.
W. J. Bryan.)
 Third daughter of Joseph Bryant married second time,
Jones Greer, Grassy Creek, North Carolina; son and
daughters.
 Third daughter of Dudley Hale, Jestin, married Martin
Hale and settled in Leesburg, Cherokee county, Ala.
(See history of Stephen Hale, Sr., and Frances Bourne's
descendants.)
 Fourth daughter married Rufus Hale (see history of

LUCINDA BOURNE
Daughter of William Bourne, Jr., and wife, Mary Johnston, and wife of Stephen Friel Nuckolls

Lewis Hale and Elizabeth Bourne's descendants). They also settled in Cherokee county, Ala.

Fifth daughter, Olive, married Levi Cornett (see Canute), and they lived and died on Elk Creek, where Dudley Hale first settled; their first son, Franklin, married first, Miss Austin; they had sons and daughters. Second time, married Miss Daniel; they had sons and daughters; lived at Summerfield, Elk Creek.

Nancy, daughter of Dudley Hale, married Rufus Hale, son of Capt. Lewis Hale; lives in Cherokee county, Alabama; has children.

Francis Hale married Elizabeth Burroughs; they had two daughters; first daughter, Nancy, married Washington Hale, son of Capt. Lewis Hale and wife, Elizabeth Bourne. They moved to Cherokee county, Ala.; they had one daughter, Jane, who married Mr. Stiff, an editor in Center, Ala. Mr. and Mrs. Stiff have a son, Washington Stiff, who lives in Center, Alabama. He married Miss Martha Senter. Washington Stiff is editor of The Harmonizer, Center, Alabama. Second daughter of Francis Hale married Mr. Massensmith. Francis Hale had five sons: first, Thomas, married Sallie Sutherland; second, Wicks, married Miss Delp; third, Fontaine, married Miss Martin; fourth, Dudley, married Miss Wright; fifth, Frank, Jr., married Betsy Huddle, of Wythe county, Virginia; their first son, Lee, killed in the Confederate war; second, Lindsey; third, Nicholas, married Hale; have children.

First daughter, Amanda, married Churchill Boyer; their first son, Watson, married Ellen Boyer; second son, Samuel, is a practicing physician; first daughter, Bettie, married Mr. Herrington; second Luzana, married Mr. Schuler; they have one daughter, married Mr. Neff, Rural Retreat, Va.

Lewis Hale (2) married Miss Cantrell of Tennessee; they have two sons, Granville, and William, who went to Texas and married; and two daughters, first, Martha, married William R. Dickey, Independence, Va. They have one son, James, who married Miss Taylor, Mt. Airy, N. C.; they have two daughters; first, married Charlie Bourne, son of Capt. R. G. Bourne; second, married Thos. Dobyns, of Patrick county, Va. Their first daughter, Mary, married John Wiley; went west; have children. Second daughter, Cynthia Dickey, married William Warren of North Carolina; they have one daughter, who married Rev. Terry Fulton.

Second daughter of Lewis Hale, Ellen, married James Ballard; first son, William, married first in California; married second time, Miss Emma Ballard, of Old Town, Virginia; they have one son, James Ballard; have one daughter, Bell, who married Winfield Perkins, Hilton, North Carolina, son of W. Perkins and wife, Bell Ballard; one son, Edwin, married Zollie Bryant, Bridle Creek, Virginia.

Third son of William Hale, William J., married Sarah Porter, of Cripple Creek, Wythe county, Va. One son, Stephen Porter Hale, the only child, was a cripple from a boy. Following is a copy of a letter written by him to the author:

"I, Stephen P. Hale, son of William and Sarah Hale, was born Nov. 1st., 1825, and married to Elmira Cantrell, Jan. 1st, 1856. From this union, were four children, to-wit: Sarah Alice, Nov. 25th, 1856; William, Dec. 17th, 1858; Mary Elmira, Jan. 25th, 1861; Stephen Porter, born Feb. 13th, 1863, and died, Sept. 5th, 1863. My wife, Elmira C. Hale, departed this life on April 1st, 1863, and on Oct. 2nd, I was married to Miss Cornelia V. Yearwood, of McMinn county, Tenn., who died June 9th, without issue; and on April 7th, 1870, I was again

SOPHIA P. HALE
Daughter of Stephen Hale, Sr., and wife, Frances Bourne, and wife of Dr. William M. Mitchell

married to Mrs. Susan A. Palmore, formerly Miss Susan A. Price, of Cumberland county, Va. From this union have been born five children, to-wit: Lillie Hale, May 6th, 1872; Charles P. Hale, May 7th, 1874; Stephen P. Hale, Oct. 10th, 1876; Susan Albina Hale, born Feb. 7th, 1879, and died Oct. 22nd, 1880. Thomas Newton Hale was born, April 21st, 1881.

"My oldest daughter, Sarah, spent about seven years in Mexico as a missionary in the service of the foreign missionary board of the Baptist Church, but her health failing, she returned home to recuperate, and is now at Carson and Newman College at Jefferson City, Tenn., teaching a class in Spanish. She expects to go back to Mexico when her health will permit.

"Thomas N., the youngest, is still with us and has charge of the farm. All the others are married and settled on farms in the county. Lillie is the wife of George G. Florida; is the mother of five living children. Mary Elmira is the wife of Dr. W. N. Bicknell, and the mother of six living children; William is living at the place where I lived when you were at our home. These seventeen are all the living grandchildren I have.

"My three oldest children are members of the Baptist Church. The four youngest, of the Presbyterian Church. My wife and myself belong to the Presbyterian Church.

"You request that I state what has been my profession or vocation through life.

"About twenty-two years—from 1843 to 1865—I spent in teaching school; twelve years as Clerk and Master of the Court of Monroe county, from 1865 to 1877; about ten years in pretending to practice law. The balance of my time and attention has been devoted to looking after my farming and other interests.

"For the last few years, I have been mostly confined to my rolling chair, though I am still able to ride little a in the saddle or buggy. I was born in McMinn county, Tenn., and most of my life, my home has been in the two counties, McMinn and Monroe."

Following is a copy of part of a letter from Miss Sarah A. Hale, written to the author from Jerusalem, Palestine, Dec. 6th, 1906:

"I returned to Mission Field, Mexico, after my father's death, but my eyes, after one and a half years work, became so weak that I decided to come abroad for a year or two.

"I sailed last March from Galveston, Texas; spent two days in Bremen, a few hours in Hanover, two days in Berlin, and two days in Dresden, sight-seeing, continually; then on to Vienna, where I spent one night, then through Servia, Bulgaria, and ancient Macedonia, through the historic City of Phillippi to Constantinople. There I spent a week, then came down the Mediterranean to Athens, Greece, in a steamer crowded with Greeks going to the Olympic Games. I stopped a few hours at Athens, then went on same steamer to Alexandria, Egypt, from there to Jaffa and to Jerusalem, arriving here last April. I soon determined to spend a year here, to know the country in all seasons.

"I made the overland journey to Nazareth and the sea of Galilee last spring, seeing Jacob's well, the ruins of Samaria, on the way; then visited Damascus and Baalbec, going and returning by way of Hafia and Beyroot.

"It was after my return to Jerusalem that I learned that Mr. P. L. Stanton and I have the same great-grandfather, Lewis Hale. It was a great pleasure for me to meet a relative in this land, so far from home. He has traveled a great deal in America, Europe, and the East. He is a voluminous writer and a fine conversationalist.

"His piety and sound judgment have enabled him to accomplish good during his sojourn in this city, and he

MAJOR PEYTON G. HALE
Son of William Hale and wife, Lucy Stone. He was one of the "Big Four"

has won for himself the confidence and esteem of all he meets."

Following is a copy of a letter the author received from Peyton L. Stanton, who was then living in Jerusalem, Palestine, November 27th, 1906.

"I graduated at Emory and Henry College, in the class of 1876. In 1875 I was licensed to preach there in Washington county, Emory Circuit; was received on trial in the North Georgia Conference in 1877, ordained Deacon in 1879, and Elder in 1881. I was transferred to Denver Conference in 1882, and spent ten years in New Mexico and Colorado; then transferred to California, and two years later went back to North Georgia Conference, of which I was a member until two years ago, when I was located at my own request.

"On the 25th of this month, November, four years ago, I left New York for the East. I was first in Egypt for about three months, and then came over land from there in March. Jerusalem has been my headquarters since March 11th, 1903. I came here for some special study in connection with the land, the Book, and the people; I do not know when I will finish my work."

Charles Hale was the fourth son of William Hale and wife, Lucy Stone. Charles Hale married first, Jane Sutherland of Elk Creek; first son, Fielden, married Tibitha Tomblin; they have one son, James, who married a Bryant; one daughter, Mary, who married Mr. Gaither, of North Carolina.

Second son, Creed Hale, went to Texas; married there, and has children.

Third son, Johnston, married, first time, Caroline Osbourne, Bridle Creek; one daughter who married William Hampton and moved to Oregon; one son went west. Johnston married second time; has children. First daughter, Elvira Hale married Geo. W. McGuire, teacher, from

North Carolina; they moved to Missouri; have children.

Second daughter, Rosa Hale, married Orville Moore, son of Isaac Moore and wife, Euphamia Jones; both died; no children. Fourth, Elizabeth Hale, married Alfred Mallory; sons and daughters.

Third daughter, Sarah Hale, married Harvey Vaughan, of Knob Fork. They have sons and daughters.

Charles Hale's second wife was Rosa Comer, daughter of Harvey Comer and wife, Elizabeth Bourne; their first son, Reese, married Theresa Cornett, of Elk Creek; three sons, Charles, a Methodist minister; second, died; third, June, married a Reeves.

Second son, Elbert Hale, married Nannie McLean, daughter of John M. McLean and wife; they have three daughters who live in Missouri.

Lucy, first daughter of Charles Hale and Rosa Comer, married Rev. Thomas C. Vaughn, Spring Valley; their first son, Marvin, married Clyde McCamant, daughter of T. J. McCamant and wife, Ellen Hale; second son, John Vaughn, married Miss Rhudy; first daughter married Jack Porter; second daughter married Phillip Herington, lawyer, of Independence, Va.; they have one son, Thomas; third, Rosa Vaughn, married Sidney P. Whitman, of Wythe county, Va.

Second daughter, Charlotte Hale, married George Delp, of Elk Creek; one daughter, married Roscoe Phipps, Elk Creek, Va.

Charles Hale's third wife, Mrs. Tabitha Bourne Hale, widow of Tivis Hale, had two daughters; Flora, who married Martin Cornett, Elk Creek; one daughter, married; second daughter married Leonidas Ward, son of Ballard E. Ward and Amelia G. Nuckolls; sons: Everett, Gwyn, Leonidas; daughter, Ruth; one son, Basil.

Montgomery Hale married Sarah Ann Anders, of Washington county, Va.; they had one son, Leonidas, who died young; one daughter, Margaret Ellen, married William J. Cornett, of Elk Creek. They have one son, Leonidas, who married Minnie Kiesling, Wythe county, Va., daughter of Emory Kiesling.

Mrs. Amanda Hale married the second time, John M. McLean, of Guilford county, North Carolina; had four daughters and one son. First daughter, Mary, married Robert Clarke Hale, son of Eli C. Hale; one daughter, Gussie, married Jelane Rhudy.

Second daughter, Nannie, married Elbert Hale, son of Charles Hale, of Knob Fork; they have two children; live in Missouri.

Third, Sena, married Charles Bryant, son of Joseph Bryant, Bridle Creek, Va.; first daughter Zollie, married Ed Perkins, Hilton, N. C.; Ada, Sena, Rosa, single.

Fourth daughter, Sallie, married Edgar Phipps; lives on Bridle Creek.

One son, John M., (2) married Miss Young; they have three children; live at Fries; he is cashier of Fries Bank

The first son of Col. Eli Cornett married Miss Ellen Scott, of Smyth county, Virginia; they have children and live in Missouri.

Second son of Col. Eli Cornett, Winton, went to Missouri. He is a merchant and banker; yet single. Winton accumulated a considerable amount of money, lived a quiet, industrious life. His health failed, and he is now in Grayson county; has retired from business and is spending his time with his relatives.

Maj. Peyton G. Hale, youngest son of William Hale, married Jane Bourne, daughter of William Bourne, Jr., and wife, Mary Johnstone: one son, William, died single in Oregon; first daughter, Nannie, married Fielden Hale, son of Warner Hale and wife, Mary Cox. In the "Foot, prints on the Sands of Time," I find this sentence, "Esq. David Cox, married Miss Jane Doughton, a patient, quiet.

good Christian, and faithful, good and affectionate wife, Hon. Fielden J. Hale, state Senator from Madison. Nebraska, is their grandson." They have one daughter, Miss Lee.

Second daughter of Maj. P. G. Hale, Mary Ann, married Emory Kirby; they have two sons, Judge Robert Lee, and William Hale. Judge Kirby married Mary Boyer, of Elk Creek.

Third daughter, Lucy, married William Perkins, of Hilton, N. C., they have two daughters; first, Catharine, married Maurice Hale, son of Eli Hale; live at Blue Springs, Va., and have two children; second daughter, Gertrude Perkins, single; two sons, James.

The fourth daughter of Peyton G. Hale, Ellen, married Thomas J. McCamant; they had five daughters; first daughter, Blanche, married Clayton Higgins; they have one son, McCamant, and live in the old McCamant homestead in Old Town, Va. Second daughter, Lizzie, married Mr. Fred Armfield of Fish River, N. C.; they have two daughters and live in North Carolina on what was the old Gov. Franklin farm. Third daughter, Clyde, married Marvin Vaughn, son of Rev. T. C. Vaughn. They live at Spring Valley, Va. Fourth and fifth daughters Josie Hale, and Myrtle Lee, died young. The fifth daughter of Peyton G. Hale, Lucinda, married Robert Garland Nuckolls; they live at the old William Hale homestead on Elk Creek; no children.

Garland

THE GARLAND COAT OF ARMS

CHAPTER VI

THE GARLAND FAMILY

(Copied from the genealogical column of *The Times-Dispatch*, Richmond, Va.)

"There were in England three Garland families entitled to bear a coat of arms: one in York, one in Lincolnshire, and one in Sussex.

Family tradition says that the Sussex branch moved into Wales. Their common ancestor was a warden of the cinque ports, and as such was a lord entitled to a seat in Parliament, had entire jurisdiction, civil, military and naval, over the five ports, and lived in Dover Castle.

The history of this distinguished family in America dates far back to Colonial times, beginning about the year 1650. Their descendants have wrought well, filling positions of honor and trust in the history of both church and state. They have intermarried with the chief families of the Commonwealth.

The Garlands were in New Kent county in the seventeenth century. The records of New Kent county are mostly destroyed, but there is one parish register preserved and in it is a record of Edward, son of Edward Garland, born May 20th, 1700. This baby, Edward, was the father of John Garland (5), who lived at Garland's Neck, Hanover county, Va. His children were, in the order of their birth, as follows: Thomas (4), who inherited the Neck by the law of primogeniture, and founded the Goochland branch of the family.

Edward (4), Robert (4) (founder of the Louisa branch), James (4), John (4), Lucy (4), and Peter (4).

The third son (Robert) of John Garland (5) was the progenitor of men who did much in their day and generation. James (4) (1722-1812) married Mary Rice, of Hanover county, whose mother was a Howlett, and soon thereafter, moved to Albemarle. He was acting magistrate of Albemarle county, Va., in 1753, was associated with Gov. Nelson, and accumulated a fortune.

Nathaniel (5) was born in 1750; married a Miss Rhodes.

John (5) (born 1751) died of camp fever in the Revolutionary war.

James (5) (born 1753) married Annie Winfield, whose mother was a Hudson. He commanded the company detailed to guard the surrendered troops of Burgoyne. When officer of the day at Charlottesville he was shot by the sentry at night as he did not give the pass word. He had four children: Hudson (6), Henrietta (6), Spottswood (6), and James (6).

Mary Garland was born March 20th, 1755, and married John Nuckolls, 1777. To them were born nine sons and one daughter. Mary Garland was a member of the Episcopal Church, and in her prayer-book (printed in MDCCLXI) are recorded the births of her children. (See Nuckolls chapter.)

Charles Garland, a brother of Mary Garland, who married John Nuckolls, died single, and is buried in the Nuckolls cemetery in Grayson county, Va. Charles and Mary Garland were of the Louisa branch of the Garland family, and were born in Louisa county, Va. In the latter years of their life, John Nuckolls and Mary Garland went back to Louisa county, died, and are buried there.

Charles Garland was a Baptist minister. There is a story that he got upon a barrel one day to preach, and in the course of his remarks, he said that the faith of the Baptists was on a firm foundation, that they would never fall; he stamped his foot to emphasize the remark and the head of the barrel fell through, and he fell with it. This circumstance, of course, broke up the meeting, but he no doubt continued to preach about the firm foundation of the Baptist faith. He was a good man, died with consumption about 1830, near Grayson C. H., Va.

Hudson (6) Garland was father of Hudson (7), and also of General John (7) Garland, whose daughter married General Longstreet, and of Spottswood (7) Garland.

Hudson (6) Garland represented Amherst county in the House of Delegates, was captain in the war of 1812, and an intimate friend of Andrew Jackson, who presented him with a cane made of a fragment of the Constitution, and, what was more valuable, a lucrative office which he held until Tyler's administration.

Spottswood Garland (6) married Lucinda, daughter of Colonel Hugh Rose and Caroline Jordon, and had Hugh A., who married Anna Powell Burwell; Caroline, who married Maurice H. Garland; Landon Cabell, who married Louisa F. Garland.

Landon C. Garland, LL.D., was president of Randolph-Macon College, president of University of Alabama and chancellor of Vanderbilt University, for a quarter of a century. His sister, Caroline, married Maurice H. Garland, whose son was General Samuel Garland, of Confederate war fame. Hugh A. Garland was author of the life of John Randolph of Roanoke.

Mrs. Rose Garland Lewis, daughter of the late Chancellor Landon C. Garland, of Vanderbilt University, died at her home in Birmingham, Alabama, October 29th, 1913, aged seventy-four years. Her husband, Dr. Burwell B. Lewis, was at the time of his death, some years ago, President of the University of Alabama. Mrs. Lewis was a devout Christian and faithful member of our church.

Many who knew and loved her sorrow because of her death.

There were twelve children born to Samuel Meredith Garland and wife, Mildred Jordan Powell. The daughter, Mildred Irvin, married Col. John T. Ellis. Martha Henry married Col. Thomas Whitehead. First son, Rev. James Powell, married Lucy Braxton, of Fredericksburg, Va., a great grand-daughter of Carter Braxton, signer of the Declaration of Independence. Narcissa E. married Mr. Dillard, of Lynchburg, Va. Lucy Lee married Mr. Richardson, of New Kent county, Va. Ella Rose married Henry Wills; Jane Meredith married Willis Wills; Sally died in infancy; David Shepherd died single; Walter died in childhood; Paulus Powell married Lucy Ellis.

Issue of the marriage of David Shepherd Garland to Jane Henry Meredith: Jane Meredith, who married Dr. Jno. P. Cobbs and moved to Indiana in 1840; Anne Shepherd, who married Dr. Gustavus A. Rose and moved to Indiana in 1840; Sally Armistead, who married Captain William Waller; Samuel Meredith, who married Mildred Jordon Powell; Mary Rice, who married Edward A. Cabell; William Henry, who married Frances Eubank; Patrick Henry, who married Miss Floyd; Eliza Virginia, who married George K. Cabell; Louisa Frances, who married Dr. Landon C. Garland; Caroline died single; Martha Henry died single. It is worth while to note that the average age of these eleven children was seventy years, while a majority, or six of them, lived to be eighty or over.

David S. Garland was a man of ability and prominence. He represented his state in Congress during Madison's administration, represented his county (Amherst) in the

LANDON CABELL GARLAND, LL. D.
Son of Spottswood Garland and wife, Lucinda, Daughter of Col. Hugh Rose

(Members of the Nuckolls family say that this picture of Landon C. Garland is an exact likeness of the author's grandfather, Robert Garland Nuckolls)

Legislature with distinction, for twenty-nine years; was a man of great public spirit and enterprise, and by his industry and great business capacity amassed a large fortune.

His mansion, built for and owned by him, is now standing in a fair state of preservation in the village of New Glasgow, about five miles from Amherst court house. In proximity to and in sight of the old Garland home, stands "Winton," the home of Colonel Samuel Meredith, whose daughter David S. Garland married.

Col. Meredith was born in Hanover county, Va., in 1732, and was captain in Colonel Byrd's Regiment, 1758, and for his services was granted to him July 11th, 1774, 2,000 acres of land in Kentucky. In 1775 he was captain of an independent company from Hanover county, which on May 2nd he resigned in favor of his brother-in-law, Patrick Henry, and accepted a lieutenancy in the company.

He was a member of the Convention of May, 1776, and in 1778 he subscribed £500 to old Washington-Henry College in Hanover Town, and for several years was president of the board of trustees of the college.

Rice (2) Garland was a distinguished member of Congress from Virginia, and afterwards Judge of the supreme court of Louisiana.

Robert, born in 1768, and Clifton, in 1769, concluded the children of James Garland and his wife, Mary Rice.

William Garland, born 1746, married Ann Shepherd of Amherst county; issue: David Shepherd; James, died single; Frances, married Mr. Pendleton; Mary, married Mr. Camden.

David Shepherd Garland, born 1769, married Jane Henry Meredith on March 4th, 1795, the daughter of Colonel Samuel Meredith and Jane Henry, his wife, who was a sister of Patrick Henry, the great orator and patriot.

In the family graveyard at Winton are buried Jane Henry Meredith and her husband, Hon. David S. Garland, and four other members of the Henry family.

Samuel Meredith Garland, born November 15th, 1802, married Mildred Jordan Powell, July 8th, 1830. He was by profession a lawyer. When quite young he represented Amherst in the Legislature, was a member of the Reform Convention of 1850-51, and of the Secession Convention of 1861. He advocated the sovereignty of the States, and voted for the Ordinance of Secession. In his later years he was clerk of the Amherst court. He was universally beloved; was a lay reader in the Episcopal Church. He died in 1880, and is buried at Kenmore, Va.

We cannot close this incomplete sketch of the Garlands without some reference to Hon. Hugh A. Garland and Hon. Augustus H. Garland.

Hugh A. Garland was a brother of Dr. Landon C. Garland; was a member of the Virginia Legislature, clerk of the United States House of Representatives, a man of vast and varied learning and a writer of distinction; author of the life of John Randolph.

Augustus H. Garland was a scion of the Lunenburg branch, was a lawyer of national reputation, Governor of Arkansas, United States Senator, and attorney general in Cleveland's Cabinet.

Garland Connection With the Pendletons and the Cabells

Lettie B. Pendleton married Hudson Martin Garland; she was the daughter of Micajah Pendleton and Mary Cabell Horsley. Micajah Pendleton was a son of Philip Pendleton, and nephew of the famous jurist, Edmond Pendleton.

Phillip Pendleton had fifteen children, and Micajah (so tradition has it) addressed Mary Horsley seventeen

THE GARRETT CEMETERY
On the Banks of Coosa River, Near Centre, Alabama

times before she would consent to marry him. Mary Horsley was the daughter of William Horsley, who was the son of William Horsley and Mary Cabell, only daughter of Dr. William Cabell and his wife, Elizabeth Burkes Cabell. Bessie Powell married Rev. R. F. Wilson, D.D.

Rev. James Powell Garland, D.D., graduated at Emory and Henry College, June 10th, 1857, and joined the Virginia Methodist Conference in 1858, and was forty-seven years in the active ministry of this church, holding positions of honor and trust in that body. His long and useful life came to a close January 13th, 1906.

CHAPTER VII

THE JONES FAMILY

(The author is indebted to *The Richmond Times Despatch* and *The Toledo Blade* for a good deal of the following information in regard to the Jones family.)

The Despatch says: "James Jones is presumed to have been the first settler in Spottsylvania county, Va., and the question might be raised if he could have been the brother of Admiral Paul Jones, who visited him in 1750, and after his brother's death, 1773, is said to have taken charge of his estate near Fredericksburg."

The first name of Paul Jones' brother is not given, and indeed the name of Jones was assumed by Paul in 1773; yet we may presume that the Jones family of Spottsylvania were some of his Scotch family, who had preceded him to Virginia, and that this James Jones was the immigrant." Paul Jones' father's name was John Paul and James Jones may have assumed the patronymic of Jones as his brother Paul did. This custom which is of classical authority has long been prevalent in Wales, and in various other countries, although it is not practiced in that part of the island in which John Paul Jones was born.

The life of Paul Jones has given rise to much romance. Cooper, Dumas and Allan Cunningham have celebrated him in their novels; and scarcely less fictitious are some of his so-called biographies.

Every school boy is familiar with John Paul Jones as the founder of the American Navy, and the hero of many naval engagements. His is a most interesting character, and the following short sketch of his life is inserted, as it will no doubt be of interest to the readers of this book.

John Paul Jones (1747-1792) was born July 6th, 1747, on the estate of Arbigland, in the parish of Kirkbean, and the stewartry of Kirkcudbright, Scotland, where his father, John Paul, was a gardener. At twelve, he went to sea as apprentice to a merchant of Whitehaven, in whose ships he visited America several times. He became a skilful sailor, and was for some time mate of a slaver in the West Indies. On his way back to England, after leaving the slave trade in disgust, the captain and mate of the ship in which he was, both died; and the skilful manner in which he brought the ship safely into port induced the owners to appoint him captain. In 1771, or thereabouts, he added the name of Jones to John Paul.

There is a tradition that he and an old man by the name of William Jones, of South Carolina, had become fast friends. William Jones was a planter and owned a large estate. He wished to leave his estate to John Paul, and the latter added the name Jones to his name in order that he might inherit the estate and because William Jones wished him to assume the name of Jones. It is more than probable, however, that both John Paul and his brother James assumed the name Jones, as has been before explained in this chapter, because their father's name was John and they followed the established custom of assuming the patronymic.

In 1773, Paul Jones inherited the estate of his brother, James Jones, in Spottsylvania county, and settled on it. When the American war of Independence broke out two years later, Paul Jones took up arms for the colonies, and accepted a command in the navy of the new republic. His engagement with the English ship, "Serapis," which, after a long and bloody battle, he compelled to strike, raised his fame to its acme. Later, he became a

Rear Admiral in the Russian Navy during the reign of Empress Catharine, but the jealousy and rivalry of the Russian commanders brought about his recall in less than eight months. He retired to Paris, where he died in 1792, at the age of forty-five years, and was laid in an unmarked grave, only discovered a few years ago.

He writhed under the suspicion of being an "adventurer;" once and again he eagerly repels the charge. His character is illustrated by an incident told of his conduct in one of the hottest fights of the Revolution when he heard one of his officers cursing,—"Do not swear, Mr. Stacy," he said, "in another moment we may be in eternity; but let us do our duty." When called upon by the commander of the British frigate Serapis to surrender the battered American ship, Bonhomme Richard, he said, "Surrender? I have not yet begun to fight."

When General Horace Porter, of New York, was United States Ambassador to France, he found the remains of Commodore Jones in an abandoned cemetery in Paris. Through General Porter's efforts, the remains were brought to the United States in 1908, and they now rest in a vault in the chapel of the United States Naval Academy at Annapolis, Md.

JOHN PAUL JONES' STATUE UNVEILED

"Washington, D. C., April 17, 1912—With impressive military and civic exercises the magnificent memorial to John Paul Jones, the naval hero of the American Revolution, was dedicated in this city today. Congress appropriated $50,000 for the memorial, which occupies a conspicuous site at the main entrance to Potomac Park.

"The President of the United States and members of the Cabinet, the diplomatic corps, justices of the Supreme Court of the United States, distinguished officers of the navy and the army, senators, representatives in congress and many others prominent in official life, as well as a large concourse of citizens, were present. Thousands of blue jackets of the navy, United States marines, soldiers of the regular army and of the National Guard and delegations representing patriotic and other civic organizations were assembled in parade as a tribute to the famous naval hero.

"The memorial, the work of Paul H. Niehaus, the New York sculptor, was admired by everyone who saw it. In many respects it differs from other similar memorials erected in the national capital. It consists of a marble pylon of classic design as the back-ground for a colossal bronze figure of the intrepid naval commander of the early days of the republic. The pylon is a massive rectangular tower about fifteen feet in height. It occupies the center of an ornamental fountain, the water for which will come from the bronze heads of dolphins at each end of the pylon. On the back of the shaft is a large panel containing a bas relief representation of Commodore Jones raising the American flag on the historic ship Bonhomme Richard.

"The Jones statue stands at the base of the monument in front of the pedestal. It is of heroic proportions, being about ten feet high. The great naval commander is shown in full uniform, with an expression and pose suggestive of his indomitable will and unconquerable spirit. Apparently he is watching a naval engagement. His right hand is clenched and his left hand clutches his sword.

"In the die under the statue is inscribed:

"1747   First   1792.
To compel foreign men of war to strike colors
to the Stars and Stripes.

"There are two inscriptions on the rear of the pylon. The first of these is on the stone forming the cap of the shaft. It embodies the language popularly attributed to Commodore Jones when called upon by the commander of the British frigate, Serapis, to surrender the battered American ship, Bonhomme Richard. The inscription is as follows:

"—Surrender?—
"I have not yet begun to fight.

"The second inscription is just below the bas relief representing Commodore Jones raising the United States flag for the first time on an American warship. It reads:

"In Life he honored the Flag
"In death the Flag shall honor Him.

"Secretary of the Navy, Meyer, presided at the dedication exercises and the memorial was unveiled by Admiral Dewey. President Taft addressed the assemblage and pronounced a splendid tribute to the valor and genius of the sailor and patriot and told of his daring deeds on the high seas. The exercises concluded with the oration of the day delivered by General Horace Porter, of New York, who, while United States ambassador to France, found the remains of Commodore Jones in an abandoned cemetery in Paris and had them brought to their present resting place in a vault of the chapel at the United States Naval Academy at Annapolis.

"The United States Marine Band furnished the musical features of the dedication program. At the conclusion of the exercises a vessel of the navy stationed in the Potomac opposite the statue fired a regulation salute."

The following names are given by the *Times-Despatch* as being, many of them, sons and grandsons of James Jones and their descendants:

Bartholomew, Bathurst, Churchill, etc.

From Churchill we trace the Jones family that came

as pioneer settlers to what is now Grayson county, Virginia.

Churchill Jones married a Miss Minitree; issue: Minitree Jones who married a Miss Spottswood; issue: Rosamond Jones, Minitree Jones (2) and Spottswood Jones, and Churchill Jones (2) all of Revolutionary fame. A number of this Jones family moved into this Southwestern part of Virginia, and settled in the forests on the waters of New River and its tributaries.

William Bourne married Rosamond Jones, daughter of Minitree Jones and wife, Miss Spottswood, in Hanover county, Virginia. They emigrated to Southwestern Virginia, coming as far as Fort Chiswell in wagons. From Fort Chiswell, they packed their household goods across the Iron' Mountains on horses, and settled on Knob Fork of Elk Creek, not far from where Elk Creek empties into New River. (See Bourne chapter.)

(We insert the following clipping: "Announce wedding eleven years after," taken from the *Washington Herald*, as interesting in this connection.)

"After keeping the news of their nuptial secret for more than eleven years, announcement was made yesterday of the marriage on August 1st, 1901, of George C. Lafferty, official reporter at the House of Representatives, and a prominent local clubman, and Miss Rosamond E. Jones, of 816 Fifteenth street, N. W., daughter of the late Chrechill Jones, of Westmoreland county, Virginia.

"Although the first formal announcement of the marriage was not made until yesterday, many of the close friends of the couple knew of the affair. For eleven years Mr. Lafferty and his wife lived separately and tried to keep the fact of their marriage a secret. The husband called daily at the Fifteenth street residence to see "Miss Jones," and spent much of his time there, but neighbors were of the opinion that he was merely the fiance and not the husband of the young woman.

IN ATLANTIC CITY

"Mr. and Mrs. Lafferty are now at Atlantic City, N. J., supposedly on their long delayed honeymoon. Why the marriage should have been kept a secret for so many years, and why the couple should have undergone such long separation, although man and wife, is a mystery which will probably be solved only by a statement from Mr. and Mrs. Lafferty. Friends of the couple said last night that they were unable to tell the cause of the secrecy.

"Mr. Lafferty is in the neighborhood of fifty-five years old. His bride is considerably younger, it is said. Mr. Lafferty comes from an old Virginia family. His home was originally in Richmond, and his father, Dr. Lafferty, was well known as a newspaper man of ability. For a time the son was employed as a stenographic reporter for the Virginia legislature at Richmond.

"His father finally succeeded in obtaining for him a position in congress, and about twenty-five years ago he came to Washington as official reporter of debates in the house. He has held the position ever since. About twenty years ago he was married, but his wife died. According to the announcement made yesterday, he married Miss Jones in New Jersey, August 1st, 1901.

WERE CHILDHOOD CHUMS

"He had known Mrs. Lafferty from childhood in Virginia. She was the daughter of the late Churchill Jones, who was well known in Westmoreland county. At the time of the marriage it is said that Miss Jones was living here.

"Mr. Lafferty is a prominent Washington clubman. He is a member of the Metropolitan Club and makes his residence there. For the last five or six years Miss Jones has been living in apartments at 816 Fifteenth street. Mr. Lafferty was frequently seen at the apartments, although he did not live there."

William Jones came from Eastern Virginia, and settled on New River below the mouths of Elk and Meadow creeks, at a place where there was an island in the river.

A road was made passing Jones' place, and a ford was made through the river, crossing the island. This was named "Jones' Ford," and was two miles from where the town of Greenville and Grayson Old Court House was located when the county of Grayson was formed in 1792.

William Jones' daughter married Isaac Garrison. From this union there was one son, David, who married Sally Bourne, daughter of Stephen Bourne who had also moved from near Richmond and settled on Knob Fork.

Isaac Garrison had one daughter who married Benjamin Shoupe. They lived on Elk Creek and have children.

Elizabeth B., daughter of David Garrison and Sally Bourne, married Hastings Fulton, son of Samuel Fulton and wife, Martha Powell Jones. After the death of William Jones, Isaac Garrison and wife lived at the old homestead, and the name of the Ford was changed to "Garrison's Ford."

Afterwards, the land passed to David Garrison, and for two generations this was known as "Garrison's Ford"— for years the only ford on the river for crossing with wagons.

After the death of David Garrison, the land passed to Hastings and Elizabeth Fulton's heirs, but was soon sold to Robert L. Dickenson. The ford is still used, but a ferry-boat is operated at the same place.

Hastings Fulton and wife settled at the old Wm. Bourne Furnace, "Point Hope," at the falls of Peach Bottom creek. They had one son and three daughters.

The son, Columbus, married Rosamond D. Edwards, granddaughter of Morgan Bryant and wife, Susan Hale, daughter of William Hale and wife, Lucy Stone, of Elk Creek. The son, Columbus, and wife live near the old "Point Hope" Furnace (now the site of an electric plant). They have one son, Robert S., who married Miss Bryant of Saddle Creek, a great grand-daughter of Joseph Bryant and wife, Sarah Hale. One daughter married Hicks Rhudy, attorney at Independence, Va., and one daughter married a Mr. Couch.

Major Minitree Jones married Miss Martha Powell in Eastern Virginia. Their son, Major Abner Jones, also married Miss Hannah Fawbush of Eastern Virginia.

Maj. Minitree Jones and family moved out and settled on New River, near the mouth of Elk Creek.

His home place is now owned by John Dickenson, Jr.

Maj. Minitree Jones was one of the pioneer settlers, aided in forming Grayson county in 1792, and was named as a magistrate in the commission given by Henry Lee, Governor of Virginia to organize the first court for Grayson county. The oath of office as a magistrate was administered to him by Flower Swift. (See "Proceedings of first court.")

Minitree Jones, Jr., and wife, Martha Powell, had a son, Powell Jones, who settled in Georgia. Powell Jone's son, Samuel Jones, was the father of the well known evangelist, Samuel Powell Jones, of Cartersville, Ga. Sam P. Jones was well known all over the United States as a preacher and lecturer.

Maj. Abner Jones who was sheriff of Grayson county in its early formation was a son of Minitree Jones, Jr. Abner Jones lived on Steven's creek. He was appointed county surveyor, and held office in Grayson county for a number of years.

Abner Jones and Hannah Fawbush, his wife, had two sons, Spottswood and Churchill, and seven daughters. First daughter, Charlotte, married David Atkins and lived on Steven's Creek. One son, Greenberry Atkins, died single. One daughter, Elvira Atkins, first married a Hackler; two daughters of this union; one married a Mr. Neel, of Bland county, Va. Elvira married second time, Fletcher Boiles, of North Carolina. They have children; live on Stevens Creek, Va.

Euphemia, second daughter of Abner Jones and Hannah Fawbush, married Isaac Moore, and lived near the old homestead. To them were born three sons, Spottswood D., Orville, and Churchill Fawbush. Spottswood married Miss Matilda Bayless of Tennessee; issue, two sons, one daughter.

Orville Moore married Rosamond Hale, daughter of Charles Hale and wife, Jane Sutherland, of Knob Fork. No issue from this union. Churchill Fawbush Moore married Mary A. Nuckolls, daughter of Clarke Nuckolls and wife, Rosamond B. Hale; issue, three sons, William, Arthur N.; William died when he was about twenty-five years old. Arthur married Miss Moore, daughter of Orville Moore, and lives at the old homestead with his father and mother.

Five daughters were born to Churchill and Mary Moore; Celia died single; Amelia married Mr. Miller, and lives in Winston, N. C.; Rosamond B. married Mr. Lawson; they live in Ivanhoe, Va., and have one son; Lura, single; Leona, single.

To Isaac Moore and wife were born two daughters.

First daughter, Matilda, married Joseph Cornett; they had three daughters, and two sons. First daughter, married John Cooper, of Dobson, N. C. Second daughter, married Harvey Atkins; Third daughter, married.

First son, Heath Cornett, married a Miss Tomlinson and moved to Illinois.

Second son, Orville, married Miss Bartlett, and moved West.

Isaac Moore's second daughter Minerva, married Creed L. Hanks. They live at Piper's Gap, Va. One son, Emmett Hanks, married Miss Lula Todd of Galax, Va.; issue, one son, died in infancy; one daughter.

Emmett died in 1909.

Flora, daughter of Creed Hanks and Minerva Moore, married Stephen Wilkinson, son of John Wilkinson and wife, Elizabeth Anderson, of Hillsville, Va.

Stephen Wilkinson and wife, Flora Hanks, have one son and one daughter, Robert and Retta. They live in Galax, Va.

Stephen Wilkinson is manager of the Galax Furniture Factory, and interested in the various enterprises of the town.

Nancy Hanks was born and brought up near Flour Gap, (now Piper's Gap) Va., on Blue Ridge, then Grayson county. When a young woman she went to Kentucky, married Mr. Thomas Lincoln, and was the mother of Abraham Lincoln.

Nancy Hanks was of the same family as Creed L. Hanks. She was a woman of fine physical organization, and of great force of character, and possessed of shrewd practical common sense, combined with deep religious feeling and great gentleness of manner. She taught Abraham Lincoln to read and write, and although but nine years of age when his mother died, Lincoln had received the lasting impress of her power for good in his deepest life. Three favorite maxims she had thoroughly instilled into his mind—never to swear, never to touch liquor, and never to lie. These three things he never did.

He said when President, "All that I am or hope to be, I owe to my sainted mother."

Celia, third daughter of Abner Jones and wife, married Andrew Nuckolls, of Wythe county, Virginia, son of Nathaniel Nuckolls, born in Louisa county, Virginia, January 3rd, 1739.

From this union there were three sons and four daughters.

One daughter, Cynthia, married James Johnston and lived in Hillsville, Va. (See Nuckolls chapter.)

Olive, daughter of Maj. Abner Jones, married John Worrell about the year 1820. The history of the Worrell family dates back as far as 1066, when Sir Herbert Worrell lost two sons at Hastings and was presented with two coats of arms in recognition of their merit. The Worrell's came to this country during its early settlement and became prominent factors in its development. Records in Philadelphia show that Richard and John Worrell were deeded lands, where Philadelphia now stands, by William Penn.

Richard and John had a brother named James, who settled in what is now Carroll county, Va. (then Montgomery), about the year 1780. This James was the father of Esau, Sr., who was the father of a large family, of which was Captain John Worrell, who married Miss Olive Jones about the year 1820.

In 1910, Malcolm Lee Worrell was appointed to the U. S. Naval Academy by Congressman C. B. Slemp, and the following article appeared in the *Tazewell Republican*:

"Following his appointment to the Naval Academy, Malcolm Lee Worrell, of Pulaski, has just passed all entrance requirements, and now wears the brand of Uncle Sam in a midshipman's uniform.

"Young Worrell's ancestry dates back to James Jones, a brother of Admiral Paul Jones, the founder of the

United States navy. In 1773, Paul Jones took charge of his brother James's landed estate near Fredericksburg, Va. James Jones' wife was a Churchill. They had a son named Churchill, who married a Miss Minitree. From this union we have Minitree Jones, who married a Miss Spottswood. From this union we have Rosamond Jones, Minitree Jones, Jr., Churchill Jones, Jr., and Spottswood Jones, all of Revolutionary fame. Maj. Minitree Jones married Miss Martha Powell, a highly educated lady, and from this union we have Abner Jones and Martha Powell Jones. Martha married Samuel Fulton, and their son, Creed Fulton was an eminent teacher and evangelist, and founded Emory and Henry College.

"Abner Jones married Miss Hannah Fawbush. From this union were two sons, Churchill and Spottswood, and six daughters.

"One daughter, Olive, married Captain John Worrell about the year 1820. From this union we have Churchill Fawbush Worrell, Maj. C. Columbus Worrell, Carinne, and Minerva E. Worrell. Carinne died single; Minerva married Harbert Kenney. Churchill Worrell married Mary Ann Ballard. From this union, one son, Dexter, A. L., who married Rose E. Lyons; their third son, Malcolm Lee, is the young midshipman of this sketch.

"It was Isaac Worrell, Sr., who delivered the address of welcome to Gen. Lafayette and the veterans of the Revolution at their Reunion in Philadelphia in 1824. Isaac Worrell, Jr., son of Isaac, Sr., was commissioned brigadier general in the British war of 1812.

"Malcolm Lee Worrell was born in Hillsville, Carroll county, Va. He was educated at Roanoke College, Salem, Va., and V. P. I., Blacksburgh, Va. Previous to his present appointment, he was in the employ of the Norfolk and Western R. R. at Bluefield, W. Va."

Maj. C. Columbus Worrell, son of Capt. John Worrell

and Olive Jones, is a worthy and useful citizen of Carroll county. He married first, Miss Latitia Ward; from this union, three sons, two daughters. His second wife was America V. Watson; from this union, four sons, one daughter. His third wife was Mrs. Rosa Beamer, nee Cox.

Minerva E. Worrell, daughter of Capt. John Worrell and wife, Olive Jones, married Harbert Kenney of Crooked Creek, Carroll county, Va. From this union, one daughter married Thomas Jones and lives near Woodlawn, Carroll county, Va. They have one son, Elmer Jones.

One son of Minerva Worrell and Harbert Kenney, married and lives near Woodlawn, Va.

Jessee P. Worrell, brother of Capt. John Worrell, married Rebecca Cooley, daughter of Benjamin Cooley and wife, Jane Dickey. He lived a while on Little Reed Island, but later moved to Missouri.

Esau, Jr., and Amos Worrell, brothers, lived on Little Reed Island, and reraed families. Two sisters, Nancy and Sallie. Nancy married Joel Franklin; lived near Hillsville; one daughter, Tima Franklin, married Mr. Staples. Two sons, Esau and Powatan Franklin live near Hillsville, Va.

Sally Worrell married Mr. Paul; kept hotel in Hillsville; married second time, James Crockett. They had no children.

CHAPTER VIII

THE CORNETT FAMILY

Up to about the year 1871, the Cornett family of Grayson spelled their name Canute; in all their business transactions it was written Canute, and some of the older people still spell it and pronounce it that way. The family tradition is that they are descended from King Canute of England. The following is copied from Montgomery's English history:

Canute (1017-1035) Seveyn the Dane, conquered England (1013). "All the people," says the Chronicle, "'held him for full king.'" He was succeeded by his son, Canute, (1017). He was from beyond the seas, but could hardly be called a foreigner, since he spoke a language and set up a government differing but little from that of the English.

After his first harsh measures were over, he sought the friendship of both Church and people. He gave the country peace. He rebuked the flattering of courtiers by showing them that the in-rolling tide is no respecter of persons; he endeavored to rule justly, and his liking for the monks found expression in his song:

"Merrily sang the Monks of Ely,
As Canute the King was passing by."

CANUTE'S PLAN; THE FOUR EARLDOMS.

Canute's plan was to establish a great Northern empire, embracing Denmark, Norway, Sweden, and England.

To facilitate the government of so large a realm, he divided England into four districts: Wessex, Mercia,

East Angelo, and Northumbria, which, with their dependencies, embraced the entire country.

Each of these districts was ruled by an Earl invested with almost royal power. For a time the arrangement worked well, but eventually discord sprang up between the rulers. Their individual ambitions and their efforts to obtain supreme authority imperiled the unity of the country.

William Canute, Sr., was an early settler on Elk creek, now Grayson county, Virginia, and is said to be a descendant of King Canute, of England.

He married Jennie Sutherland, a daughter of John Sutherland, Sr., and wife, Elizabeth Bryan.

In the history of the Bryan family, written by the wife of William Jennings Bryan, she states, "The great grandfather of William Jennings Bryan had a brother, Francis Bryan, and a sister, Elizabeth Bryan, that moved west from Eastern Virginia, and the family has lost trace of them."

In the early settlement of Southwest Virginia, Francis Bryan and his sister, Elizabeth Bryan, came to Fort Chiswell and the Lead Mines; from there they crossed the Iron Mountain and settled on Elk Creek. Elizabeth Bryan married John Sutherland, Sr., and brought up a family of sons and daughters. Francis Bryan married Phoebe Woodruff, and moved from Elk Creek to Ashe county, North Carolina.

John Sutherland's family were originally from Scotland.

William Canute, Sr., and wife, Jennie Sutherland, had a large family; all settled on Elk Creek.

Their first son, Col. Eli Canute, married Sena Hale, daughter of Richard Hale and wife, Elizabeth Stone. They have two sons: first, Capt. William Cornett; second, Wiley Winston Cornett. They also had six daughters: Matilda, Elizabeth, Amanda, Elvira, Theresa, and Jennie.

The second son, Levi Cornett, married Olive Hale, daughter of Dudley Hale and wife, Mary Burroughs. They had seven sons: first son, Francis Cornett, married first, Miss Austin, of Elk Creek, Virginia; had sons and daughters; his second marriage was to Miss Jane Daniels, of Elk Creek; they also had sons and daughters.

The second son of Levi Cornett and wife, Olive Hale, George W. Cornett, married first, Miss Herbert; they had one son, Thomas. He married the second time, Miss Sarah Gentry, daughter of Col. Allen Gentry and wife, Rebecca Reeves. Judge Cornett is a lawyer, represented Grayson county in the Legislature, and was judge of the county court. He has been a useful and worthy citizen of Grayson county for many years.

He has four daughters and one son, by his second wife. His son, Munsey, is a lawyer; married and has children. First daughter, Myrtle, married Rev. Kelly Boyer, member of the Western North Carolina Conference.

Second daughter, Rebecca, married first, Mr.———, of Richmond, Virginia.

The second time married Frank Sanders, son of John L. Sanders, Chilhowie, Virginia.

Third daughter, married Prof. Morgan Cheek, Principal of Elk Creek High School.

Third son of Levi Cornett, William, first married Callie Delp; had one daughter, who married a Mr. Copenhaver, of Smyth county, Virginia. William second time, married Miss Fisher Asbury, Wythe county. One son, Thomas, married Miss Lundy, daughter of Ellis Lundy and wife, Alice Hale.

Fourth, Zach. M., married Gazilda Cecil, of Pulaski county, Va. and lives there; has children.

Fifth, Miles Foy, was a noble young man; died single.

Sixth, Lewis K., married Nannie Warrick; he was representative in Legislature of Virginia from Grayson county the second time; has two children.

Friel, the youngest son, who lives at the old homestead, is a worthy citizen; he married Miss Hester Ring; one son, Romulus Ring; four daughters; first, Isabella, married Col. William Mitchell; two daughters; Martha married John Cecil, of Pulaski county; moved to Texas; have children. Nancy married Mr. Steffy, Wythe county, Virginia.

Second, Nancy, married Lewis Perkins; no children.

Third, Elvira, married James Cornett; live on Elk Creek; have children.

Fourth, Theresa, married Carson Andis; one daughter, married Robert Carson; one married Noel Tomlin, Jr.

The third son of William Canute and wife, Jennie Sutherland, was Francis Cornett, Sr. He married Miss Catherine Fulton, daughter of Samuel Fulton and wife, Miss Martha Powell-Jones. (See Fulton and Jones families.)

There were three sons: First, Samuel Monroe Cornett, married Jane McCarty, of Elk Creek. Prof. Fielden R. Cornett married Malissa Copenhaver, of Smyth county, Virginia.

The third son of Francis Cornett and wife was Peyton H. Cornett, who married Amelia Cox, daughter of Enoch Cox and wife, Susan Thomas, of Bridle Creek, Virginia.

There are also two daughters of Francis Cornett and wife: the first, Amanda, married Van Buren McCarta; the second, Martha Powell, died single.

The fourth son, Col. Alexander Cornett married Jemima Rhudy. Their sons: Friel N., James P., William J., Stephen H., and Eli C.; daughters: Martha, Elizabeth, Theresa, Charlotte, and Nancy.

William Cornett, Sr., and wife, had three daughters: First, Charlotte D., married William Rhudy; had a family of sons and daughters.

Lucy H. married Andrew Porter; they had sons and daughters; lived on Elk Creek.

The third daughter of William Cornett and wife was Margaret. She married Rev. Abraham Elliott, a local Methodist preacher. Mr. Elliott and his wife first settled on Meadow Creek, near Grayson C. H.; afterward moved to Elk Creek to the Cornett mills; from there to Independence, Virginia. For some time they kept Hotel Elliott at Independence. Mr. Elliott was a tinner by trade; was a useful, industrious, good man; he and his wife both died and are buried at Independence. They brought up a family of sons and daughters; all settled in and around the town of Independence. Their youngest daughter, Margaret, married William Wright, editor of the "Grayson Journal." Mr. Wright has been editor of this paper for over forty years at Independence, Virginia.

William Cornett, Sr., was an energetic, enterprising citizen, and brought up and trained his family for useful, industrious citizens of their country.

Elk Creek is a bold, swift mountain stream, flowing through a beautiful valley, and emptying into New River, furnishing fine water power.

William Cornett, in the early days, built a mill for grinding grain, also a saw mill, and a carding machine for carding wool. These mills were on the banks of Elk Creek, and were used by the settlers for many miles around.

CHAPTER IX

THE COX, OSBORNE, PHIPPS, HASH, AND REEVES FAMILIES

In the time of the early settlement of this country, there were, of course, few families, and they so inter-married one into the other that it is hard to write of them separately, so I will, in this chapter, give these families together.

About the year, 1740, David Cox and John Cox, two brothers, came from Scotland to Virginia. They both located in what is now Grayson county, on New River, about ten miles west of Grayson Old Court House.

John Cox was captain of the Home Guard, or Regulators, during the Revolutionary war. He built a fort on a ridge at the mouth of Peach Bottom Creek, overlooking New River; supplies for the Fort were packed on horses from the Lead Mines in Wythe county.

It is said that there is yet a tree marked at a point on New River, near the mouth of Meadow Creek, showing the Old Trail from the Fort to the Lead Mines. This is on the farm of John Austin, who is a descendant of John Cox. After the Revolutionary war, Capt. John Cox moved up the river to the mouth of Cranberry Creek, on the South Fork of New River, opened up a large farm there, and is buried there in the family graveyard. Most of his family settled in Ashe county, N. C.; he had two sons, James and Joshua, and five daughters.

David Cox, brother of Captain John Cox, moved his family and located on the river near where his brother first settled, near what is now Cox's Ford, ten miles west of Grayson Old C. H. David Cox's wife was a Miss McGowan; they had eleven sons and three daughters.

One of these sons, Samuel, known as Sheriff Sam Cox, married Rebecca Osborne, and reared a large family on the New River farm. Two of his daughters married brothers, John Blevins and Samuel Blevins. Three of his sons married sisters, Alexander married Miss Polly Osborn; Calloway married Miss Nancy Osborn; Samuel, Jr., married Miss Phoeba Osborn, and lives at the old homestead where Samuel Cox, Sr., lived. They, and their families, live in the same neighborhood, near the mouth of Little River; they are true types of their patriotic ancestors.

Another son of David Cox and wife, Miss McGowan, Joshua Cox, married Miss Ruth Osborne, and settled on Bridle Creek, in a rich and fertile valley, which industry and enterprise have developed into fine farming lands. Joshua Cox was a good citizen, and did much towards advancing the best interest of his neighborhood. They reared five sons, John, David, Harden, Samuel, and Isom; also three daughters, Hannah, Jennie, and Margaret. John Cox married Miss Nellie Ward; Esquire David married Miss Jane Doughton, and lived on New River; his daughter, Mary, married Warner Hale. Harden Cox married Miss Nancy Reeves, a zealous Christian, and active worker in the Methodist Church.

Harden Cox served his country as a justice of the peace for many years, and was assessor when Grayson and Carroll were all one county; their eldest son fell in the Confederate Army, a brave soldier.

Esquire Elbert Sevier Cox lived near the old homestead; he first married Rebecca Hale, daughter of Mastin Hale and wife, Susan Perkins, of Elk Creek; his second wife was Miss Jane Hampton, daughter of Alexander Hampton and wife, Jestena Fulton, who was daughter of Samuel Fulton, Sr., and wife, Martha Powell-Jones.

Joshua McGowan Cox and family ived at the old family residence, near Independence. Enoch Cox, another brother, married Miss Susan Thomas, an amiable, good woman; their daughter, Mollie, married Zachariah Osborne, Jr.

Samuel Cox married Miss Elizabeth Thomas, daughter of Jonathan Thomas and wife, Patience Bourne; they lived on Bridle Creek; he and his amiable Christian wife reared an intelligent and worthy family.

Capt. Meville B. Cox, their son, a prominent citizen, contributed much for the improvement of society and his country. His wife was Miss Martha P. Fulton, a lady of cultivated intellect and refinement. Capt. M. B. Cox and wife, were both members of the Methodist Church, South, having been brought up in the nurture and admonition of the Lord. Their example in the family circle will live when they are gone from this life. Their sons and daughters are following the example of their parents.

Emeline, daughter of Samuel Cox and Elizabeth Thomas, married Harden Cox, Jr., and lived on Potato Creek. They were active and exemplary members of the Methodist Church, built an elegant home, and have done much for the community and county in which they live. Their son, Charles, and wife, live with their mother, in their happy home of beauty and comfort, the fruit of their labor.

Caroline, another daughter of Samuel Cox and wife, married Mr. Bridges; they had one daughter, Miss Virginia Bridges, who married Verda Hampton; they have one son, Samuel Cox Hampton. Mrs. Hampton died young, but she had accomplished her work, and died in the triumph of the Christian's hope; she leaves an influence that will live while she sleeps. Her mother lives with Mr. Hampton and his little son, Samuel C., and will train the little boy for usefulness in this life.

The youngest son of Samuel Cox, and wife, McGowan, died suddenly at the old homestead when a young man. His death was a shock to the family, but he rests in peace. Thomas Cox married Miss Ransom of Washington county, Va.; he was sheriff of Grayson county; he and his wife were Christians, and brought up a nice family of sons and daughters, who reflect honor on their parents.

Dr. Everett Cox was a practicing physician; also a Methodist preacher. He married Miss Scott, daughter of Rev. Andrew Scott, of Rye Valley, Smyth county, Va. They have two daughters.

Miss Jinsey Cox, daughter of Samuel Cox and wife, married Mr. Bartley, of Eastern Virginia; they have one daughter, Bessie, who married Dr. Halsey, of Wilson.

Margaret married Enoch Reeves, of Grayson; they had sons and daughters. Ruth married John Calloway and they lived on New River; had one son.

Isom Cox married Miss Jincy Phipps, daughter of Joseph Phipps and wife, Miss Nancy McMillan; Mrs. Cox was an intelligent, energetic lady, and a blessing to her family. They were among Grayson's best citizens, and largest farmers. Isom Cox owned the land where Bridle Creek Academy and Methodist Church are located. He did much for church and state; was ever ready to assist in any laudable enterprise for the good of society. He and his faithful wife were members of the Methodist Church, South. Their example is a priceless heritage to their children, and the children have honored their parents by following their example.

Third daughter, Ruth, married Thomas Worth, son of David Worth and wife, Elizabeth Thomas.

Third daughter, Bena, married Alexander P. Bryant, son of Lewis Hale Bryant and wife, Miss Drucy Phipps.

Their two sons, Haywood and Joseph, fell in the Confederate Army. Nobler young men and better soldiers never honored an army or country. Joseph married Miss Emma Phipps, daughter of Alexander Phipps and wife, Ludema Thomas; no issue.

There were five daughters of Isom Cox and his wife. Emeline married William H. Bryant, son of Joseph Bryant and wife, Sarah Hale. They brought up a nice family. Nannie married Columbus Phipps, of Bridle Creek, Va. (See Phipps family.) Elizabeth married Preston Reeves; lives on New River.

THE OSBORNE FAMILY

Esquire Enoch Osborne settled on New River, near Bridle Creek; this for many years was known as the Osborne settlement. Enoch Osborne had three brothers, Solomon, Ephriam, and Johnathan, who came to this country with their families about the same time, and settled on New River, near together.

A fort was built on the farm now occupied by Joshua Osborne and son, John, at Ancella Post Office. Indian depredations were common on the border settlements, and preparations for protection and defence were necessary.

It was fortunate for society that the first settlers were people of moral worth and piety.

Enoch Osborne's wife was a Miss Hash. He and his wife were Christians, and aided very much in planting the standard of Christian civilization over the land that was so recently inhabited by savages.

Their home was a resting place for the wayworn traveling preachers. The venerable Bishop Asbury called with them, rested, and took refreshments, as he was making his ministerial tours through this newly settled country, preaching the gospel.

It was at the old Fort where Esquire Enoch Osborne, Sr., first located a home.

An incident occurred with the Osborne brothers, in their newly occupied territory, that tells of the dangers and exposures to which pioneer settlers were subjected.

Enoch Osborne and brothers, Solomon and Ephriam, went into what is now Watauga, N. C., on a hunting trip, deer being plentiful in that section. Getting wet by a shower of rain, and wet bushes, they struck up camp in the evening, and lay down to sleep and rest, hanging up their clothes by the camp fire to dry. The Indians surprised them by shooting into the camp and killing Solomon Osborne; an Indian chased Enoch some distance, and lost him in the dark. Ephriam, after fleeing from camp carefully crept back in the dark to his horse that was fastened with a hickory bark halter to a tree, loosed him and rode home. Enoch returned home without shoes, and in his night clothing. These facts are gathered from Mrs. Mary McMullen, wife of Hon. Lafayette McMullen, member of Congress, from Scott county, Va., for several sessions. Mrs. McMullen, before her marriage, was Miss Mary Woods, granddaughter of Solomon Osborne, who was murdered in the camp by the Indians.

Up to the present day, the Osborne family have lived in Grayson county; some have moved to the West, while quite a number have remained as worthy, industrious citizens of their native county.

Solomon Osborne, Jr., married Hannah Cox, lived at the old fort on New River, and on the same farm his son Joshua now lives; others of this family live in the same community.

Zachariah Osborne married Miss Jincey Burton, a lady of deep piety, a faithful wife and affectionate mother. Zachariah Osborne and wife brought up a large family on the river near the fort; three daughters, Mary, Nancy, and Phœbe, married three brothers, Alexander, Galloway, and Samuel Cox, Jr. Mahala married Joshua Cox;

Biddie married David Cox; one married Daniel Boyer; Caroline married Johnston Hale. Margaret married John Phipps, of Saddle Creek.

Their son, Enoch Osborne, married Miss Cox; Allen married; Floyd married Miss Rosa Hale, daughter of Warner Hale and wife, Miss Mary Cox; Preston married Miss Isabelle Cox; Zachariah, Jr., married Miss Mollie Cox; both the above Isabelle and Mollie were daughters of Enoch Cox and wife, Miss Susan Thomas.

Floyd Osborne and Preston Osborne both settled on Meadow Creek, near Old Town, and have brought up their families there. Emmett P. Osborne, son of Floyd Osborne, married Miss Mary Williams, daughter of Hyram Williams and Miss Jane Brown. He lived on the old Brown farm on Meadow Creek; died at the Jefferson Hospital, Roanoke, Va., from an operation for appendicitis; he leaves a wife and six children.

Thomas H. Osborne, youngest son of Floyd Osborne, lives at the old homestead on Meadow Creek.

John H., another son, lives on Rock Creek, Va.

THE PHIPPS FAMILY

Benjamin Phipps came from Rowan county, N. C.; settled on Bridle Creek; his brother, Isaiah, and the Hash family, came also about the same time. Benjamin Phipps married Miss Jane Hash, an excellent, good woman; she lived to be nearly one hundred years old; lived to see her children and grandchildren to the fourth generation.

Their son, Captain Joseph Phipps, married Miss Nancy McMillan, daughter of John McMillan, a native of Scotland, and a man of letters. He came to Ashe county and settled on Elk Creek. He brought his excellent wife with him from Scotland. He was an extensive farmer and good citizen, and was first clerk of Ashe county. His family had the industry and watchfulness in business affairs peculiar to their nationality.

Captain Joseph Phipps and wife settled on Saddle Creek, Va., and he was one of Grayson county's best farmers,—a man of great energy, and a successful manager of business. He acquired a handsome amount of property, and reared a worthy family. He and his excellent wife went down to their graves, honored, loved and respected.

They had three sons, John, Alexander, and Joseph Phipps, Jr. John Phipps married Miss Margaret Osborne and settled on Saddle Creek; they reared a nice family.

Alexander Phipps married Miss Ludema Thomas, daughter of William Thomas, and settled at the old Field's place, Bridle Creek; they have two sons, Columbus and Stephen Phipps; they live on Bridle Creek.

Columbus Phipps married Miss Nannie Cox, daughter of Isom and Jincey Cox. Mr. Phipps has used more than ordinary energy in all that pertains to temporal, business and religious duties. His faithful services as the superintendent of the Sunday School have done much to advance the number of its members and interest. The home of Mr. Phipps and excellent family shows what industry and economy can do. He has a fine farm, improved stock, and stately dwellings. He and his son are also doing a good business in the mercantile line, selling dry goods. His youngest daughter, Rosa, married Rev. French Wampler of the Holston Conference, now at Fountain City, Tennessee.

Stephen Phipps married Miss Mattie McMillan; has a nice home near the old homestead, and has a nice family.

Alexander Phipps and wife had three daughters; first, Rosamond, married Mathew Dickey, Jr.; second, Martha married Dr. Martin Dickenson; lived at Independence, Va.

Emma married Joseph Cox, son of Isom Cox and wife. He died in the army and his wife died soon after he did; no issue.

Joseph Phipps, Jr., married Miss Cynthia Bourne, daughter of Stephen Bourne, of Knob Fork; they had two sons: Dr. John Phipps, who married Miss Cora Miller, daughter of Rev. Charles K. Miller and wife, Miss Mattie Young. They lived at Rural Retreat, Va.

Second son, Con Phipps, lives at the old homestead, which his father inherited from his father, Captain Benjamin Phipps, on Saddle Creek.

There were two daughters, first Etta, married Ken Bryant; lives on Saddle Creek; their daughter married Dr. Robinson; they live at Woodlawn, Va.; one daughter married Robert C. Fulton.

One daughter of Joseph Phipps and wife married Mr. Miller, of Rural Retreat.

Capt. Joseph Phipps had seven daughters. Rena married Fielding Young; Jincey married Isom Cox; Emily married Dr. Fleming Thomas; Mazy married Stephen H. Bryant; Jane married Stephen M. Dickey; Drucey married Louis Hale Bryant, and Nancy married John M. Dickey. This family of Capt. Joseph Phipps has been a great benefit in the settlement and improvement of Grayson county.

When we look around over this country and see the highly cultivated and well-stocked farms with splendid buildings; when we count the prosperous towns and villages, with their schools and churches and good government, and then contrast the present conditions with those of the early days, when there were only a few white settlers in a wild Indian country, with just a few forts and block houses for defense, we appreciate all the more the courage and bravery and industry of our ancestors, and the heritage of peace and the comforts of life which are ours as the result of their labors and their economy.

The Reeves family were also pioneer settlers, and as they are so blended with the Cox, Osborne, Phipps and Hash families, we will give a short sketch of them in this chapter.

George Reeves and family came from Drewry's Bluff, below Richmond, Va., and settled on New River, about six miles from Independence. He, like all the other pioneers, used good judgment in selecting the situation for his home, and lived there until the close of his life, and his home, like many others has remained in the hands of his posterity.

The sons of George Reeves, and wife are Jesse, William, George, and John. Their daughters, Anna, Charity, Mary, and Susan. Jesse married Miss Terrill, moved up the river to mouth of Peak Creek; William married Miss Terrill; George married Miss Jane Osborne, a woman of high order of talent, kind, industrious, and pious. He moved up the river, and lived where Esquire Charles Doughton lived. He was an energetic business man, and while serving his county as an officer, he was shot and mortally wounded. He left a widow and seven children: Jesse, Enoch, George, Mary, Nancy, Rebecca, and Cynthia.

John Reeves married Miss Phœbe Osborne, of whom it may be said she was a true type of womanhood in all that was good and lovely. John Reeves and family occupied the old homestead; their son, Osborne Reeves, married Rebecca Osborne, of whom it may be well said she was truly a helpmeet. Mr. Reeves was an elder in the Protestant Methodist Church. His son, John Reeves, Jr., fell in the Confederate army. The testament in his left vest pocket was cut through with the bullet that took his life. Osborne Reeves and family moved to Georgia.

Col. George W. Reeves married Miss Caroline Thomas, daughter of Esquire Stephen Thomas and wife, Miss Rebecca Perkins. Col. George W. Reeves lived near Jefferson, Ashe county, N. C.

Jesse A. Reeves married his cousin, Charity Reeves.

John Reeves, Jr., the youngest son of John Reeves, Sr., married Miss Mary Reeves, an amiable lady, and resided at the old homestead. They had the honor, and pleasing task of taking care of their parents in the evening of life. Mr. Reeves died when comparatively a young man. His body, with his father, John Reeves, Sr., and his sainted wife and mother, rests in the family graveyard, awaiting the trumpet to call them in the resurrection morning.

Preston Reeves, son of John, Jr., and widow, Mary Reeves, married Miss Elizabeth Cox, daughter of Isom and Jincey Cox of Bridle Creek. Mr. Reeves and wife by prudence and economy have provided well for the home comforts of life, following the example of their noble and praiseworthy ancestors.

The daughters of John Reeves, Sr., were Lucy, who married Esquire James Gambill; Miss Mahala, who married Rev. Samuel Plummer; Miss Polly Reeves, who married Marshall Calloway.

Enoch Reeves, son of George Reeves and wife, Miss Jane Osborne, was a Primitive Baptist preacher, reared a nice family; his sister, Nancy Reeves, married Esquire Harden Cox; another sister, Rebecca Reeves, married Colonel Allen Gentry. He and his wife were devoted members of the Methodist Church, South. Their son, Capt. George W. Gentry, married Miss Caroline Whitman; their daughter, Cynthia, married Capt. James H. Parks; another daughter, Sarah, married Judge George W. Cornett, of Elk Creek, Grayson county, Va.; the third daughter, Martha, married Rev. Joseph B. Doughton; the fourth, Miss Ellen, married William Hardin. Dr. L. C. Gentry married Miss May Hamilton; Reed Gentry married Miss Ludema Thomas, daughter of Dr. Fleming Thomas and wife, Miss Emily Phipps. Reed Gentry had one daughter, Miss Reed Gentry, who married Judge James Padgett, of Independence, Va.

The Hash family came from Rowan county, N. C., about the same time that Enoch Osborne, Benjamin and Isaiah Phipps came and settled on New River. Enoch Osborne married a Miss Hash; Benjamin Phipps married Miss Jane Hash. (Their decendants are given with the Osborne and Phipps families.)

There are quite a number of citizens of this Hash family living in the west end of Grayson county, and they were men and women of prominence in the early settlement of the county, but time and space forbid us tracing this and many other families.

CHAPTER X

The first attorney for the court of Grayson county, Virginia, was Alexander Smyth. I will give a copy from the first records of the Courts of Grayson.

"Alexander Smith, gent., produced license signed by Richard Carey, Henry Tazewell and Edmond Winston, permitting him to practice as an attorney in the inferior and superior courts within this commonwealth and having taken the oath prescribed by law is admitted to practice in the courts."

ANOTHER COPY

"Alexander Smith is appointed Deputy Attorney for the Commonwealth in this Court which is ordered to be certified to and it is further ordered that he be allowed the sum of twenty pounds in the levy the present year as a compensation for his services for one year from this time."

A COPY FROM THE OBITUARY OF MRS. J. M. MCTEER.

"Mrs. McTeer was first Miss Frances Stuart Smyth, daughter of General Alexander Smyth (for whom Smyth county, Virginia, was named), an officer of the war of 1812 and a member of Congress from 1817 to 1825 and 1827 to 1830. General Smyth was the mover in organizing the county of Wythe and was the first representative in the Legislature from Wythe county, Va.

General Smyth was son of Rev. James Smyth, clergyman of the Episcopal Church, who was sent by the authorities of England to take charge of Botetourt Parish, which embraced all the country lying west of the Blue Ridge.

Rev. James Smyth's mother was Frances Stuart and her husband was of the nobility of the house of the Stuarts, and held quite a large landed estate in the north of Ireland. General Smyth was born on the Island of Rathlin twelve miles from the north coast of Ireland and brought to this country when only five years of age. Young Smyth, at the proper age, obtained license to practice law and soon rose to distinction at the bar. He was located at Fincastle and attended the courts at Abingdon, Va.

There were no railroads then and traveling was done on horseback and stage. It was on one of these trips to attend Court in Abingdon that the young lawyer stopped at a cabin three miles below Wytheville to warm, it being a cold and most disagreeable day.

His temporal wants were attended to by the bright, rosy cheeked, beautiful daughter of the mountaineer with such queenly grace and modest manner that the young lawyer was entrapped by her.

After this he made Mr. Pinkley's house a convenient stopping place and in due course of time the young lawyer, Smyth, married Miss Nancy Pinkley and their marriage license was the first to be recorded in Wythe county court, 1791.

General Smyth after his marriage settled on Cripple Creek, in Wythe county, Va., on the Mountain Park farm, and his daughter, Miss Frances Stuart Smyth, was born there December 2nd, 1806. She was married to Col. James H. Piper, of Culpeper county, Va., the 9th day of February, 1824.

Col. Piper and wife settled on Cripple Creek on a part of the Mountain Park farm at Speedwell Furnace. He for years represented his district in the Senate; also was a man of sterling worth; did much for the development of his country, especially Wythe and Grayson counties. He was a civil engineer, finely educated; was called to locate roads across our mountains; located the road across Blue Ridge at Piper's Gap, leading from Grayson C. H. to Mount Airy, N. C. He was on the location of the Wytheville and Raliegh turnpike through Wythe and Grayson, when he was taken sick and died at the Grayson Sulphur Springs on the 8th day of September, 1854.

On the second day of March, 1857, Mrs. Piper was married to Rev. John M. McTeer, of the Holston Conference. Mrs. Piper joined the Methodist Church at Asbury Camp Ground, Cripple Creek, Va., 1840. When she joined the church she consecrated all to the Lord and for forty-two years was a devoted, exemplary Christian. Her house was opened for preaching and in the parlor at Speedwell regular services were held, until the church was built on the Ward farm, at Speedwell. Col. Piper is buried at the Speedwell Church.

There was no issue, but Mrs. McTeer brought up from childhood, three boys, Piper Catlett, son of Rev. Thos. K. Catlett, and Canari D., and James Piper McTeer, sons of Rev. J. M. McTeer. These are sons of McTeer's first wife, Miss Kelly. This daughter of General Smyth did much for the welfare of her country and for the church in all the adjoining counties.

Gen. Smith had another daughter, Miss Malvina Smith, who married —— Mathews. They also settled on the Mountain Park farm, Cripple Creek, and raised a large and very interesting family of sons and daughters, who did much for Wythe, Smyth and Grayson counties. One daughter, Miss Nancy Mathews, married Benjamin Rush Floyd. Another daughter, Miss Dorthula Mathews, married Dr. James Robertson, of Culpeper county, Va. They settled at Grayson C. H. and lived there a number of years. Dr. James E. Robertson was a nephew of Col. James H. Piper.

One son, Richard Mathews, was an attorney, lived at Grayson C. H., and practiced law in Grayson; also Carroll county, after Carroll county was cut off from Grayson.

One son, Alexander Mathews, married Miss Pierce, of the Lead Mines. He settled on Cripple Creek and raised and introduced thoroughbred stock cattle into Southwest Virginia. Did much for Wythe and Grayson counties in improving the grazing stock of short-horn cattle.

While General Alexander Smyth lived in Wythe county he did much for the county of Grayson, aided very much in establishing in the county her laws and her office holders in its early formation, and the citizens of Grayson were devoted to his memory.

Also Col. Samuel McCamant, to whom we refer in these sketches, was a lawyer and life-long friend of Gen. Smyth. McCamant did much for Grayson and Wythe counties. He lived and died in Grayson, a worthy man.

CHAPTER XI

THE DICKEY FAMILY

Mathew Dickey came over from North Carolina in the early days, and settled on Peach Bottom Creek, in what is now Grayson county.

He was one of the magistrates of the first court of Grayson county, held at the house of William Bourne, May 21st, 1793 (see copy of court record. He and William Bourne were both interested in the old Point Hope Furnace at the falls of Peach Bottom Creek. (See Bourne history.)

Mathew Dickey lived on the west side of the creek, and William Bourne on the east side.

Mathew Dickey married Miss Rebecca Wiley, and a number of his descendants are still living in Grayson and other portions of the country—useful and prominent citizens.

His son, James Dickey, Esq., married Elizabeth Bourne, daughter of Stephen Bourne, son of William Bourne and wife, Rosamond Jones. (See Bourne family.)

There were eleven children of this family, six sons and five daughters. William R. married Martha Hale, daughter of Lewis Hale; their son, James, married Miss Taylor, of Mt. Airy. N. C., whose first daughter married Charlie Bourne; second daughter married Thomas Dobyns.

James' second wife was Miss Vaughn, daughter of Col. Wiley Vaughn, of Independence, Va.; no issue. William Dickey's first daughter, Mary, married John Wiley; second daughter, Cynthia D., married William Warren; issue: one daughter, married Rev. Terry Fulton.

Stephen Dickey married Miss Jane Phipps, daughter of Benjamin Phipps and wife, Nancy McMillan. Stephen Dickey was a Baptist minister, and a major. He and his wife were very useful citizens. They built a comfortable home on Peach Bottom Creek near Independence, Va., and reared a family of three sons. Dr. John R. Dickey, and Dr. James Alexander Dickey, both live in Bristol, Tenn. They are successful business men and men of influence, both in church and state.

Friel Dickey, the youngest son of Stephen Dickey, married Miss Nannie Cornett, daughter of Col. Alexander Cornett and wife, Mina Rhudy. They had two daughters, Rosa and Eunice. Friel Dickey and his wife lived on Peach Bottom Creek, near Independence, Virginia. Both died young.

Matterson Dickey married a Miss Wiley of North Carolina. They moved to Texas, and some of their children live in Texas. One daughter married J. Hurst Dickey of Marion, Va.

Mathew Dickey, Jr., married Miss Rosamond Phipps, daughter of Alexander Phipps and wife, Lucinda Thomas; issue: two sons and two daughters. Alexander Phipps was quite successful in business, but died in Florida while still a young man. He never married.

John Mc., youngest child, lives at the old homestead on Peach Bottom Creek. He is a successful farmer and stock raiser; still single.

The first daughter, Miss Allie, married Mr. W. T. Berry, of Lynchburg, Va. They live in Lynchburg, and have one daughter, Rosamond; one son, Steele.

The second daughter, Martha, married Garnett Davis, only son of Col. Alexander M. Davis and wife, Mary Dickenson. Garnett Davis inherited his father's home place in Independence, Va., and lives there. His wife, Martha, died in 1910, leaving a family of four sons.

John M. Dickey married Nancy Phipps, daughter of Joseph Phipps, Sr., and wife, Nancy McMillan; issue: four daughters. First daughter, Minnie, married Alexander M. Dickenson, attorney at law at Marion, Va., youngest son of John Dickenson and wife, Rosamond Hale. Second daughter married Mr. Porterfield, of Washington county, Va. Third daughter married Joseph Delp, of Elk Creek, Va. Fourth daughter married Mr. Lincoln, of Marion, Va.

Ellis Leftwich Dickey married Miss Dillard, of Eastern Virginia; issue: one son, Albert, one daughter. For a number of years, the office of county clerk was held by the Dickey family, at Independence, Va., and Ellis Dickey was, for several years, deputy clerk.

Jane, the first daughter of James Dickey and wife, married Samuel Thompson, of Alleghany county, North Carolina.

The second daughter, Cynthia, died single.

Third daughter, Nannie, married Stuart Mathews from Wythe county, Va. They moved to Texas; issue: two sons. Stuart Mathews was a grandson of General Alexander Smyth.

The fourth daughter, Martha, married Lee Fredericking (a German) and lived at Independence, Va.; issue: two sons, one daughter. They afterward moved to Hinton, W. Va.

The fifth daughter, Elizabeth, married Fielden J. Lundy, son of George Lundy and wife, Miss Thomas; issue: two sons, one daughter.

First son, Ellis L. Lundy, married Alice Hale, daughter of Rev. Wiley D. Hale and wife, Martha Mitchell; issue: two sons, four daughters. First son of Ellis Lundy, Clarence, married Maud Sutherland, daughter of Capt. Wm. M. Sutherland, of Hillsville, Va.; is a clothing merchant at Mt. Airy, N. C.; issue: three children. Second son, Fielden Hale, married Miss Busic.

Second son of Fielden J. Lundy and wife, Fitzhugh Lee, married Rosa Busic. They live at the Lundy homestead in Independence, Va.

One daughter of Fielden J. Lundy and wife, Leona, married Dr. Koontz, a prominent physician. They live in Independence, Va. Fielden J. Lundy was county court clerk for nearly forty years. He was faithful and competent and knew more of the business of the courts than any other man. He was well known and honored by all. He lived a Christian life, and died in the triumph of a Christian faith, and the hope of an eternal life in heaven. (See Lundy history.)

Mathew Dickey, Sr., and wife, Rebecca Wiley, had a daughter that married Benjamin Cooley, Esq. Dr. Aras B. Cox, author of "Footprints on the Sands of Time," says, "No modern Tubal Cain could have excelled him as an artificer in his superior skill in working metals. He made some of the finest clocks in the United States. One of these clocks was purchased by John McMillan, of Alleghany county, N. C., and it not only kept the usual order of time, but the days of the week and the month, and the changes of the moon. Esquire Cooley was a useful and honored citizen, and had an intelligent and highly respected family."

Benjamin Cooley, Esq., was among the early settlers of that part of Grayson that is now Carroll county. He lived on Coal Creek.

There were but few clocks or time pieces in the country at that time. The twelve o'clock mark for the sunshine in the open door on the floor, was the only way many of the pioneers could tell the time of day. Esq. Cooley decided that he would go to Salem, N. C., and get the Moravians to teach him how to make clocks. Upon arriving there he found that they demanded what he thought a big price to teach him, and he swore that he would not pay the price, but would learn to make clocks by himself.

William Bourne, living on Knob Fork, owned a fine Grandfather Clock. The works were brass, and in addition to the time of day, the changes of the moon were shown. It was the first clock ever brought into Grayson county. After Mr. Cooley returned from North Carolina, he went to see Mr. Bourne and asked him if he might take the pattern of his clock. Mr. Bourne consented, and Mr. Cooley took the clock to pieces and made patterns of all the running works. From these patterns he made clocks and sold them all over the country. The old Bourne clock is still running, and is owned now by Mrs. Ruth Nuckolls Johnston, of Cleveland, Tenn.

She is the sixth generation from William Bourne and Rosamond Jones. Mrs. Johnston has other timepieces, but she says the old Grandfather Clock keeps the best time of them all.

The case of the clock is rosewood veneer, with inlaid blocks of different kinds of wood, and brass trimmings. It is an eight-day clock with heavy iron weights, and is wound up with a key.

Benjamin Cooley and his wife, Jane Dickey, had two sons; first son, Martin Cooley, married Catherine Currin, daughter of Maj. George Currin and wife, Martha Swift. They had two sons; moved to Oregon. Second son, James Cooley, married Caroline Higgins, daughter of Thomas Higgins and wife, Mary Edwards. Their first daughter married Robert Jones, and lives in Galax, Va. One daughter, Fannie, married Henry C. Nuckolls; died at Quinton, Oklahoma, 1911.

One son, Frank, single; one son, Rufus, a minister in

the Christian Church; two sons, teachers; one son, George, teacher and farmer.

Rebecca Cooley married Jesse P. Worrell. They moved to Texas, and have sons and daughters. Amanda Cooley married Logan Roberts of Mt. Airy, N. C.; died without issue.

Julia Ann Cooley married Mr. Price; was for a number of years a teacher; no issue.

Benjamin Cooley had a brother who married Mary Hanks, and lived on Coal Creek near Benjamin Cooley's. This brother had a large family of children. One daughter, Matilda, married John Carico, son of Rev. William Carico. They established a home near Providence Camp Ground, and reared a large family of sons and daughters, who made useful citizens.

One daughter married Peter Beamer; lived near Fancy Gap, Va. Andrew Cooley, a son.

Harden Cooley, a Methodist minister. Andrew and Harden lived in Knoxville, Tenn.

James Cooley, son of Andrew Cooley, married Laura Johnston, daughter of James B. Johnston, of Hillsville, Virginia.

Benjamin Cooley, Jr., lived and died at the old home. All of these were useful men, had nice families, most of them members of the Methodist Church, and died in the Christian faith, and their posterity show to the world the benefits accruing from good ancestry and parental training.

A COPY FROM LINEAGE BOOK

"NATIONAL SOCIETY OF THE DAUGHTERS OF THE AMERICAN REVOLUTION

"John Dickey commanded a company of Carolina Militia at Ramsour's Mills. His widow applied for pension, 1844, in Rowan county, and it was allowed for 17 months actual service in North Carolina line."

Mathew Dickey, Sr., married Rebecca Wiley, in North Carolina; moved to Grayson county, Virginia; died in Grayson county, Virginia. Date on tombstone—"Died June 15, 1827, age 75 years."

CHAPTER XII

THE GOODYKOONTZ FAMILY

The following is copied from a manual compiled and pen-written by Jasper Goodykoontz; published by Jasper Goodykoontz, Atlanta, Indiana, 1908.

DESCENDANTS OF DAVID GOODYKOONTZ

"Sometime before the Revolutionary War, about 1765, David Goodykoontz (formerly spelled Gutekunst) and a brother emigrated from Wurtemburg, Germany, to the United States, settling in the vicinity of Chambersburg, Pa. David subsequently removed to Virginia and settled near the present town of Floyd, which is the county seat of Floyd county, and his brother went farther southward, but was never afterward heard from. David was born in Germany about 1740, and died near Floyd, Va., about 1815. About 1768 he married Margaret ———, who died in March, 1819, and was buried in the home cemetery four miles from Floyd.

The following are their children: First, Mary M. Goodykoontz (1769-1850), who married George Phlegar (1762-1839) about 1789.

Second, Polly Goodykoontz (1771-1867), who married William Gilham (1775-1831).

Third, George Goodykoontz (April 23, 1773-September 13, 1824), P. O., Floyd, Va., who married Mariam Beaver, September 4, 1800.

Fourth, Margaret Goodykoontz (January 25, 1775-September 8, 1851), P. O., Floyd, Va., who married Abram Phlegar (1776-1865), December 12, 1797.

Fifth, Elizabeth Goodykoontz (1776-October 6, 1858), P. O., Floyd, Va.; never married.

Sixth, Jacob Goodykoontz (1780-1818), who married ―――― Beaver.

Seventh, Eva Goodykoontz, (1786-1867), P. O., Floyd, Va., who never married.

Eighth, Daniel Goodykoontz, (1784-September 16, 1843), P. O., Anderson, Indiana, who married ―――― Beaver.

Another authority (a great-grandson of David Goodykoontz), said that David Goodykoontz had nine daughters, that three of the daughters married Phlegars, and one married a Mr. Stipes. He also said that the brother who went southward went to New Orleans, and that David Goodykoontz is buried at Chambersburg, Pa., but his wife, Margaret, is buried at the old Lutheran Church, near Floyd C. H. There are Goodykoontz's at Rocky Hollow, S. C.

The three brothers, George, Daniel and Jacob, bought a large tract of land near Floyd, Va. George's portion of the tract was one thousand acres.

The Goodykoontz home (five miles from Floyd C. H., on the West Fork of Little River) was originally an old Indian block house, built between 1775 and 1790. The remodeled house, as it now stands, was built in 1854. David and Isaac Goodykoontz, sons of George Goodykoontz and Mariam Beaver, inherited the home place, and lived there together for sixty-six years. After David's death (in 1871) Isaac, who was a bachelor, continued to live at the home place. He afterwards married Mrs. Amanda Cecil, and lived until 1884. The estate then passed into the hands of William Goodykoontz, third son of David, who lived there until about 1900. William sold the estate and removed to Roanoke, Va., so the estate has passed out of the hands of the Goodykoontz family, after having been owned by them for over one hundred years.

David and Isaac Goodykoontz were equal partners in business—farming and buying and selling cattle, and Isaac was a member of the State Senate of Virginia. They are both buried in the family burying-ground near the old home.

David Goodykoontz gave two sons, George and William, to the Confederate army. Both were desperately wounded, but recovered and lived many years after the close of the war, and reared large and useful families.

During the war, the Goodykoontz family suffered much from the demands of the soldiers, but more from that unprincipled band that infested all neighborhoods—the Bushwhackers.

There was a large barn near the house, the first story of which was of stone. The Bushwhackers burned this barn. At the time of the burning, there were thirteen horses in the barn, wagons, farming tools, grain, hay, etc. Everything was lost.

The marauders came another night, and attempted to rob and burn the dwelling-house. Two or three old guns had been left in the house, and after a number of shots had been fired into the house, the family fired from the inside and wounded one of the men of the party. After this, they left without doing any further damage.

The children of George Goodykoontz and Mariam Beaver are as follows: first, Catherine; second, Rebecca; third, David; fourth, Archibald; fifth, Isaac; sixth, George; seventh, Alfred M.; eighth, Rachel; ninth, Nancy; tenth, Adeline; eleventh, Washington; twelfth, Polly.

Catherine married Moseby Le Seuer; P. O., Camp Creek, Va., children: first, Martel, married Sarah Phlegar; P. O., Camp Creek, Va.; children: Elbert J. Le Seuer, Belle Fontaine, South Dakota. Alice Le Seuer married

Mr. Hawety, P. O., Camp Creek, Va. Flora Le Seuer, married Mr. Van Fleet, Neasho, Mo. Second, James W., married Nancy C. Yearout, P. O., Floyd, Va.; children: first, Ellen (Le Seuer) Turner, River, Va.; second, Eliza A. (Le Seuer) Sowers, Floyd, Va.; third, Charles W. Le Seuer, Johnson City, Tenn.; fourth, John R. Le Seuer, Wallace, Va.; fifth, Catherine C. (Le Seuer) Shell, Elizabethton, Tenn.; sixth, Jennie V. (Le Seuer) West, National Soldier's Home, Tenn.; seventh, Thomas Le Seuer, River, Va.; eighth, Crockett Le Seuer, Bristol, Tenn.; ninth, Foster Le Seuer, Bristol, Tenn.; tenth, Lucy C. (Le Seuer) Weaver, Elizabethton, Tenn.; eleventh, Richard Le Seuer, Bristol, Tenn.; twelfth, Mary Le Seuer (died in infancy); thirteenth, Edwin F. Le Seuer (died in infancy).

Rebecca Goodykoontz married James Le Seuer, P. O., Alumine, Va.; children: George W., Mary F. (Le Seuer) Spillsman, Elizabeth, Catharine, and Dollie.

David Goodykoontz (December 8, 1805—March 15, 1871) married Ruth Harter, (November 8, 1830). They lived at the old Goodykoontz homestead, and their children are as follows:

First, Henry M.; second, Mary Fletcher; third, Elizabeth; fourth, Julia; fifth, George W.; sixth, William; seventh, Alfred; eighth, Adeline; ninth, Nancy Rosetta; tenth, Ellen; eleventh, David; twelfth, Millard.

Henry M. Goodykoontz married Amanda Wade, P. O., Santoo, Va.; children: First, Winton Goodykoontz, San Antonio, Texas; second, Lou Ella Goodykoontz, Sweet Springs, W. Va.; third, Webster Goodykoontz, Sweet Springs, W. Va.; fourth, Edward Goodykoontz, Sandy Bluff, W. Va.; fifth, Flora Goodykoontz, Sweet Springs, W. Va.; sixth, Ida H. (Goodykoontz) Allison, Allisonia, Va.

Mary Fletcher Goodykoontz married Rev. B. F. Nuckolls, of Holston Conference, M. E. Church, South (author of this book), November 6, 1865; P. O., Galax, Va.; children: first, Willie David; second, Rosa Ellen; third, Ruth Frances; fourth, Isaac Clark. (See Nuckolls history for further data.) Mary Fletcher Goodykoontz Nuckolls died at Galax, Va., November 21, 1910. Elizabeth Goodykoontz died young of scarlet fever.

Julia Goodykoontz married Rev. B. W. S. Bishop, of Holston Conference, M. E. Church, South. They owned a home at Emory, Va.; children: first, Charles McTyiere Bishop; second, Lucy; third, Mattie; fourth, David Horace Bishop.

Charles McTyiere Bishop graduated at Emory and Henry College, joined the Holston Conference, married Miss Phœbe Eleanor Jones of Asheville, N. C., and transferred to the Missouri Conference in 1888. In 1911, he was elected president of the Southwestern University at Georgetown, Texas., and resides there with his family. He is an able man and an eloquent preacher; is a member of the Commission on the Federation of the Methodist Churches of America.

His children are as follows: First, Phœbe Eleanor; second, Mary Martha; third, Charles (died young); fourth, Roseboddie; fifth, Hendrix.

Lucy Bishop died when she was about twenty-two years old. Mattie Bishop married Mr. John Price, son of Dr. R. N. Price, of Holston Conference. Mr. Price died in 1903, leaving three sons, Charles, John, David. The three sons reside with their mother at Welch, W. Va. David Horace Bishop was educated at Emory and Henry College and Vanderbilt University. He now occupies the chair of English in the University of Mississippi. He married Miss Mary Hartwell Somerville, of Oxford, Mississippi.

Benjamin Floyd Nuckolls and wife, Mary Fletcher Goodykoontz, and Eldest Son, William David Nuckolls

Julia Goodykoontz Bishop died at Emory, Va., in 1882. B. W. S. Bishop married the second time, Mrs. Mary Dickey; no children; Mr. Bishop died at Tazewell, Va., in 1894; Mrs. Bishop (2) died at Glade Springs, Virginia, in 1911. George W. Goodykoontz married Mary Williamson, P. O., East Radford, Virginia. He was a soldier in the Confederafe army, and was badly wounded.

Their children were: First, Nancy; second, William; third, Alfred; fourth, John; fifth, Ida; sixth, Charles; seventh, Lena; eighth, Harry. Nancy married; lives at———.

William married Miss Pope of Mason City, Iowa; one child, Ruth Evelyn. William held responsible positions as train-despatcher; he was only thirty-five years of age when he died at Mason City, Iowa. His wife and child reside there.

Alfred married Miss Sadie Bosang of Pulaski, Va. They live in East Radford, Va., and have children. Alfred holds a responsible position with the N. & W. R. R.

John married Miss Williams, of Roanoke, Va. They live in Roanoke and have children. John is one of the Division Superintendents of the N. & W. R. R.

Ida married Charles Caldwell, of East Radford, Va. They live in East Radford and have children.

Charles married Miss Rhea, of Bristol, Tenn. They live in Bluefield, W. Va.; have one child. Charles is a druggist.

Lena married. They live in East Radford, Va., and have children.

Harry (single) is in the drug business with his brother, Charles, in Bluefield.

William (1862-1910) was a Confederate soldier. He was badly wounded, and carried a minnie ball in his arm till the day of his death. He married Lucy Woolwine. They lived at the old Goodykoontz homestead until about 1900, when they sold it and moved to Roanoke, Va. They have seven children: first, Horace Wells; second, Arthur Emmett; third, Oscar Wilmer; fourth, Oakey B.; fifth, Robert S.; sixth, a daughter, Willie C.; seventh, a daughter, Lake E., married Mr. Samuel Fishburne Woody.

Horace Wells married Miss Hooper, of New Orleans, Louisiana; he is a successful lawyer, and lives in Williamson, West Virginia. Arthur Emmett, single, lives with his mother on the home place. Oscar Wilmer is married and lives in Chicago. They have children. Oakey B. is married; lives in Roanoke, Virginia. Robert I., single, lives in Roanoke, Virginia.

Willie C., single; lives at the home place with her mother. Lake E. married Mr. Samuel Fishburne Woody, and lives in Roanoke, Virginia. William Goodykoontz died in 1910, at his home near Roanoke, Virginia.

Alfred (1844-1872) married Ellen Cecil in 1870; one son, John, born April, 1871, died in 1897; never married.

David (3), son of David (2), (1853-1853).

Millard F., born 1855, married first, Mary Howery, second, Lizzie McCauley; P. O., Graham, Va.; children: Julia May, married J. D. Williams, P. O., Roanoke, Va.; Mattie Myrtle, married W. D. Bower, P. O., Camp Creek, Va.; Minnie Ruth, married M. L. Snead, P. O., Carloover, Bath county, Va.; Glen P., P. O., 1016 Kindle Avenue, Portsmouth, O.; Second marriage children: Clarence F., Robert E., Harry L., Roy F., Nannie A., William D., Bernard Ellis.

Elizabeth Goodykoontz (1834-1842), Adeline J. (1846-1855). Nancy Rosetta (1851-1856).

Ellen Goodykoontz, youngest daughter, married S. Zechariah Cecil. They live near Newbern, Va., and have five children: Samuel, Linnie, Ruth, Mary, Estell. Samuel is married and lives in Newbern, Va.; has children. Linnie, single, lives at home. Ruth married Isaac Walton McClure; they live in Texas, and have three sons and four daughters. Mary married Mr. E. H. Southern; they have two children; live in Pulaski, Va. Estell, single.

Washington Goodykoontz (1882-1895), P. O., Floyd, Va.; was never married; was in Confederate army.

George Goodykoontz (2), (January 30, 1812-April, 1888) married Sarah Williamson., P. O., Caledonia, Mo. His children: Redmond, Letitia, Clark, Mary (January 9, 1855) married Mr. Bland, P. O., St. Louis, Mo. Thomas (18....-........), P. O., Caledonia, Mo.

Rev. Alfred M. Goodykoontz was a member of Holston Conference (November 3, 1813-November 15, 1857). He married Mary A. Kirkpatrick, October 8, 1846, P. O., Ross, Tenn. He died in Abingdon, Va., while preaching the gospel. One daughter, Margaret Emma, (single) P. O., Prosise, Tenn. One son, George E. (April 7, 1854), married Sarah J. Loving, March 26, 1878, P. O., Prosise, Tenn. Children: Minnie Andrews, Charles Franklin, Edgar Marion, William Loving, Thomas K. Beaver, James Richard, Joseph Wiley, Mary Margaret (October 14, 1894.)

Rachel Goodykoontz (October 14, 1815) was drowned June 17, 1818.

Nancy (July 27, 1817-September 9, 1842) married Pascal Baber who died September 23, 1842; first daughter, Arabella Baber (October 27, 1837-March 20, 1883.), married William Hall, August 9, 1870; children: Washington C. Hall, October 3, 1872; Mae Adda (January 3, 1874), married Crockett Le Seuer, Bristol, Tenn.; Nannie Luther (September 26, 1876-March 10, 1883), William Rush Hall (March 8, 1878-July 23, 1905).

One son, John W. Baber (April 5, 1840-August 6, 1861), was in Confederate army.

Second daughter, Clementine Baber (July 15, 1842), P. O., Floyd, Va.; never married.

Adeline Goodykoontz (December 24, 1820) married Johnathan Hall; no children, Riner, Va.

Polly Goodykoontz (March 13, 1824), died when a little girl.

GOODYKOONTZ—PHLEGAR FAMILY

Two of the daughters of David Goodykoontz, Sr., married Phlegars.

Mary M. Goodykoontz (1769-1832) married in 1789, George Phlegar (1762-1834). Their son, Benjamin Phlegar, married first, Mary ———, second, Sarah ———. They lived at Floyd, Va., and had a large family. Their son, George, was a Confederate soldier, and was killed in the battle of Gettysburg; Andrew was a bachelor; Ellen married David Willis, Floyd, Va.; Mary married Judge Merritt; Adeline, maid; Thomas, bachelor; Abram, bachelor; Henrietta married Rev. George W. Summers, of Holston Conference; John N.; Nancy married Mr. Smith; Lillie, maid; Dora married Mr. Irving Rooney, New York; Estella married Dr. Smith, Radford, Va.; Benjamin; Jesse M.; William married Miss Smith; Mattie married Mr. Brown.

Rev. G. W. Summers and wife, Henrietta Phlegar, had six daughters: first, Pearl, married Mr. Thompson Asbury; they live in Glade Spring, Va.; no children. Second, Bane, married Mr. Paul Dulaney of Bristol, Tenn.; they live in Washington City; have two children, Benjamin Bane and Paul Summers. Third, Mary, married Mr. George Penn, Jr., of Abingdon, Virginia. They live in Abingdon; have one daughter. Fourth, Dora, single, Washington, D. C. Fifth, Lois, single, Bristol, Tennessee. Sixth, Bessie, single, Bristol, Tennessee.

Mrs. Henrietta Summers died while the family lived in Cleveland, Tenn., and is buried in the Cleveland cemetery. Dr. Summers is a professor in Sullins College, Bristol, Tenn.

Grandchildren of Mary M. Goodykoontz and George Phlegar:

Elizabeth Phlegar (1790-1850) never married.
Lydia (1792-18) married.
Joseph (1794-18,) married.

Great grandchildren:

Isaac Phlegar, Calvin, John, Margaret, Eliza, married Mr. Simmons; Sarah, married Martel Le Seuer; Jacob, David, and Joseph.

Margaret (1775-1851), third daughter of David Goodykoontz, married Abram Phlegar, December 12, 1797, P. O., Floyd, Va. Their son, Eli Phlegar, was born in 1808; died in 1864; P. O., Floyd, Va.

Following is a sketch of Eli Phlegar's son, Judge Archer A. Phlegar:

DEATH COMES TO JUDGE PHLEGAR

DISTINGUISHED JURIST SUCCUMBS TO BRIGHT'S DISEASE AFTER BRIEF ILLNESS.

Bristol, Tennessee-Virginia, December twenty-second—Judge Archer A. Phlegar, distinguished Virginia lawyer and jurist, died at his home here at ten forty-five o'clock Sunday morning. He had been ill but one week, death resulting from acute Bright's disease, following an attack of grip.

It was Judge Phlegar's oft-expressed wish that he might die "in harness," and this wish was virtually fulfilled, for he had just concluded the argument in an important civil suit in the corporation court here, when he became ill and had to hasten to his home.

Judge Phlegar's rather sudden death removes one of the most distinguished lawyers and jurists, not alone of his own State, but of the entire South. He was an authority upon all important questions of law, and during many years of active work he made for himself a reputation which only high merit could possibly have attained. He was never placed in any position of trust or responsibility during his long career as a lawyer and jurist that he did not meet the demands of the occasion with masterly ability, and his success was emphasized by the extensive clientage which he had represented for so many years. In recent years he had been at the head of the law firm of Phlegar, Powell, Price and Shelton, of this city, which firm had an important clientage extending over portions of Virginia, Tennessee, and West Virginia, and embracing clients among important financial and corporate interests in New York City and other financial and commercial centers.

Judge Phlegar continued in his activities with his wonted vigor until seized with his fatal illness a week ago, and up to that time no man in Virginia had been more zealous in the attention to important duties.

During the last fifteen years, Judge Phlegar had not only represented various important corporations in the capacity of legal advisor, but aside from his service in this capacity to the Norfolk and Western Railway Company, the Carolina, Clinchfield and Ohio Railway Company, and kindred corporations, he had served as receiver for the Virginia Iron, Coal and Coke Company, which has a capital stock of ten million dollars, and after having by his wise business methods, brought its company out of a state of financial embarrassment by adding largely to its earnings, he was made general counsel for the company. This compliment to his energy and ability had not been long thrust upon him until he received the appointment at the hands of Governor Hoge Tyler to a position on the State Supreme Court bench. He was named to fill out the unexpired term of the late Judge Riley. His desire to serve his state was such that he immediately resigned as general counsel for the Virginia Iron, Coal and Coke Company, thus surrendering a handsome income that he might be of direct service to the people of his State.

Judge Phlegar was a son of Eli and Ann C. Phlegar. He was born at Christiansburg, in Montgomery county, Virginia, February twenty-second, eighteen and forty-five and was therefore, in his sixty-eighth year. His early education was received at the Montgomery Male Academy, at Christiansburg. He later took the course at Washington and Lee University.

He left the University to enter the Confederate Army. He served as a soldier in the Fifty-fourth Virginia regiment of which his uncle, Robert C. Trigg, was colonel. At the close of the civil war he studied law under the late Judge Waller R. Staples, of Christiansburg. He was admitted to the bar at Christiansburg in eighteen and sixty-nine. He rapidly attained to eminence in his profession. One of the first positions held by him after being admitted to the bar was that of commonwealth's attorney for Montgomery county. He served as a member of the Virginia State Senate in eighteen and eighty-one. He was again elected to that body in nineteen and three, and between that year and nineteen and five had a conspicuous hand in shaping the legislation necessary to make the code of Virginia conform to the new State constitution.

Judge Phlegar was tendered an appointment on the corporation commission of Virginia by Governor Montague, but declined this honor.

Judge Phlegar's death is not only a distinct loss to the profession which he honored through so many years of successful practice, but to the State and community, and to the Presbyterian Church, of which he had been an humble and consecrated member since he was a young man. He was the teacher of the men's Bible class of this city, and that class met this Sunday afternoon to do honor to his memory.

He took special pride in Sunday school work, and as an instructor on Bible topics, was distinguished for his aptness and ability.

At the time of his death, Judge Phlegar was general counsel for the Virginia and Southwestern Railway Company, having succeeded Judge Joseph L. Kelly in that position upon the promotion of the latter to the corporation court judgeship in October, nineteen and ten. He had also served as first vice-president and a director in the Carolina, Clinchfield and Ohio Railway Company, but resigned those positions some time ago. He was president of the Bank of Christiansburg, a position which he had held for fifteen years. He was always deeply concerned in the welfare of Christiansburg and its institutions, and although long a resident of Bristol he had never changed his place of legal residence from Christiansburg, nor had he transferred his church membership from there.

Judge Phlegar was especially noted for his philanthropic work. He was one of the trustees of the Thronwell orphanage at Clinton, South Carolina, and for years had contributed to the expense of that institution. It was a rule of his life to contribute ten per cent of his earnings to charity, and from year to year he wrote numerous checks at this season of the year in conformity with his plan of giving. He had given many thousands of dollars for charity, and in so doing he was always unpretentious, preferring that nothing be said concerning his giving. The poor of this and other communities will miss his annual contributions to them at this season, as it was his custom to mail these checks on the first of each year.

Judge Phlegar is survived by his widow, who, prior to her marriage, was Miss Susan Shanks, of Salem, and by the following children: David S. Phlegar, of Norfolk, Virginia; Mrs. E. B. Crosley, Philadelphia; Miss Mary Phlegar, of Bristol, and Hunter Phlegar, of Christiansburg.

All members of the family were at his bedside when the end came, it having become apparent late Saturday that he had small chance to recover.

The funeral party will leave Bristol for Christiansburg Monday evening, and the burial will take place there Tuesday afternoon. The funeral service will be conducted from the Presbyterian church of Christiansburg at two o'clock Tuesday afternoon, at which time it is expected that many prominent persons from over the State will be in attendance. The Bristol bar, of which Judge Phlegar had been a distinguished member for a number of years, will be largely represented at the funeral.

Numerous messages were sent from here Sunday to notify friends and relatives throughout the State of the death of Judge Phlegar.

The news of the death spread rapidly among the people in the churches of the city, thousands having assembled for the worship of the morning service just at the hour when death had claimed the beloved lawyer and citizen, whose noble Christian life and high ideals had impressed the people of this community of his great worth. The funeral party left Bristol this evening and occupied a private car of the Virginia and Southwestern Railway. Officials of the railway and members of the Bristol bar accompanied the body to Christiansburg.

One daughter of Eli Phlegar, Ellen (born 1848), married Mr. Johnston; their first daughter, Anna Johnston (born in 1868), married Mr. Campbell; second daughter, Susan (1870) married Mr. Price; their sons were Richard, Lennie Archer P. (1876).

CHAPTER XIII

THE KENNEY FAMILY

William Kenney and wife, Miss Dunn, were early settlers in this country. They came from Frederick county, Va., and settled in the Valley of Crooked Creek, now Carroll county, Va. His sons were Robert, Hance, and William. Robert married Miss Mallory; her mother was Rosa Bourne, daughter of Stephen Bourne. William married Fidella Wells, of Wilson, Va. Their son, John A. Kenney, still owns part of the old homestead. There were three daughters: Eliza Kenney married Dr. James Worrell; Eleanor married Robert N. Anderson, and Jane married James Early. Amos Ballard, of Grayson Old C. H., married Jane Kenney, sister of William Kenney, Sr.

John Early was also an early settler of English ancestry. He married Miss Rhoda Stevens, of Reed Island, Va.; lived near what is now Hillsville. Their sons were James, John, Peter. James married Jane Kenney; Peter married Jane Worrell; John married Ann Johnston, sister to Mrs. Martha Johnston Thornton, wife of William Thornton, who for many years has kept the hotel, "Texas House," Hillsville, Va. Mrs. Rhoda Stevens Early married second time, Dr. Straw, of Wythe county, but is buried at Hillsville, Va.

Dr. Joshua Stoneman, a Quaker from Pennsylvania, was for a long time the only doctor in this country. He was a very prominent and useful citizen and had one son, Mark D. Stoneman. Dr. Stoneman moved to Illinois. His daughters were well posted in vegetable medicines, and very useful and attentive in sickness.

One of Dr. Stoneman's daughters, Elizabeth, had her horse and saddle bags always ready, and travelled all over this country at night, or in daytime, whenever called. Another daughter, Mary who married Louis LaRowe, would go to attend the sick whenever called for.

There are a number of the Stoneman descendants here, and we find them solid and firm. They are as the name indicates, "Stone Men."

There are other families worthy a place in history of this upper New River Valley, but time and space forbid the record. I hope some one in the future will write up this country and its people better than I have been able to do. At any rate the history has been known, and will continue to be written on memories pages, and is known and will be known to the great God of the universe, unto whom we all shall render up the final account, for the manner and use we have made of the time, opportunities, and talents given to us.

INDEX

-A-

Adams, Clara 63
Aimy, - 24
Alexander, (Miss) 83
Allin, William 9
Allison, F. 120
    Ida H. 193
Anders, Sarah Ann 138
Anderson, (Miss) 24
    Alex Chapman 103
    Alexander Chapman 77
    Catharine/Catherine
        78, 103
    Charles 78, 103
    Dan 103
    Daniel 78
    Edward 78
    Elizabeth 158
    Ellen 85
    Evalina 117, 121
    Frank (Major) 96
    Friel Nuckolls 77, 78,
        103
    Garnett 78, 103
    Grey 78, 103
    James 6
    James (Major) 67, 117
    Lucy B. 75
    Lula 78, 103
    Ned 103
    Orville 10
    Paulina 78
    Pauline 103
    Rhuby 103
    Robert Garland 85
    Robert N. 205
    Ruby Elizabeth 77
    Virginia 78, 103
Andis, Carson 53, 165
    Margaret Ellen 56
Andrews, Rebecca 26
Armfield, Fred 60, 140
Asbury, (Bishop) 171
    Fisher 164
    Thompson 198
Ashworth, Parks 16
Atkins, David 157
    Elvira 157
    Greenberry 157
    Harvey 157
    James 112
Austin, (Miss) 133, 164
    John 167

-B-

Baber, Arabella 197
    Clementine 198
    John W. 197

Baber, Pascal 197
Bacon, - 12, 13, 15
Bagwell, Burt 131
Baker, - 7
Baley, J.D. 11
Ballard, (Miss) 58, 103
    Amos 205
    Bell 134
    Edwin 134
    Emma 134
    James 134
    Mary Ann 160
    William 134
Ballock, Agatha 93
Bamblett, Wm. (Dr) 78
Banner, (Mr) 77
Barnett, (Mr) 116
    Bessie 116
Bartlett, - 11, 12
    (Miss) 158
    Alfred G. 12, 13, 14,
        15
    Frances 102
    Matilda 12
    Samuel 12, 13, 14,
        15
    William 12
Bartley, (Mr) 170
    Bessis 170
Barton, (Mr) 64
Bayless, Matilda 157
Beamer, Peter 188
Beaver, - 191
    Mariam 190, 191, 192
Beck, Granny 24
Bedsaul, Elisha 9
    Mary 72, 99
Benson, Abner 93
Berry, Rosamond 184
    Steele 184
    W.T. 184
Bicknell, W.N. (Dr) 135
Bishop, B.W.S. (Rev)
    194, 195
    Charles 194
    Charles McTyiere 194
    David Horace 194
    Hendrix 194
    Julia Goodykoontz 195
    Lucy 194
    Mary Martha 194
    Mattie 194
    Phoebe Eleanor 194
    Roseboddie 194
Black, Mary 67
Blair, (Miss) 103
    A.Sidney 45
    Catherine 45
    Celia 46
    Elizabeth 46, 48, 49,

Blair, Elizabeth (cont)
    50, 52
    Emma 52
    Gladys 51
    Hazel Claudine 51
    Ivy Earl 51
    John 15, 18, 20, 26,
        45, 46, 50, 51, 113
    John Harold 51
    L.D. 45
    Lorenzo Dow 51, 52
    Lucinda 46, 50
    Polly 46
    Rebecca 46
    Robert 57
    Rosa 113
    Rosa B. 45
    Rosa Bourne 46
    Thomas 3, 6, 9, 26,
        45, 102
    Walter 51
    William 51
Bland, (Mr) 197
Blevins, John 168
    Nancy 79
    Samuel 168
Bobbitt, Calvin 13
    Lacy 16
    William 3, 4
Boiles, Fletcher 157
Bolen, D.W.(Judge) 107
Booher, (Mr) 117
    Mary 116
Bosang, Sadie 195
Bourne, Addie 64
    Amanda 53
    Andrew 54
    Callie 64
    Celia 18, 61
    Charity 18, 20, 26,
        45, 46, 50, 113
    Charles 64
    Charlie 134, 183
    Chloe 62, 63
    Cleveland 62, 63
    Creed 64
    Cynthia 53, 54, 131,
        132, 175
    Elizabeth 18, 53, 54,
        61, 112, 113, 127,
        133, 138, 183
    Emmett 63
    Ephraim 130
    Etta 63
    Floranza 53, 62
    Frances 18, 22, 61,
        73, 74, 84, 112,
        117, 132
    Harvey Gordon 62, 88
    Houston 62

207

Bourne, Houston Gordon 88
  Jane 60, 62, 73, 139
  Jane B. 53
  John A. 54
  Johnston(e) 53, 62
  Julia 63
  Julia Ann 53
  Julia Fulton 64
  L.W. 62, 63, 64
  Linnie 130
  Lucinda 62, 84
  Lute 63
  Malinda 62, 101
  Martin 21, 53, 62
  Mary 18, 54, 55, 62, 88, 114
  Mary Ann 64
  Mary Johnstone 62
  Matilda 54
  Matterson 53
  Midge 63
  Milly 18, 25
  Milton 63
  Minnie 63
  Montgomery 21, 53, 130
  Nancy 53
  Patience 18, 20, 24, 25, 169
  Pearl 88
  Pinkie (A?) 62
  R.G. (Capt) 64, 134
  Rachel 62
  Rex 64
  Richmond G. (Capt) 64
  Robert 62, 63
  Rosa 102, 112, 128, 205
  Rosa B. 61
  Rosa Jones 112
  Rosamond 17ff.
  Sally 155
  Stephen 17, 18, 21, 52, 155, 175, 183, 205
  Tabitha 74
  Talitha 113
  Talitha B. 53
  Thomas 63
  William 2, 3, 4, 7, 8, 17ff., 45, 53, 54, 61, 62, 63, 64, 73, 75, 84, 88, 89, 98, 101, 102, 112, 117, 127, 139, 153, 183, 187
  William Stephen 62, 63
Bower, W.D. 196
Boyer, Bettie 133
  Churchill 133
  Daniel 173
  Ellen 133
  Kelly (Rev) 164
  Luzana 133
  Mary 140
  Samuel 133
  Watson 133
Bradley, (Miss) 88
Bramblett, Wm.H. (Dr) 64
Braxton, Carter 144
  Lucy 144
Brewer, James 131
Bridges, (Mr) 169
  Virginia 169
Brown, (Mr) 198
  Amelia 81
  Creed 81

Brown, George 81
  Jane 82, 173
  John 81, 82
  Nathaniel 81
  Sena 81
Bryan, Elizabeth 132, 163
  Francis 81, 132, 163
  Morgan 132
  William Jennings 132, 163
Bryant, - 137
  (Miss) 83, 130, 156
  Aaron 132
  Ada 139
  Alexander 132
  Alexander P. 170
  Allie Rose 110
  Charles 139
  Gideon 128
  Haywood 170
  I.B. 132
  Jennie 131
  Jestin 131
  Jestina 130
  John 132
  Joseph 102, 131, 132, 139, 156, 170, 171
  Ken 175
  Lewis Hale 132, 170
  Lewis Preston 132
  Louis Hale 175
  Lucy 128
  Morgan 128, 156
  Olive 131
  Phoebe 132
  Rosa 131, 139
  Sallie 128
  Sarah 128
  Sena 139
  Shadrack 128
  Stephen 131
  Stephen H. 175
  William 131
  William H. 171
  Zollie 134, 139
Bryson, (Miss) 57
Buchanan, - 1
Burke, Minnie 77, 115
Burroughs, Elizabeth 112, 133
  G.T. (Mrs) 125
  Mary 111, 112, 117, 130, 164
  Thomas 112
Burrus, Alverda 103
Burt, Elizabeth S. 121
Burton, Jincey 172
Burwell, Anna Powell 143
  Mary 73, 106, 111, 113
Busic, (Miss) 186
  Dan 131
  Rosa 115, 131, 186
  Walter 115
Byrd, (Col) 145
  (Mr) 113
  John P. 53
  Sallie 53

-C-

Cabell, Edward A. 144
  Elizabeth Burkes 147
  George K. 144
  Mary 147
  William (Dr) 147

Caldwell, Charles 195
Calloway, John 170
  Marshall 177
Camden, (Mr) 145
Campbell, (Capt) 107
  (Mr) 204
  Wm. (Gen) 118
Cantrell, (Miss) 133
  Elmira 134
Canute Eli (Col) 163
  William 163, 165
Carden, (Mr) 112
  Sarah 112
  .C. (Rev) 112
Carey, Richard 4, 179
Carico, John 188
  William (Rev) 188
Carr, Crockett (Prof) 73
Carrico, William 100
Carroll, Charles 15
Carroll/Carl, John 26
Carson, Adolphus 113
  Ellen 77
  Robert 165
  Samuel 113
Carter, (Rev) 60
  Madison T. 16
Catlett, Piper 181
  Thos.K. (Rev) 181
Catron, (Miss) 130
  S.S. (Rev) 71
Cecil, Amanda 191
  Ellen 196
  Estell 196
  Gazilda 164
  John 165
  Linnie 196, 197
  Mary 196, 197
  Ruth 196, 197
  S.Zechariah 196
  Samuel 196
Chaffin, William 6
Chatam, (Mr) 54
Cheek, Henderson 128
  Morgan 164
Choate, Sarah 114, 118
Claig, Mitchell 105
Clark, (Miss) 59
Clarke, Oscar 113
  Stephen 113
  Walter 113
Clements, Franklin 16
  John 12, 13, 14
Cleveland, Elize 93
Cobbs, Jno.P. (Dr) 144
Cock, James 6
Cocke, John 15
Cody, Redmond 6
Collins, (Dr) 57
  (Miss) 56
Coltrane, I.B. 119
  Ira B. (Col) 123ff.
Colyar, Jacob 4
Comer, Harvey 138
  Rosa 138
Cook, - 12, 15
  William H. 16
Cooley, Amanda 188
  Andrew 188
  B.F. 118
  Benj. 102
  Benjamin 15, 161, 186, 187, 188
  Fannie 187
  Frances 83
  Harden 188
  James 69, 187, 188

Cooley, Julia Ann 188
  Martin 102, 187
  Matilda 188
  Rebecca 161, 188
Cooper, B.F. (Dr) 77, 78, 103, 114, 115
  Brutus Fleming (Dr) 77, 78
  Eddie Forest 77
  Emma 77, 115
  John 157
  John (Dr) 78
  Johnnie 77
  Lillie Rosa 78, 103
  Lockett 53
  Lula 77, 114
  May 103
  Nannie 78
  Sarah F. 78
Copenhaver, (Mr) 164
  Malissa 165
Corn, Ella 63
Cornett, Alexander (Col) 165, 184
  Amanda 113, 127, 164, 165
  Bessie 117
  Charlotte 165
  Charlotte D. 165
  Eli 127
  Eli (Col) 113, 139
  Eli C. 165
  Elizabeth 113, 164, 165
  Elvira 114, 164, 165
  F.A. 109
  F.R. (Prof) 20
  Fielden R. 165
  Francis 164, 165
  Franklin 133
  Friel 165
  Friel N. 165
  George W. 177, 164
  Glenn 20
  Heath 158
  Isabella 165
  James 165
  James P. 165
  Jennie 164
  Joseph 157
  Leona Mitchell 80
  Leonidas 139
  Levi 133, 164
  Lewis K. 165
  Lucy H. 166
  Margaret 166
  Martha 165
  Martha Powell 165
  Martin 138
  Matilda 113, 114, 164
  Miles Foy 164
  Monroe 117
  Munsey 164
  Myrtle 164
  Nancy 165
  Nannie 184
  Orville 158
  Peyton H. 165
  Rebecca 164
  Romulus Ring 165
  Samuel Monroe 165
  Stephen 113
  Stephen H. 165
  Theresa 138, 164, 165
  Thomas 109, 115, 164
  Wiley Winston 163
  William 164, 166

Cornett, William (Capt) 80, 117, 163
  William J. 139, 165
  Winton 139
  Zach. M. 164
Cornute, Rubin 6
Couch, (Mr) 128, 156
  Hazel 79
  Ruby 79
  Rudolph 79
Cox, - 13
  (Miss) 173
  Alexander 168, 172
  Amelia 165
  Aras B. (Dr) 186
  Bena 132, 170
  Calloway 168
  Caroline 169
  Charles 131, 169
  David 4, 114, 139, 167, 168, 173
  Elbert Sevier 168
  Elizabeth 171, 177
  Em(m)eline 131, 169, 171
  Emmett 131
  Enoch 25, 165, 168, 173
  Everett (Dr) 170
  Florence 103
  Galloway 172
  Hannah 168, 172
  Harden 131, 168, 169, 177
  Isabelle 173
  Isom 131, 132, 168, 170, 171, 174, 175, 177
  James 6, 167
  Jennie 168
  Jincey 174, 177
  Jinsey 170
  John 167, 168
  Joseph 175
  Joshua 8, 167, 168, 172
  Joshua McGowan 168
  McGowan 170
  Margaret 168, 170
  Mary 103, 113, 139, 168, 173
  Melville B. 169
  Mollie 169, 173
  Nannie 132, 171, 174
  Newton 117
  Rosa 161
  Ruth 170
  Samuel 25, 168, 169, 170, 172
  Thomas 170
  Thos. 103
Crockett, (Miss) 61
  James 161
  Walter 107
Crosley, E.B. 203
Currin, Ann 102
  Catherine 102, 187
  George 102
  George (Maj) 62, 100, 101, 187
  Hugh 15, 102
  John 101
  Mary 101
  Mary J. 62
  Robert 62, 101
  Seraphina 45, 61
  Surphina 101, 102

Currin, William 101
  William B. 62

-D-

Dalton, Thomas 16
Dameron, Pearl Bourne 88
Daniel, (Miss) 133
Daniels, Jane 164
Daugherty, Charles 127
  Lindsey 127
Davenport, (Mr) 127
Davidson, (Miss) 92
Davis, Alex M. (Col) 56
  Alexander M. (Col) 184
  Garnet(t) 56, 184
  Joseph 56
Dawkins, Benjamin 93
  Benjamin F. 92, 93
  Elijah 92, 95, 96
  Elizabeth 92, 93
  James B. 92, 93
  Joshua P. 92
  Morgan (Maj) 96
  Nancy 92, 93, 94, 97
  Nannie 93
  Ophelia 96
  S.M. (Maj) 96
  Susan 92, 93, 95, 96
  Thomas N. 92, 93
Delp, (Miss) 133
  (Mr) 46
  Callie 164
  George 138
  Horace 56
  Joseph 185
  Minitree 46, 56
Dickenson, A.M. 110
  Alexander M. 185
  Alexander Martin 55
  Amelia 54
  Blanch 46
  Blanche 56
  Charlotte 54, 57, 114, 115
  Elizabeth 55
  Elizabeth Caroline 54, 57
  Ellen 57
  Eugenia 57
  James 54
  James Piper 55
  Jane 54
  Jestena 54, 59
  John 54, 56, 57, 129, 130, 156, 185
  John (Col) 46, 55, 56
  Lelia B. 55
  Leon 109
  Lucy 55, 128
  McCamant 55
  Martin 7, 9, 18, 54, 114
  Martin (Col) 55, 57, 59
  Martin (Dr) 55, 174
  Martin D. 57
  Mary 24, 54, 56, 184
  Matilda 54, 59
  Mattie 57
  Nannie 57
  R.L. 11
  Robert 57
  Robert L. 56, 155
  Rosa 55
  Rosa B. 60

Dickenson, Rosamond B. 54
  Rush Floyd 55
  Sallie 54, 56
  William 54, 57
  William B. 56
Dickey, (Miss) 64
  Albert 185
  Alexander Phipps 184
  Allie 184
  Cynthia 134, 185
  Cynthia D. 183
  Elizabeth 115, 185
  Ellis Leftwich 185
  Eunice 184
  Friel 184
  J.Hurst 184
  James 53, 134, 183, 185
  James Alexander (Dr) 184
  Jane 102, 161, 185, 187
  John 188
  John M. 55, 175, 185
  John Mc. 184
  John R. (Dr) 184
  Martha 184, 185
  Mary 183, 195
  Matterson 184
  Mat(t)hew 2, 3, 4, 5, 6, 8, 9, 53, 174, 183, 184, 186, 189
  Mattie 56
  Minnie 55, 185
  Nannie 185
  Rebaca 9
  Rosa 184
  Stephen 184
  Stephen M. 175
  William R. 134, 183
Dickinson, see Dickenson
Dillard, (Miss) 185
  (Mr) 144
Dixon, (Mr) 131
Dobyns, Aileen 49
  Alma 49
  Ben 114
  Ben W. 77, 114
  Benjamin E. 77
  Benjamin S. (Dr) 49
  Brutus Fleming 114
  Charles 80
  James Wiley 77, 114
  Mary 134
  Ruth 49
  Samuel Green 80
  Stephen Brutus Fleming 77
  Thomas 183
  Thos. 134
  William 49
Dodd, Edwin 79
  Edwin Nuckolls 79
  John 79
  Robert 79
  Ruth Nuckolls 79
Doughton, Charles 176
  Jane 114, 139, 168
  Joseph B. 178
Drope, William 4
Dufphey, Ella 49
  Isabella 81
  John B. 81
  Joseph 81
  Josephine 49
  William R. (Dr) 49, 50

Duke, (Dr) 90
  (Miss) 90
Dulaney, Benjamin Bane 198
  Paul 198
  Paul Summers 198
Dunkley, (Dr) 114
  J.H. (Dr) 47
  Ruth Waugh 47
Dunn, (Miss) 205

-E-

Early, Bernard 69
  James 55, 69, 205
  John 205
  Marian 55
  Marion 69
  Peter 205
Edmondson, (Mr) 59
  Caroline 59
  Mary 56
Edwards, Archibald 128
  C.H. 56
  John Murphy 128
  Mary 187
  Morgan 128
  Robert 56
  Rosa Bryant 128
  Rosamond D. 156
  William 55, 128
Elliott, Abraham (Rev) 166
  Margaret 166
Ellis, John T. (Col) 144
  Lucy 144
Engledow, (Mr) 71
  Allie J. 71
English, - 7
  Judy 7
Eubank, Frances 144
Eversole, Robert 52

-F-

Farley, Mathew (Capt) 105
Farmer, (Miss) 52
Fawbush, Amelia Nuckolls 79
  Arthur Neal 80
  Celia 79
  Glen 80
  Hannah 68, 79, 156, 157, 160
  Leona Nuckolls 79
  Lura 80
  Rosa Bourne 79
  William 80
Felts, Gordon 52
  Laura E. 51
  Leander 51
  Thomas L. 52
Fielder, Dennis 6
  Donna 11
  John 9
Fields, Hugh 102
  Joseph 6, 102
  William 102
Finn, Sarah Ann 82
Fisher, Melville 70
Fleet, Van 193
Florida, George G. 135
Floyd, (Miss) 144
  Benjamin R. 16
  Benjamin Rush 181
  Rush 55

Foley, Moses 2, 3
  Moses (Rev) 6
Foster, John 54
Franklin, Esau 161
  Joel 161
  Powatan 161
  Tima 161
Fredericking, Lee 185
Freeman, Thomas N. 91
Fries, (Col) 11
Frisbie, Nathaniel 2, 3, 4, 9, 99
Fulton, (Miss) 25
  A.S. 16
  Andrew (Judge) 69
  Betsy 69
  Catherine 165
  Columbus 128, 156
  Creed 160
  Hastings 155
  Jestena 168
  Julia 62
  Martha P. 169
  R.S. 132
  Robert C. 175
  Robert S. 156
  Samuel 155, 160, 165, 168
  Terry (Rev) 134, 183

-G-

Gage, (Dr) 20
Gainer, Phillip 7
Gaines, Phil(l)ip 2, 3, 4, 5
Gaither, (Mr) 137
Gallagher, Elizabeth 128
  Emmett 128
  Marvin 128
  Mary 128
  Nannie 128
  Patrick 128
  Peter 128
Galloway, (Mr) 129
Gambill, James 177
Gardner, (Miss) 57
  Thomas 60
Garland, (Miss) 67
  Anne Shepherd 144
  Augustus H. 146
  Caroline 143, 144
  Charles 67, 84, 100, 142
  Clifton 145
  David Shepherd 144, 145, 146
  Edward 65, 141
  Eliza Virginia 144
  Ella Rose 144
  Frances 145
  Henrietta 142
  Hudson 142, 143
  Hudson Martin 146
  Hugh A. 143, 146
  James 141, 142, 145
  James Powell (Rev) 144, 147
  Jane Meredith 144
  John 65, 141, 142
  John (Gen) 143
  Landon C. (Dr) 144, 146
  Landon Cabell 143
  Louisa F. 143
  Louisa Frances 144
  Lucy 141

Garland, Lucy Lee 144
  Martha Henry 144
  Mary 65, 66, 67, 72,
    84, 100, 122, 142,
    145
  Mary Rice 144
  Maurice H. 143
  Mildred Irvin 144
  Narcissa E. 144
  Nathaniel 142
  Patrick Henry 144
  Paulus Powell 144
  Peter 141
  Rice 145
  Robert 65, 141, 142,
    145
  Sally 144
  Sally Armistead 144
  Samuel (Gen) 143
  Samuel Meredith 144,
    146
  Spottswood 142, 143
  Thomas 141
  Walter 144
  William Henry 144
  William 145
Garrett, Susan 74, 118
Garrison, David 155
  Elizabeth B. 155
  Isaac 155
Gentry, (Prof) 128
  Allen (Col) 164, 177
  Cynthia 177
  Ellen 178
  Ephraim 117
  George W. 128
  George W. (Capt) 177
  L.C. (Dr) 178
  Martha 178
  Reed 178
  Sarah 164, 177
Gilham, William 190
Gleaves, (Miss) 118, 126,
  129
  James (Maj) 127
Goast, Stephen 4
Golahorn, Alex 59
Golden, Nancy 113
Goodykoontz, Adeline 192,
  193, 198
  Adeline J. 196
  Alfred 193, 195, 196
  Alfred M. 192, 197
  Archibald 192
  Arthur Emmett 196
  Bernard Ellis 196
  Catharine 192
  Charles 195
  Charles Franklin 197
  Clarence F. 196
  Clark 197
  Daniel 191
  David 76, 190, 191,
    192, 193, 196, 198,
    199
  Edgar Marion 197
  Edward 193
  Elizabeth 191, 193,
    194, 196
  Ellen 193, 196
  Eva 191
  Flora 193
  George 190, 191, 192,
    197
  George E. 197
  George W. 193, 195
  Glen P. 196

Goodykoontz, Harry 195
  Harry L. 196
  Henry M. 193
  Horace Wells 196
  Ida 195
  Ida H. 193
  Isaac 191, 192
  Jacob 191
  James Richard 197
  Jasper 190
  John 195, 196
  Joseph Wiley 197
  Julia 193, 194
  Julia May 196
  Lake E. 196
  Lena 195
  Letitia 197
  Lou Ella 193
  Margaret 190, 191,
    199
  Margaret Emma 197
  Mary 197
  Mary Fletcher 76, 193,
    194
  Mary M. 190, 198, 199
  Mary Margaret 197
  Mattie Myrtle 196
  Millard 193
  Millard F. 196
  Minnie Andrews 197
  Minnie Ruth 196
  Nancy 192, 195, 197
  Nancy Rosetta 193,
    196
  Nannie A. 196
  Oakey B. 196
  Oscar Wilmer 196
  Polly 190, 192, 198
  Rachel 192, 197
  Rebecca 192, 193
  Redmond 197
  Robert E. 196
  Robert S. 196
  Roy F. 196
  Ruth Evelyn 195
  Thomas 197
  Thomas K. Beaver 197
  Washington 192, 197
  Webster 193
  William 191, 192,
    193, 195, 196
  William D. 196
  William Loving 197
  Willie C. 196
  Winton 193
Gose, David 54, 129
  Jane 54
  John 129
  Matilda 129
  Rosa 129
  William 129
Goudelock, - 95
Grabill, (Miss) 25
Graham, (Miss) 132
  D. 120
Grayson, (Mr) 2
Green, (Mr) 128
  Ashby 69
  Blanche 69
  Clara 69
  Fulton 69
  Jack 69, 70
  Nancy 69
  Sallie 70
Greer, Ed 131
  Ethel 63
  James 131

Greer, Jones 132
  Shadrach 25
  Shadrack 5
Gregory, John M. 15
Groseclose, Annie 80
Gwin, Charles G. 54
  Elizabeth 59
  Ernest 54
  Hugh 54, 60
  James 58
  John 60
  Lenora 57
  Martin 60
  Mary 61
  Richard 54, 59
  Sallie 55, 59
  Thomas 54, 55
Gwyn, see Gwin

-H-

Hackler, - 130, 157
Hale, (Miss 130
  Agnes 116
  Agnes May 110
  Alexander 61, 102,
    130
  Alfred 46, 113
  Alice 77, 114, 131,
    164, 185
  Alonzo Sidney 114
  Alvirda 117
  Amanda 130, 133, 139
  Amanda J. 123, 125
  Amanda Jane 61
  Amelia 53, 113
  Ballard E. 74
  Banner 115
  Basil 138
  Bettie 113
  Blanche 77
  Burroughs 130
  Callie 116
  Caroline 114, 115,
    130
  Celia 61, 127
  Chapman G. 61, 118
  Charles 53, 74, 105,
    109, 137, 138, 139,
    157
  Charles P. 135
  Charlotte 77, 112,
    114, 138
  Chatham 117
  Clara 77, 115
  Clark 61
  Clarke 74, 118
  Clarke G. 74
  Cleveland 77, 115
  Creed 115, 137
  Currin C. 12, 13, 14
  Daniel 105
  Dudley 9, 108, 111,
    117, 127, 130, 132,
    133, 164
  E.Scott 109
  Edward 104, 105
  Edward Everett 105
  Elbert 138, 139
  Eli 130, 140
  Eli C. 25, 61, 108,
    116, 118, 139
  Eli Scott 108, 116
  Elias 105
  Elizabeth 61, 73, 103,
    128, 138
  Ella 53

Hale, Ellen 60, 74, 134,
    138, 140
  Elvira 61, 127, 137
  Emma 114, 116
  Emmett 113
  Eva 116
  F.L. 10
  F.L. (Capt) 107
  Fielden 137, 139
  Fielden J. 140
  Fielden Lewis 61, 117,
    118ff.
  Flora 53, 138
  Fontaine 133
  Forest 115
  Forrest 77
  Frances 24
  Francis 112, 127, 133
  Frank 133
  Franklin 130
  Friel 61
  Gideon 130, 131
  Granville 134
  Gussie 116, 139
  Isaac 105
  Isaiah 105
  J.C. 75
  Jackson 61, 127
  James 46, 77, 112,
    113, 114, 115, 130,
    137
  James Gwyn 115
  James R. 132
  Jane 113, 133
  Jeremiah (Rev) 112
  Jessie 105
  Jestena 78
  Jestin 117, 132
  Jo 132
  John 46, 61, 112,
    113, 130, 131
  John B. 114
  John C. 74
  John M. (Capt) 54,
    115
  John S. 113
  Johnston 137, 173
  June 138
  Keziah 130
  Laura 116
  Lee 133
  Leftrick 130
  Leon 110
  Leonidas 138
  Lewis 2, 3, 4, 8, 9,
    73, 98, 106, 107ff.,
    111, 112, 113, 117,
    118, 130, 133, 134,
    136, 183
  Lewis (Capt) 18, 61,
    127, 133
  Lewis B. 130
  Lillie 77, 115, 116,
    135
  Lindsey 133
  Linnie 128
  Lorenzo D. 46
  Lorenzo Dow 114
  Lucinda 61, 62, 73,
    84, 87, 112, 113,
    122, 140
  Lucy 60, 129, 138,
    140
  Malinda 61
  Mamie 116
  Margaret Ellen 139
  Martha 134, 183

Hale, Martin 61, 78, 91,
    117, 132
  Mary 61, 105, 112,
    116, 123, 130, 137
  Mary Ann 140
  Mary Burwell 108
  Mary Elmira 134, 135
  Mastin 61, 73, 117,
    130, 168
  Maurice 116, 140
  Millie 61, 115
  Milly 127
  Mollie 25
  Montgomery 138
  Nancy 127, 129, 133
  Nannie 61, 139
  Nathan 105
  Nicholas 133
  Norman 116
  Normon 116
  Olive 53, 133, 164
  Oscar 113
  Peyton 130
  Peyton G. 62
  Peyton G. (Maj) 60,
    73, 127ff., 139
  Peyton N. 47
  Peyton N. (Capt) 61,
    113, 127
  Phoebe 105
  Preston 130
  Rachel Holmes 116
  Rebecca 168
  Reese 115, 138
  Richard 9, 111, 112,
    113, 163
  Robert 132
  Robert Clarke 116,
    139
  Rosa 113, 130, 138,
    173
  Rosa B. 82, 101, 122,
    127
  Rosa Bourne 61, 73,
    75, 76, 78, 79
  Rosamond 55, 157,
    185
  Rosamond B. 61, 157
  Rufus 61, 127, 132,
    133
  Sallie 53, 113
  Sallie B. 114
  Sallie L. 47
  Sarah 102, 131, 134,
    138, 156, 171
  Sarah Alice 134, 135,
    136
  Scott 77, 115
  Sena 113, 127, 163
  Sidney 46
  Sophia P. 61, 80, 117,
    123
  Stella 74
  Stephen 18, 46, 61,
    73, 74, 84, 108,
    112, 116, 117, 118,
    121, 122, 132
  Stephen (Col) 54, 57,
    114, 115
  Stephen M. 61, 102,
    112, 128
  Stephen Mason 77, 115
  Stephen P. 135
  Stephen Porter 134
  Susan 116, 128, 156
  Susan Albina 135
  Susan B. 47, 78

Hale, Tabitha Bourne 138
  Talitha 112
  Theresa 115
  Thomas 105, 114, 133
  Thomas B. 46
  Thomas Newton 135
  Tivis 53, 113, 138
  Virginia 74, 114
  Vivian 116
  W.S. 109, 110
  W.Stephen (Prof) 109
  Wallace Graham 131
  Warner 46, 61, 103,
    113, 117, 139, 168,
    173
  Washington 61, 127,
    133
  Wicks 133
  William 9, 46, 55, 62,
    73, 105, 111, 112,
    115, 128, 129, 134,
    135, 137, 139, 156
  William B. 12, 13,
    14, 45, 61, 117
  William J. 134
  William Scott 110, 116
  William Stephen 116
  Willie 77
  Wiley D. 47
  Wiley D. (Rev) 185
  Wiley Dickenson (Rev)
    77, 114, 115
Hall, (Miss) 64
  Gordon 69
  Johnathan 198
  Mae Adda 197
  Nannie Luther 197
  Washington C. 197
  William 197
  William C. 16
  William Rush 197
Haller,(Dr) 129
Halsey,(Dr) 170
Hamilton, Hale Snow (Rev)
    112
  Mary 178
Hampton, (Miss) 130
  Alexander 168
  Bernard 79
  Jane 168
  Kemper 79
  Litrell 79
  Nancy 79
  Raleigh 79
  Samuel Cox 169
  Selma Frances 79
  Verda 169
  William 137
Hankley, Eliza 79
Hanks, Creed L. 158
  Emmett 158
  Flora 158
  Joshua 15, 16
  Mary 188
  Nancy 158
Hardin, William 178
Hare, Joseph 105
Harter, Ruth 76, 193
Hartwell 194
Hash, (Miss) 171, 178
  Jane 173, 178
Hawety, (Mr) 193
Hawk, (Miss) 85
Hawkins, - 130
Henick, Avery 6
Henley, Lula 63
Henry, - 13, 14

Henry, Clarissa 93
  James E. (Maj) 93
  Jane 145
  Patrick 145
  R.P. (Capt) 12
Herbert, (Miss) 164
Herington, Phillip 138
  Thomas 138
Herrington, (Mr) 133
Heuser, Carrie 129
Higgins, Caroline 187
  Clayton 60, 140
  McCamant 60, 140
  Thomas 187
Hill, Leftrick 13
Hoge, William (Dr) 59
Holmes, Rachel 126
Hooper, (Miss) 196
Horne, Basil 113
  William 113
Horsley, Mary Cabell 146
  William 147
Houk, Clara 130
Houseman, Elizabeth E. 52
  Eugenia 52
  L.A. 51
  Lorenzo 52
  Mamie 51
  Sallie 52
  Walter 52
  William 52
Howard, Charles M. (Rev) 59
  John B. 50, 51
  Lucinda 51
  Mary B. 50, 51
  Thomas 50
Howell, George 6
Howery, Mary 196
Howlett, - 142
Huddle, Betsy 133
  Margaret 130
Hudson, - 142
Huffard, (Miss) 77
Huffman, (Dr) 55
  Eddie 55
Hunt, Elizabeth 54

-I-

Isom, Catherine 127
  David 114, 118
  Margaret 118

-J-

Jack, - 13, 14
  Jennie Linn 173
Jackson, Berton 70
  Lelia 55
  Joshua 70
  Nannie 70
  Robert (Judge) 69
  Robert C. (Judge) 55, 69
James, (Miss) 130
  Emeline 45, 51
  Ezekiel (Dr) 53
  Friel 53
  John 52
  Mildred 45
  Spencer 53
  Stephen 53
Jefferson, (Gov) 107
Jeffries, - 95
  John D. 94

Jeffries, Sam 94
Jennings, William 6
Jones, (Mr) 25, 99
  Abner 6, 9, 157, 159, 160
  Abner (Maj) 68, 69, 79, 156
  Bartholomew 152
  Bathurst 152
  Celia 68, 69, 159
  Charity B. 46
  Charlotte 157
  Churchill 17, 152, 153, 154, 157, 160
  Elizabeth 113
  Elmer 161
  Euphamia 138
  Euphemia 79, 157
  James 18, 148, 149, 152, 159, 160
  James Paul 149
  John Paul 148, 149, 150
  Julia 99
  Martha 103
  Martha Powell 155, 160, 165
  Matilda 117
  Minitre(e) 2, 3, 4, 5, 6, 8, 17, 98, 99, 153, 160
  Minitree (Maj) 46, 113, 156
  Olive 159, 160, 161
  Paul 149, 159, 160
  Paul (Admiral) 18, 148
  Phoebe Eleanor 194
  Powell 156
  Robert 187
  Rosa 45, 73, 75, 117, 127
  Rosamond 17ff., 153, 160, 183, 187
  Rosamond E. 153
  Samuel 156
  Samuel Powell 156
  Spottswood 17, 153, 157, 160
  Thomas 161
  Thomas B. 46
  William 149, 155
Johnson, see also
  Johnston & Johnstone
Johnson, Alpha Heath 70
  Catherine 48
  Dora 69
  Eliza 69
  Heath 69, 70
  Henrietta 69
  James 69, 70
  James B. 68
  Viola 69
Johnston, see also
  Johnson & Johnstone
Johnston, (Miss) 60
  (Mr) 204
  Ann 205
  Anna 204
  David E. 104
  J.E. 76
  James 159
  James B. 188
  Laura 188
  Martha 116, 205
  Mary 88
  Mary Ruth 76

Johnston, Ruth Frances Nuckolls 22
  Ruth Nuckolls 21, 110, 187
  Susan 204
Johnstone, see also
  Johnson & Johnston
Johnstone, Mary 18, 61, 64, 84, 101, 102, 139
  Robert 18, 61
Jordan, A.H. 129
  Elizabeth 129
  Margaret 129
Jordon, Caroline 143

-K-

Kahle, E.F. (Rev) 11
Kegley, Caroline 129
Kelly, Joseph L. 202
Kenerly, Mazie Phipps
Kenn(e)y, Eleanor 205
  Eliza 205
  Hance 205
  Harbert 160, 161
  Jane 205
  John A. 205
  Robert 16, 205
  William 205
Keown, M. 94
Kiesling, Emory 139
  Minnie 139
Killinger 75
Kinzer, Fannie M. 78
  Michael 78
  Phillip P. (Rev) 52
  Sidney Blair 52
Kirby, Emory 140
  Robert Lee (Judge) 140
  William Hale 140
Kirkpatrick, Mary A. 197
Kitchen, Nancy 60
Koontz, (Dr) 11, 186
Kyle, (Miss) 50
  Elma 80
  Eugene 80
  Glasgow 80
  James 80
  Madison 50
  Sam D. 51
  Samuel 50
  Stella 50
  Ward 80
  William (Judge) 52

-L-

Lafferty, (Dr) 154
  George C. 153
Lambert, George 116
Lapop, (Mr) 55
LaRowe, Louis 206
Lawson, (Mr) 157
  Fred 79
  Lura 157
  Ruth 80
Lee, (Miss) 140
  Henry 3, 98, 107, 156
Lenoir, Rufus 59
  Thomas 58
  William (Gen) 58
Leonard, Catherine 102
  James 45
  Sarah 83
LeSeuer, Alice 192

LeSeuer, Catharine 193
  Catherine C. 193
  Charles W. 193
  Crockett 193, 197
  Dollie 193
  Edwin F. 193
  Elbert J. 192
  Eliza A. 193
  Elizabeth 193
  Ellen 193
  Flora 193
  Foster 193
  George W. 193
  James 193
  James W. 193
  Jennie V. 193
  John R. 193
  Lucy C. 193
  Martel 192, 199
  Mary 193
  Mary F. 193
  Moseby 192
  Richard 193
  Thomas 193
Levesy, Geo. 6
Lewis, - 13, 14
  Burwell B. (Dr) 143
  Rose Garland 143
  William 16
Lincoln, (Mr) 185
  Abraham 158
  Thomas 158
Lindsey, William 15, 16
Littlejohn, Charles 95
  T.D. 94
Long, Carroll (Rev) 76
  William 6
Longstreet, (Gen) 143
Loving, Sarah J. 197
Lundy, (Miss) 164
  Busic 131
  Clarence 115, 185
  Elizabeth D. 17
  Ella 79
  Ellis 114, 131, 164
  Ellis L. 185
  F.J. 114
  Fielden Hale 115, 186
  Fielden J. 185, 186
  Fielden Johnston 17
  Fitzhugh 131
  Fitzhugh Lee 186
  George 185
  Hale 110
  Leona 186
  William 79
Lybrook, (Judge) 127
Lynthecum, Queenie 51
Lyons, Rose E. 160

-Mc-

McCabe, Thomas 16
McCamant, Alexander Smith 59, 60
  Blanche 60, 140
  Charlotte Virginia 59
  Clyde 60, 138, 140
  Emmett 59, 60
  Hattie 60
  James Martin 59, 60
  John D. 59, 60
  Josephine 60
  Josie Hale 140
  Lizzie 60, 140
  Myrtle 60
  Myrtle Lee 140

McCamant, Samuel 16, 59, 60
  Samuel (Col) 59, 182
  T.J. 138
  Thomas J. 140
  Thomas Jefferson 59, 60
  William B. 59, 60
McCarta, Van Buren 165
McCarter, Jane 117
McCarty, Jane 165
McCauley, Lizzie 196
McClure, Isaac Walton 197
McComas, (Miss) 60
McComas/McComes, David 26
McCoy, John 6
McGowan, (Miss) 167
McGuire, Geo. W. 137
McKinney, Ada 25
  Cleveland 25
  Jessee 25
  Jessie 18, 25
  Polly 25
  William 25
  Willis 25, 116
  Winston 25
McKinzie, Greenberry 9
McKnight, (Miss) 52
McLean, Ethel 110
  James 130
  Jane 130
  John 109, 130
  John M. 138, 139
  Mary 116, 139
  Nannie 138, 139
  Olive 130
  Sallie 130, 139
  Sena 139
McMillan, Alexander 53
  Evelina 50
  John 173, 186
  Mattie 174
  Nancy 131, 173, 184, 185, 170
McMullen, Lafayette 172
  Mary 172
McNutt, Margaret 129
McTeer, Canari D. 181
  James Piper 181
  John M. (Rev) 181

-M-

Mabey, Joshua G. 16
Mackey, A.H. 91
Mahood, Nellie 74
Mallory, (Miss) 205
  Alfred 138
  Crockett 131
Marsh, C.F. 91, 92
Martin, (Miss) 133
  (Mr) 88
  Benjamin 57
  Beverly 57
  Clarence 57
  George 4, 9
  John 57
  Mary 57
Massensmith, (Mr) 133
Mathews, - 181
  Alexander 182
  Dorthula 181
  Harold 16
  Nancy 181
  Richard 182
  Richard T. 16
  Stuart 185

Mays, Patsy/Patty 17, 18, 52
Meek, James 59
  Jane 59
  Joseph 59
  Mary 59
  Sophia 59
Meredith, Jane Henry 144, 145, 146
  Samuel (Col) 145
Merritt, (Judge) 198
Metcalf, Thomas E. 88
Meyers, Thomas N. 83
Mill, Joseph 6
Miller, (Mr) 79, 157, 175
  Charles K. (Rev) 175
  Cora 175
Minitree, (Miss) 153, 160
Mitchell, Frances 117
  James L. 16
  John B. 15, 118
  Katie May 117
  Leonora Gwyn 115
  Linnie 80
  Malinda M. 117
  Martha 47, 114, 165, 185
  Martha Gwin 77
  Mary 117
  Nancy 165
  Sam (Dr) 109
  Samuel Hale (Dr) 117
  Sena 117
  Virginia 117
  W.M. (Dr) 117
  William (Col) 165
  William M. 80
  William Marshall (Dr) 123
  Zachariah (Dr) 123
Montague, (Gov) 201
Moore, (Miss) 157
  Alfred (Col) 82
  Amelia 157
  Amos 15
  Arthur N. 157
  Celia 157
  Churchill Fawbush 79, 157
  Cora 80
  Fred 79
  Isaac 79, 138, 157, 158
  Leona 157
  Matilda 157
  Minerva 158
  Orville 80, 138, 157
  Patrick (Col) 96
  Riley 129
  Rosamond B. 157
  Spottswood D. 157
  William 157
Morgan, - 95
  (Mr) 61

-N-

Nash, John 6
Natt, - 6
Neal, (Mr) 115
Neel (Mr) 157
Neff, (Mr) 133
Nelson, (Gov) 142
  W.F. 85
Newberry, (Mr) 127

Newland, Elizabeth 123
Niehaus, Paul H. 151
Norris, (Mrs) 96
  John D. 96
  Julia 96
  William (Maj) 95
Nuckolls, Adella L. 91
  Alexander 90
  Alexander Heath 79
  Allie 67, 71
  Alpha Heath 79
  Amelia 83
  Amelia Clyde 79
  Amelia G. 138
  Amelia Gwyn 73, 74
  Andrew 67, 68, 69, 72, 83, 100, 159
  Ann 90
  Annie 79
  Asa 66, 67, 100
  B.F. 75, 101
  B.F. (Rev) 69, 109, 110, 194
  Ben 83
  Ben Floyd 15
  Benj. Floyd 21
  Benjamin Floyd 76
  Benjamin Winton 80, 81
  Bertha 18, 81
  Bertie 84
  Betty 67
  Bruce 84
  C.D. (Dr) 69
  Calvin 68, 71
  Celia 70
  Charles 5, 66, 67, 73, 98
  Chester B. (Dr) 83
  Chester Reeves 83
  Clarke 75, 76, 79, 80, 82, 89, 100, 157
  Clarke Hale 80, 81
  Clarke S. 72, 73, 78, 101, 122
  Columbus 85
  Cornelia L. 91
  Creed 72, 73, 89, 100
  Cynthia 68, 159
  David 66
  Dawn/Daron 81
  Dorthula Gertrude 80
  Duke 90
  E. 85
  Earl Garland 80, 81
  Elbert L. 83
  Elisha 66, 67
  Elizabeth 71, 88
  Elizabeth A. 91
  Elizabeth B. 81
  Ellis 83
  Ellis V. 83
  Emmett 85
  Ezra 62, 66, 84, 85, 86, 87, 88, 89, 100, 122
  Fannie 79
  Fay/Gay 81
  Flora W. 83
  Frances 62, 79, 84
  Frances H. 88
  Frank 187
  Frankie 95, 96
  G. Harvey 85
  Garland 67, 68, 71
  George 72, 83, 100, 188
  George Bias 90
Nuckolls, Heath 84, 85
  Henry C. 83, 187
  Houston 85
  Hugh 72, 83, 100
  Isaac Clarke 76, 194
  J.M. 85
  James 65, 67, 72, 83, 100
  James T. 91
  Jessie 83
  John 65, 66, 67, 71, 72, 84, 91, 93, 94, 95, 96, 97, 100, 122, 142
  John Michael 79
  Kent 68
  Lafayette 85
  Laura C. 91
  Lee 67, 73
  Lelia B. 78
  Lelia Burt 47
  Linnie 81
  Louise 79
  Louisiana A. 91
  Lucinda 90
  Malinda 75
  Margaret A. 80
  Martha 67, 72, 81, 100, 101
  Martha G. 117
  Mary 90
  Mary A. 79, 157
  Mary V. 91
  Maud Forrest 81
  Melissa 95
  Nancy 67, 71, 92, 95
  Nathaniel 66, 67, 69, 70, 71, 72, 82, 83, 90, 91, 100, 159
  Nathaniel A. 91
  Patsy 66, 67
  Paul 62, 84
  Pauline 81
  Peter 66, 67
  Polly 67, 87
  Rhodes 66, 67
  Robert 9, 67
  Robert G. 66, 73, 81, 82, 89, 109
  Robert G. (Capt) 100, 101
  Robert Garland 72, 73, 122, 140
  Robert Rhodes 71, 72
  Rosa Ellen 194
  Rosamond B. 88
  Rosamond Ellen 76
  Rufus 187
  Rupert 62
  Rupert B. 84
  Ruth Frances 76, 194
  S.F. 88
  Sally 67
  Samuel 66, 67, 90
  Sarah Frances 76, 77, 103, 114, 115
  Sarah Margaret 84
  Sena 67, 70, 73, 81, 88, 100
  Sophia L. 75
  Stephen 90
  Stephen Friel 62, 84, 86, 87
  Stephen Nathaniel 80, 117
  Susan 67, 95
  Susan Viola 79
Nuckolls, Thomas 72, 83, 84, 90, 100
  Thomas Fielden 80
  Thomas J. 91
  Virginia 84
  W.T. 96
  Wm. T. 97
  William 62, 65
  William B. 84
  William David 76, 194
  William Swift 47, 78, 79, 80, 81
  William T. 91, 93, 95

-O-

Oakley, Edgar 115
Oscar 77
Oglesby, William 89
Osborn, see also
  Osborne & osbourne
Osborn, Nancy 168
  Phoeba 168
  Polly 168
Osborne, see also
  Osborn & Osbourne
Osborne, Allen 173
  Annie 82
  Bettie 82
  Biddie 173
  Callie 82
  Caroline 173
  Dean Floyd 82
  Ellis 82
  Emmett 82
  Emmett P. 173
  Enoch 171, 172, 173, 178
  Ephraim 171, 172
  Floyd 82, 173
  Hattie 82
  Jane 176, 177
  John 171
  John H. 173
  Johnathan 171
  Joshua 171, 172
  Mahala 172
  Margaret 173, 174
  Mary 82, 172
  Nancy 172
  Phoebe 172, 176
  Preston 173
  Rebecca 176
  Ruth 168
  Solomon 171, 172
  Thomas H. 173
  Zachariah 169, 172, 173
Osbourne, see also
  Osborn & Osborne
Osbourne, Caroline 137
  Enoch 2, 3, 4, 5, 8
  Rebecca 168

-P-

Padgett, (Judge) 11
  James (Judge) 178
Painter, Lydia 68
Parker, Ben B. 63
  Bryce 63
  Carl 63
  Ella 63
  Hattie 63
  Pinkie 63
  Rolla 63
Parks, James H.(Capt) 177

Parsons, John M. 131
Paschel, Elizabeth 12
Patton, Sally 45
Paul, (Mr) 161
  James 149
  John 149
Pendleton, (Mr) 145
  Edmond 146
  Lettie B. 146
  Micajah 146
  Philip 146
Penn, William 159
Perdue, Patsy 104, 105
  Uriah 105
Perkins, Bettie 54
  Catharine 140
  Celia 64, 115
  Ed 139
  Gertrude 140
  J.L.M. (Rev) 54
  James 132
  Jennie 48
  Johnson 48
  Kate 116
  Levi 115, 127
  Lewis 129, 165
  Rebecca 24, 177
  Rufus 54
  Susan 73, 117, 168
  Timothy 24, 64
  William 140
  Winfield 134
Petty, Joshua 95
Pfingsten, Josephine 63
Phipps, (Dr) 73
  Alexander 25, 171, 174, 184
  Agnes 20
  Benjamin 173, 175, 178, 184
  Columbus 132, 171, 174
  Con 132, 175
  Dodge L. 117
  Drucey 170
  Drucey 175
  Edgar 139
  Emily 175, 178
  Emma 171, 175
  Etta 131, 175
  Isaiah 173, 178
  Jane 175, 184
  Jensey 132
  Jincey 175
  Jincy 170
  John 173, 174
  John (Dr) 175
  Joseph 53, 131, 132, 170, 175, 185
  Joseph (Capt) 173, 174
  Lesbia 132
  Martha 174
  Mattie 55
  Mazie 131
  Mazy 175
  Nancy 175, 185
  Rena 175
  Rosa 174
  Rosamond 174, 184
  Roscoe 138
  Stephen 174
  Tobias 5
Phlegar, Abram 190, 198, 199
  Adeline 198
  Andrew 198
  Ann C. 201

Phlegar, Archer A. 199ff.
  Benjamin 198
  Calvin 199
  David 199
  David S. 203
  Dora 198
  Eli 199, 201, 204
  Eliza 199
  Elizabeth 199
  Ellen 198, 204
  Estella 198
  George 190, 198, 199
  Henrietta 198
  Hunter 203
  Isaac 199
  Jacob 199
  Jesse M. 198
  John 199
  John N. 198
  Joseph 199
  Lillie 198
  Lydia 199
  Margaret 199
  Mary 198, 203
  Mattie 198
  Nancy 198
  Sarah 192, 198, 199
  Thomas 198
  William 198
Pickerell, John 6
Pierce, (Miss) 182
  (Mr) 131
Pike, Albert 127
Pinkley, (Mr) 180
  Nancy 180
Piper, James H. (Col) 180, 181
Pless, Asbury Glen (Dr) 81
  Maud Forrest 81
Plummer, Samuel (Rev) 177
Poindexter, (Mr) 55
  Gwin 55
Polton, Mary 93
Pope, (Miss) 195
  Isaac 103
  Nathaniel 2, 3, 4, 6, 9
  William 71
Porter, Andrew 118, 126, 166
  Elizabeth 54, 116, 118, 126
  Horace (Gen) 150, 152
  Jack 138
  Malvina 129
  Margaret 126
  Sarah 134
  Stephen 129
Porterfield. (Mr) 185
Powell, Bessie 147
  Martha 156, 160
  Mildred Jordon 144, 146
Powell-Jones, Martha 168
Preston, (Miss) 70
Price, (Mr) 188, 204
  Archer P. 204
  Charles 194
  David 194
  John 194
  Lennie 204
  R.N. (Dr) 194
  Richard 204
  Susan A. 135
Pugh, (Mr) 53
  Frances 116

Pugh, John (Rev) 116
  Mary 25
  Robert 25
  Rosa 25
  Stephen 25

-R-

Raines, William 16
Ransom, (Miss) 170
Rapert, Robert 120
Rawley, Heath 69
  John (Maj) 69
  Kent Nuckolls 69
Reed, (Dr) 114
Reeves, - 138
  (Miss) 132
  (Mr) 25, 55
  Albert 55
  Andrew 83
  Anna 176
  Carrie 83
  Charity 176, 177
  Cynthia 176
  Edward 47, 114
  Enoch 170, 176, 177
  George 47, 114, 176, 177
  George W. (Col) 177
  Jesse 176
  Jesse A. 177
  John 13, 176, 177
  Lucy 177
  Mahala 177
  Martin 55
  Mary 176, 177
  Nancy 168, 176, 177
  Osborne 176
  Polly 177
  Preston 64, 171, 177
  Rebeca 164
  Rebecca 176, 177
  Richmond G. 64
  Susan 176
  William 176
Rhea, (miss) 70, 195
Rhodes, (Miss) 142
Rhudy, (Miss) 138
  (Mr) 115
  Hicks 156
  J.H. 128
  James 130
  Jelane 116, 139
  Jemima 165
  Mina 184
  William 165
Rice, Mary 142, 145
Richardson, (Mr) 144
Riley, (Judge) 201
Ring, Elbert 130
  George 9
  Hester 165
  Martin 9
  Olive 56
  Roy 56
  Sallie 56
Roarch, (Widow) 6
  Timothy 9
Roberts, Catherine 102
  Charles 103
  Clyde 103
  Currin 102
  Dan 103
  Elizabeth 77, 78, 103
  Frank Currin 103
  Fred 103
  Hugh 103

Roberts, James 103
  John 45, 102
  Logan 103, 188
  Lola 103
  Lucy 102
  Margaret 102
  Martha 102
  May 103
  Nancy 103
  Olive 103
  Ollie 103
  Sallie 61, 102
  Sidney 102
  Thomas F. 101
  Thomas Floyd 103
  Thompson 45, 61, 101, 102
  William 103
Robertson, James (E.) (Dr) 181
  John 10
Robinson, (Dr) 51, 131, 175
Rodgers, Robert 80
Rogers, Charles 115
  Charlotte 115
  Dawkins 93
  James (Gen) 93, 97
  John 115
  Mary 115
  Russell (Rev) 115
Rooney, Irving 198
Rose, Gustavus A. (Dr) 144
  Hugh (Col) 143
  Lucinda 143
Roth, Ethel 63
Rowe, Richard 73
Russell, (Miss) 112
Rutherford, (Mr) 127

-S-

Sanders, Frank 164
  John L. 164
Saunders, Bert (Dr) 78
Sayers, Robert 7
Schooler, Ellis 88
  Frances 88
  Houston 88
  Rice 87
Schuler, (Mr) 133
Scott, (Miss) 170
  (Mr) 114
  Andrew (Rev) 126, 170
  Ella 113
  Ellen 139
  Frances 25, 116, 118
  James 126
  Margaret 53, 54
  Mary 114
  Sallie 114
  William 54, 114, 116, 118, 126
Senter, Calvin 25
  Martha 133
Shanks, Susan 203
Shannon, (Capt) 105
Sheffy, Daniel 7, 70
  Edward 70
  Ezra Nuckolls 70
  Robert Sawyers (Rev) 70, 71
Shell, Catherine C. 193
Shelton, (Miss) 81
Shepherd, Ann 145
Shoupe, Benjamin 155
Simon, - 13, 14

Simmerman, George W. 64
  John P.M. 66
Simmons, (Mr) 199
Skinner, Alice Rosa 63
  Brooksie 63
  Christa 63
  Conda 63
  Effie Julia 63
  Ellie 63
  Elsie Bly 63
  Eunice 63
  Floy 63
  George 63
  John 63
  John (Mrs) 64
  John H. 62
  Lute 63
  Roy 63
  Verna 63
Slemp, C.B. 159
Sloan, (Miss) 129
Smith, (Dr) 198
  (Miss) 198
  (Mr) 198
  Alexander 5, 7
  Malvina 181
  Sarah 53
Smoot, (Mr) 101
Smyth, Alexander 4, 179
  Alexander (Gen) 182, 185
  Frances Stuart 179, 180
  James (Rev) 179, 180
Snapp, Phillip 59
Snead, M.L. 196
Southern, E.H. 197
Sowers, Eliza A. 193
Spalding, Joseph C. 16
Sparks, Lelia 73
Speck, Carl Thomas (Dr) 76
Spicer, (Mr) 132
Spillsman, Mary F. 193
Spottswood, (Miss) 17, 153
  Alexander (Col) 1
Spraker, (Mr) 54
  Jacob 9
Stafford, (Miss) 71
  James 16
Stanton, Celia Elizabeth 112
  Chapell Quillian 112
  Elbert Miller 112
  John Wesley 112
  Mary Irene 112
  Mathew Whitfield 112
  McClure Hale 112
  P.L. 136
  Peyton L. 137
  Peyton Lisby 112
  Sarah Jane 112
  William Lewis 112
Staples, (Mr) 161
  Waller R. 201
Steffy, (Mr) 165
Stephen, (Col) 54
Stetson, Benjn. 22
Stevens, Rhoda 205
Stiff, (Mr) 133
  Washington 133
Stipes, - 191
Stone, Charlotte Jestina 83
  Elizabeth 46, 111, 163
  George 46

Stone, Hamilton 46
  Jane 46
  Jeremiah 3, 6, 111
  John 3, 46, 83
  Lorenzo Dow 46
  Lucy 46, 55, 62, 111, 137, 156
  Mary 46
  Susanna 111
  Thomas 46
  William 46
Stoneman, Elizabeth 206
  Joshua (Dr) 205
  Mark D. 205
  Mary 206
Straw, (Dr) 205
Strother, (Col) 59
Stuart, Archabald 16
  Frances 180
Sullins, David (Dr) 87
Summers, Bane 198
  Bessie 198
  Dora 198
  George W. (Rev) 198
  Lois 198
  Mary 198
  Pearl 198
Sumner, Jonathan R. 16
Sutherland, (Miss) 130
  Jane 137, 157
  Jennie 163, 165
  John 132, 163
  Leonard 129
  Maud 185
  Minnie 115
  Sallie 133
  William (Capt) 115
  Wm. M. (Capt) 185
Swecker, (Miss) 71
Swift, (Miss) 101
  Alfred 99
  Elisha 99
  Flower 2, 3, 4, 5, 6, 7, 8, 9, 98ff., 156
  Flower (Col) 72
  Jestena 99
  John 99
  Louisa 72
  Margaret 72, 82, 100, 101, 122
  Martha 62, 187
  Mary 6, 9
  Thomas 99
  William 99

-T-

Taswell, Henry 4
Taylor, (Miss) 134, 183
  Carrie 93
Tazewell, Henry 179
Terrill, (Miss) 176
Thomas, (Miss) 185
  Amelia 25
  Ann 25
  Caroline 47, 114, 177
  Cora 130
  Elizabeth 25, 169, 170
  Fleming (Dr) 175, 178
  Jacob 130
  Jo 130
  Jonathan 18, 24, 25, 169
  Lucinda 184
  Ludema 25, 171, 174, 178
  Mary 25
  Randolph 25

Thomas, Rosa 25
   Rufus 117
   Stephen 24, 25, 177
   Susan 25, 165, 169, 173
   William 25, 174
Thompson, (Mr) 132
   Abner 71
   Samuel 185
Thornton, Bertie 83
   Lillie 116
   William 116, 205
Thurman, (Mr) 57
Thurmon, Julia 54
Tipton, (Dr) 51
Todd, Emmon 81
   Geo. W. 81
   George W. Clarke 81
   Ila 81
   Lance 81
   Lula 158
   Mebus 81
   Rosa B. 81
Toler, Martha 71
Tomblin, Tibitha 137
Tomlin, Noel 165
Tomlinson, (Miss) 158
Tompkins, W.D. 69, 70
Tompson, (Miss) 95
   Bill 95
Trench, Nannie 93
Trigg, Robert C. 201
Trimble, Evaline 103
Troy, Susan 113
Tunner, Annie 79
Turner, Ellen 193
Tyler, Hoge (Gov) 201

-U-

Umberger, Albert G. 80
   Keller Yonce (Rev) 80
   Kenneth 80
   Susan 129

-V-

Vance, Charles 77
   Ethel Louisa 77
Varney, Alice 74
Vaughan, see Vaughn
Vaughn, (Miss) 183
   (Mr) 130
   Alma 116
   David 5
   Emmett (Dr) 116
   Harvey 138
   John 16, 138
   Marvin 60, 138, 140
   Nathaniel W. 16
   Rosa 138
   Rosamond 129
   T.C. (Rev) 11, 129, 140
   Thomas C. (Rev) 60, 138
   Thomas Jefferson 60
   Wiley (Col) 183
   William 6
Vaught, - 130

-W-

Wade, Amanda 193
   Robert 84
Wagoner, David 64
   Mary 64
Walden, John 106
Wall, (Miss) 83
Waller, William (Capt) 144
Walsh, Ella 73
Walters, Effie 73
Wampler, French (Rev) 174
Ward, Amelia Gwyn 75
   Annie 80
   Ballard 138
   Ballard E. 20, 73, 74, 75
   Ballard Ernest 75
   Basil 74
   Charles 80
   Clarence 74
   Eli Hale 74
   Ella 80
   Ellis William Clarke 73
   Ethel 73
   Everett 138
   Everett Hale 74
   Floyd 73
   Floyd Harvey 73
   Frances Laura 74
   Gwyn 74, 110, 138
   Herbert Gwyn 75
   Ida 74
   James Brown 80
   James Stuart 74
   John A. 80
   Jonathan 6
   Latitia 161
   Laura 73
   Lena 80
   Leonidas 74, 138
   Leonidas Hicks 74
   Lilburn 80
   Lilburn (Dr) 74
   Mamie 73
   Nellie 168
   Robert N. Kent 80
   Rosa Bourne 80
   Ruth 74, 138
   Ruth Nuckolls 80
   Stella H. 80
   Susan 80
   Varney Stuart 74
   William 73,
Warren, William 134, 183
Warrick, Bertie 77
   Claude S. 77
   Ethel 77
   James 113
   James Lafayette 77
   John Wesley 77
   Nannie 165
   Paul 77
   Thomas 77
Watson, America V. 161
   Martha 51
Waugh, Berta Carson 48, 49
   Charles P. 48
   Dan Blair 48
   Elizabeth 47, 50
   Elizabeth B. 114
   Emma Amelia 50
   Emmett 47
   Eugenia 47, 114
   Flora 49, 50
   James 46, 48, 49, 50, 89
   James P. 62
   John B. 89
   John B. (Capt) 48
   Laura 47, 114
   Lenora 47, 114
   Martha 47
   Martha M. 114
   Mary 50
   Richard G. 48
   Sue 110
   Susan 78
   Susan B. 47
   Swift 47, 78
   William P. 78, 89, 114
   William Peadon 47
Weaver, Lucy C. 193
   Noah 131
Webb, John 16
Webber, Augustus 9
Welch 53
Wellington, (Mr) 82
   Susan Nuckolls 82
Wells, Fidella 205
West, Jennie V. 193
Wheeler, Lucinda 130
White, (Miss) 70
   Celia 112
   Susan 112
   W.R. 63
Whitehead, Thomas (Col) 144
Whitman, Blanche 129
   Caroline 128, 177
   Clarke 129
   Clay 129
   David 61, 128, 129
   George 129
   Gertrude 129
   Jennie 129
   John A. 109, 129
   Lillie 129
   Margaret 129
   Nancy 128
   Nannie 129
   Sidney 129
   Sidney P. 138
   Stephen 61, 128
   William 129
   William H. 129
Wilcox, Cyrus 12, 13, 14
Wiley, (Miss) 64, 184
   John 134, 183
   Rebecca 53, 183, 186, 189
   William 105
Wilkinson, John 158
   Retta 158
   Robert 158
   Stephen 158
Willard, Aaron 22
   Yaron 22
Williams, (Miss) 195
   (Mr) 127
   Bessie N. 83
   E.L. (Mrs) 125
   Frank 114
   Hiram 82
   Hyram 173
   J.D. 196
   Jessie 9
   John 9
   Leona 114
   Mary 173
   William 6
Williamson, Mary 195
   Sarah 197
Willis, David 198
Wills, Henry 144
   Willis 144
Wilson, (Miss) 55

Wilson, John 6
  R.F. (Rev) 147
Winfield, Annie 142
Winston, Edmond 4, 179
Witherow, B.G. 76
  Benjamin 76
  Charles 76
  Eugene 49
  Fred 49
  James 49
Wolfe, A. Edwin 114
  Edwin A. 47
  Eugene 47, 114
  Gladys 47, 114
  Juanita 47, 114
Wood, James 9
  Martha 81, 82
Woodruff, Phoebe 132, 163
Woods, (Mr) 1
  Mary 172
Woody, Samuel Fishburn 196
Woolwine, Lucy 195
Worrell, Amos 161
  C. Columbus (Maj) 160
  Carinne 160
  Churchill Fawbush 160
  D.A.L. 118
  Dexter A.L. 160
  Esau 159, 161
  Herbert (Sir) 159
  Isaac 160
  James 159
  James (Dr) 205
  Jane 205
  Jessee P. 161, 188
  John 159, 160, 161
  Malcolm Lee 159, 160
  Minerva E. 160, 161
  Nancy 161
  Richard 159
  Sallie 161
Worth, David 170
  Thomas 170
Wright, (Miss) 133
  Ellen 83
  Hugh 54
  Julia 54
  Richard 6
  William 166

-Y-

Yearout, Nancy C. 193
Yearwood, Cornelia V. 134
Yontz, James 130
Young, (Miss) 102, 139
  Andrew 25
  Ezekiel 50
  Fielding 175
  Fields McMillan 50
  Floyd 25
  James 50
  Mary 73
  Mattie 50, 175
  Robey (Dr) 25
  S.E. (Dr) 25
  Virginia 50
Zumwalt, Alice 63
  Annie 63
  Bowen 63
  Chloe 63
  Clifton 63
  Floy 63
  Murray 63
  Wayne 63

Addenda

Bourchees, (Mr) 88
Penn, George 198

www.ingramcontent.com/pod-product-compliance
Lightning Source LLC
Chambersburg PA
CBHW052153300426
44115CB00011B/1649